Taking Sports Seriously

Taking Sports Seriously

Law and Sports in Contemporary American Culture

Jeffrey Standen
WILLAMETTE UNIVERSITY COLLEGE OF LAW

CAROLINA ACADEMIC PRESS
Durham, North Carolina

Library of Congress Cataloging-in-Publication Data

Standen, Jeffrey.
Taking sports seriously : law and sports in contemporary American culture / Jeffrey Standen.
   p. cm.
Includes bibliographical references and index.
ISBN 10: 1-59460-458-4
ISBN 13: 978-1-59460-458-4 (alk. paper)
1. Sports--Law and legislation--United States. I. Title.
KF3989.S73 2008
344.73'099--dc22
                              2008027708

CAROLINA ACADEMIC PRESS
700 Kent Street
Durham, North Carolina 27701
Telephone (919) 489-7486
Fax (919) 493-5668
www.cap-press.com

Printed in the United States of America

*This sports book is dedicated to
my sports-loving boys,
Jonathan and Trevor,
and my book-loving daughter,
Emily.*

Contents

Preface

I have been taking sports seriously, applying the tools of legal analysis to sports issues. My writings have been in the form of scholarly articles, book reviews, legal—and popular—press editorials, and in blog entries, both on my own website (The Sports Law Professor) and as a guest commentator on others. This book collects many of these materials, along with some new contributions and essays. Each piece has been amended to explain certain terms and events, to detail references, and to omit to the extent possible all unnecessary technical jargon. The pieces have also been grouped roughly according to subject matter, although, as you will see, lawyers connect the dots of the world in ways that may seem very odd to the non-lawyer mind. In the end, while modifying the pieces to facilitate easy reading, I tried to maintain the form and style of the original materials as much as feasible. You will notice that, at times, my writing style is offhand and colloquial. Sports is fun, and in my view writing about sports should try to capture and try to reflect the inherent good feelings all of us have when enjoying a sports contest, either as a player or as a spectator. At other times, the writing devolves to the lawyer's structure, with cautious paragraphs building arguments slowly and carefully. Some readers may find this latter stylistic approach strange; but if we're going to take sports seriously, we might as well get used to the analytical, logical writing style of the lawyer. This book should prove useful to stimulate thought in a law class on sports law, a college seminar on athletics or exercise science, or for the educated reader willing to reconsider and perhaps revise one's perspectives on the many "sports law" topics that permeate the daily news. In any event, right or wrong, I hope my thoughts provide a contribution to the betterment of the field. I do want us to take sports seriously.

Welcome to the practice of law, sports-style.

Acknowledgments

I am grateful to Ms. Amanda Keller for research and editorial assistance. I am also indebted to Mr. Lonn Johnston, whose technical expertise was invaluable in establishing my website, *The Sports Law Professor*, on which many of these essays first appeared. Thanks also to Ms. Elizabeth Engdahl for encouraging me to combine my offbeat perspectives and deep and abiding interests in law and sports in a series of essays published in Legal Times. Finally, I wish to acknowledge a debt to Willamette University for its continued support of my work.

The following essays, in slightly different form, appeared first in Legal Times, which reserves its copyright: *Why Can't Michael Play?*, *Don't Play Pro Se*, *How A Lawyer Plays Golf*, and *Can You Hear Them Now?*

Introduction

Often one hears the complaint that people take sports far too seriously. Youth sports coaches care too much about winning, we're told, and the result is disappointed children, hurt feelings, arguments with parents, or worse. Parents take it too seriously too, and become deeply angered when their little hero doesn't get to play quarterback or merely comes off the bench on the basketball team. Even young players, subtly pressured by anxious parents to strive for stardom in high school or the rare college scholarship, overdo it, spending too much time on sports, and devoting too much of their sports time to one sport, basically trading away childhood fun for endless drills, private sports lessons, and overbearing and constant parental advice.

Taking sports too seriously continues into higher echelons. Collegiate "student-athletes" are barely students any more: the unending demands of practice, tournaments, travel and other team obligations leave little time for today's Division 1 athlete to maintain even a plausible educational commitment. Even at the professional level, times are bad. The "off-season" is now a misnomer: "serious" players train constantly, seeking improvement, even through illicit means, and the added compensation that improvement generates. The days of colorful athletes setting down their cigarette and swatting a home run are long past. Fans too take sports too seriously, wasting endless hours in sedentary solitude watching games and reviewing fantasy rosters. Wild rooting, including body painting, day-long tailgating, excessive boosterism, and even hooliganism or worse all are common attributes of today's mad fandom. To become part of the contemporary sports landscape, from youth player to professional, from fan to manager, the job requirement is clear: only serious people need apply.

This common perception is wrong. Our problems with sports stem not from taking these games too seriously, but from not taking them seriously enough. Often people dismiss sports as "childhood games," implying that this multi-billion dollar industry is little more than kids goofing around after school. Others chide sports for being mere "entertainment." This view leads to mistakes, as it unnecessarily aligns the slick, scripted productions of Hollywood and the gambling games of Las Vegas with hard-fought sports contests of skill and determination, thus missing important distinctions. A casual regard for sports leads to casual diagnosis of and remedies for sports ills. It leads to sloppy thinking and ill-considered solutions. It leads us to ignore or overlook analyses and solutions of the kind that we routinely consider and adopt in more "serious" pursuits, such as the law or public policy. Ultimately, our dissmissive attitude toward modern sports leads to inattention, and inattention allows those who are paying attention, those are who taking sports seriously, to have their way with sports with but slight hindrance. Taking sports seriously is a necessary response to the importance of sports in the modern world. Taking sports seriously is the cure, not the illness.

What do I mean by "taking sports seriously"? I mean taking the rules of sports games and the constitutions of sports leagues as seriously as a lawyer takes the law. When lawyers examine a particular rule of law, or a proposal to change or amend a particular rule of law, they look at a number of aspects of the rule. They consider the relevant body or area of law, estimating how the changed rule would fit into the overall scheme. They consider the law's history, and its purpose and structure. At a minimum the lawyer will make sure the new rule doesn't violate or contradict other legal rules within that area. Lawyers also examine a new rule of law for its comportment with similar rules in other areas of law in order to see if the new rule presents a consistent and principled approach to solving what might seem a similar set of problems. As much as possible, the lawyer will make sure that the new rule carries as minimal an adverse impact or causes the minimum in untoward consequences to the other body of law and to other important interests. Finally, the lawyer will conduct a purposive analysis, asking if the rule of law will further the overall goals of legal regulation. Such goals include creating incentives for good behavior, deterring harmful conduct, and promoting equality, justice, and other broad norms and goals. Taking law seriously is serious business, one which demands a level of care and thoroughness that is the hallmark of the successful lawyer. Taking sports seriously would require the same level of care.

Sports has never received this kind of attention, and it needs it. Not because sports is big business. Lots of industries are huge, but they're not the focus of scores of books and magazines, dedicated newspaper sections and omnipresent television networks. Sports deserves serious treatment because sports has an importance in contemporary society that transcends the dollar value of the business. We are moving toward a nation and world whose citizens are increasingly splintered among an endless array of television stations, internet sites, video games, and specialized jobs. Network television shows compete for a fractured viewership, and local newspapers, waning in the face of the "free-information" society, no longer form the locus of the community. What does bring us together, on both a national and more local scale, are the sporting contests and sports teams that captivate our interest. From major golf tournaments, to college basketball's "March Madness," to major league baseball seasons that involve teams from around the country, to scholastic football, sports stands as perhaps our last major repository of community spirit and togetherness. Major cataclysms, such as terrorist attacks or natural disasters, can sporadically unite us in a more profound, if temporary, way. But sports provides a persistent, regular and inextricable thread to the fabric of American society. As other sustaining elements of a common culture have been marginalized by the dawn of the information age, sports has filled the vacuum, growing in importance to our contemporary social discourse. By taking sports lightly we place at risk a vital aspect of American culture, perhaps even one of the centers of American culture.

Another center of contemporary American culture is law. To think that a mere body of statutes could have any cultural ramifications at all seems strange. Yet "the law" today means so much more than rules that constrain wayward behavior. "The law" connotes the august trappings of the courtroom, whose captivating dramas formed the precursor to today's fascination with "reality" television programming. "The law" suggests a certain reverence for rules, especially for Americans whose regard for the founding constitution approaches mythical status, providing the document a deference that far exceeds the quality of its provisions and the limited foresight of its drafters, whose most important contribution (in contemporary terms), the Bill of Rights, was at best a briefly considered afterthought to the main document. Finally, in practical terms, for better or worse American law has just grown. The modern administrative state has become an uncontroversial feature of contemporary life. Legal regulation to varying degrees pervades nearly every meaningful aspect of our lives. Much of our contemporary culture is filtered through law. The lawyer, as mediator for much of this filtering, has taken on a role analogous to the medieval priest, explaining the hidden meanings of dimly understood provisions and proscriptions to the assembled congregation.

The importance of the lawyer, and the fascination with him or her, fills our law schools and law firms with amazingly bright, serious people. That these trained, capable people should fail to direct their attention to the problems of sports leaves sports shortchanged. The study of "sports law" was once considered a remote outpost in the field of law. In the wider culture, it was thought limited to particular problems of certain athletes, typically those who had earned themselves a criminal prosecution. Little in this traditional conception seems even relevant to sports law today. Sports law today includes a complex and pervasive set of problems concerning a unique and multi-layered industry. Sports law has moved into the curriculum and into the mainstream of contemporary American culture.

Taking sports seriously means bringing to bear the carefulness and purposive analysis of the lawyer on issues of sports. From Little League to Major League Baseball, Pop Warner to the NFL, our carelessness about the rules of sport has yielded predictable results: our sports landscape is littered with problems, misbehaviors, bad incentives, misunderstandings, and inapt rules. No competent lawyer would have written such rules for a client or proposed such rules to a court of law or to a government. Yet we have thoughtlessly adopted many of the rules of sports without a proper concern for the incentives they create, the abuses they permit, or the collateral harms they occasion. We just haven't cared. It's time we do.

Taking Sports Seriously

Chapter One

Our Sports Culture

Sporting contests often seem to bring to the public attention very fundamental questions about what it means to live and get along in today's world. Sports help us decide how we should go about treating others, including those less fortunate than ourselves. Sports make us think about how we should conduct ourselves, both in private and in public. Sports makes us decide when even legal conduct is impermissible, because it gains us undue advantages. Questions like these might also be raised in a college course on ethics. But unlike the abstract environment of the classroom, sports does not permit the luxury of an equivocal answer. For example, say your team leads by one in a championship youth baseball game, and the opponent's best hitter comes to plate. Would you, as pitcher, give him an intentional walk — even if the next batter in line is a recovering and weakened cancer survivor? You have to answer, or at least the coach does, because in just a moment or two the first pitch will be delivered.

Or try this one: you are a parent and know that by simply delaying your child's entrance into the school system for one year, you will give him nearly certain advantages, perhaps in the classroom,[1] but certainly in many sports. Yet delaying your child's en-

---

1. Evidence linking student age with test performance suggests that older students do not, as is commonly thought, gain a palpable advantage over their younger classmates. Mary C. Bounds, *Stipek Study Shows Older Students Do Not Academically Outperform Younger Peers in Early Grades* (*New York Times*, April 25, 2004).

rollment for athletic advantage would entail an athletic disadvantage to his classmates. Would you do it? Would you delay enrollment even if the presence of your large child put other children at some comparative disadvantage, not just in terms of winning or losing a game, but in terms of the risk to their physical health and well-being? Would it matter that one result of your action, combined with that of other parents, may be the actual prohibition by schools of traditional children's games?

Sports also makes us think not just about sports but about the way professional athletes perform both on and off the field. By presenting these larger-than-life figures, these formerly poor adult-children newly lavished with unspeakable riches, sports makes us question what's appropriate in our private lives. Should we dress like they do? Do drugs and carry guns like some of them do? How are these people similar to and different from us? Sports makes us think all the time. See if these materials change your mind, or perhaps demand that you make up your mind. Sports won't allow you to sit on the sideline.

Playing Little League for Keeps

In the last inning with a one-run lead in the championship game, the baseball coach in a nine- to ten-year-old league had his pitcher intentionally walk the opponent's best hitter. He did so to get to the next batter, a weaker hitter and a weakened cancer patient, who struck out to end the game. Big-time commentary ensued, and it wasn't nice. The coach was called a "jackass" on MSNBC.[2] He was called worse in the unconstrained blogosphere.

---

2. Many of the articles argued that youth sports have become increasingly competitive and kids are being taught to win at all costs, rather than develop skills and good sportsmanship. Neither team had issued a single intentional walk the entire season. Bob Cook, "When Youth Baseball Goes

I agree with the coach, though with some qualification. I've coached youth baseball at this level and others. At higher levels, the games become competitive in the sense that the score is kept. At lower levels, the score is not kept. These levels are separated by ability, not just age, so that older children with less-developed skills might play in a noncompetitive league, while more-skilled younger children might play in a competitive league.

Once the score is kept, coaching strategy matters.[3] The kids with the best arms do most of the pitching; the best fielders play infield; the weaker hitters are placed toward the bottom of the lineup and are rotated in the outfield. In a routine game at this very young level, players will rotate so frequently that most kids get a decent chance to play most positions and in roughly equal measure. But this was the championship game. If the league didn't want competitive games, why was it awarding a championship? When I coached a nine- to ten-year-old team, I usually rotated players all over the field. But some players with specific skills got to play more of the key positions during the key moments of some games than other players. It's just realistic. Not every kid can pitch a baseball for a strike, and no one enjoys a "walkathon," least of all the players. When the final game came along and we found ourselves playing the team with which we were tied for first place, I changed my strategy. Instead of my usual rotations, with most kids pitching just an inning each and playing all over the field, I chose my two

---

Bad—Really Bad," (August 11, 2006) *MSNBC Online.* http://www.msnbc. msn.com/id/14295832.

3. Team sports other than baseball have coaching decisions that are similar to baseball's intentional walk; they constitute an intentional coaching move that can take advantage of an opposing team's weaker player. In basketball, purposely fouling a poor free throw shooter takes advantage of a weakness which may result in a change of possession. In football, coaches call plays to have the quarterback throw a pass at the receiver covered by the opponent's poorest secondary defender. In hockey, a coach may juggle lines in the hope of putting his best line against the opponent's weakest.

best pitchers, each for three innings, arranged my lineup to group the best hitters at the top, and rotated the less-skilled players in the outfield. The opposing coach did the same. And we won, narrowly, and my players piled all over each other in celebration. Parents can pretend it's all non-competitive and claim only the coaches care about winning and can call these volunteer coaches jackasses, and so forth. However in my coaching experience, kids always know the score. It seems as if the parents who don't contribute are the first to call the coaches names.[4]

So I support the coach's decision, but with an important qualification: I would never order a batter intentionally walked in a youth game. One of my teams was once beaten in a key divisional game by the third home-run by a batter we couldn't get out. I had the chance to order an intentional walk. One of my coaches even suggested the walk, but I wanted our pitcher to challenge the batter and learn from the encounter. With that said, I've seen other managers order walks, and I completely support their decision to

----

4. Extreme recent actions by parents have resulted in violence, including fights with other parents and attacks on referees. This behavior fuels and encourages the increasingly competitive atmosphere of youth sports. We obsess over children finding early success in sports, especially as young athletes have made their way into the spotlight. The success of Tiger Woods, Lebron James, and Michelle Wie has caused parents to become emotionally involved in their child's athletics, forcing their kids into more competitive situations at an early age. Jane Weaver, "Being a Good Sports Parent," (April 14, 2004) *MSNBC Online.* http://www.msnbc.msn.com/id/4556244/.

An old wisdom is that parents mistakenly "relive" their childhood through their children's success in sports. What seems more prevalent today is nothing more than a parent's understandable desire to see his child succeed. Unfortunately, the valuable college scholarship, so often mentioned by parents desperately confronting the future prospect of daunting educational expenses, translates into pressure on the child athlete that is potentially debilitating to the child's performance and enjoyment of a sport. Many times I have heard a child tell me of a dream to get a college athletic scholarship. Somehow I sense that dream did not originate in the mind of the ten-year-old. Kids dream about skipping school.

do so. It's not a moral decision; it's a baseball decision that is made by balancing the team's goal of winning with the individual player's need to develop and improve. Sometimes you let the player swing on three balls and no strikes, and sometimes you do not. It's a baseball decision.

Winning games is considered bad form by some people. They're wrong; winning is a good thing. It's the best goal for the team, because it alone teaches players the importance of sublimating their personal needs for the good of the whole. Every child I've ever coached profited from trying to win. Kids always want more for themselves: part-time players want to play full-time; outfielders want to play infield; infielders want to catch; catchers want to pitch; and the pitchers want to pitch more. Without the goal of winning, why shouldn't every kid get to take turns at pitching, just throwing ball after ball until the league-limit of runs is walked home? The team goal of winning explains to children why, at this point in their development, their talents are needed elsewhere, and that the best thing for the group is that another child plays that position. It's a hard lesson but an important one. In my experience, kids easily perceive why their role on the team is what it is; it's the parents who just can't understand, no matter how patiently it's explained to them, why their little Junior doesn't get to play instead of that other boy.[5]

I don't know all the details of this game where the coach ordered the walk. I wonder, if the league was competitive, why a kid who

---

5. Some parents who perceive that their child is not getting enough playing time have more frequently opted to enroll their child in several youth teams, as opposed to just one. As a result of this, doctors have seen more frequent sports related injuries. In particular, youth pitchers have incurred arm injuries after pitching in multiple leagues without giving their arm the proper time for recovery. In an effort to combat this trend, Little League Baseball is testing out a pitch count that would limit the number of pitches per day a player can throw. For example, kids ages 10 and under are limited to 75 pitches per day. "Little League Looking at Pitch Count." 10 August, 2006. *MSNBC Online.* http://www.msnbc.msn.com/id/14293264/.

had been described as a recovering but still-weakened cancer patient
was allowed to participate. Was there no noncompetitive alternative for him? Further, why was he batting right after the team's best
hitter, nearly inviting the intentional walk strategy? Some youth
sports leagues want it both ways. They want to be egalitarian by
letting every kid play regardless of skills, while at the same time
they are making the games competitive. Someone's going to get
hurt; in this case, perhaps someone did. Maybe it was the player,
first stricken by cancer and then by the embarrassment of striking
out in a championship game. Or maybe it was the coach, surprised
to find that his seemingly innocuous decision in a Little League
baseball game brought him national condemnation.

Gunners

Owning a firearm helps prevent attacks; at least that's one doc-
umented position in the enduring gun-control debate.[6] Of course
all conclusions are provisional, but it seems obvious why many professional athletes would want to be armed when they mingle with
the general public.[7] These athletes are very wealthy young men and

---

6. John Lott, in *More Guns, Less Crime*, various journal articles and
many popular newspaper editorials, has made a statistical and anecdotal
case detailing the significance of firearms for self-defense. Lott's primary
evidence is that states with the largest increases in gun ownership have
also experienced the largest decreases in violent crimes. "Shall-issue" laws
have been passed by 31 states, guaranteeing any adult citizen, who does not
have a criminal record or history of serious mental illness, the right to
carry a concealed hand gun. Lott provided two reasons why the rate of
violent crimes decreases: first, criminals are uncertain whether potential
victims can defend themselves, and second, those who have guns can better defend themselves in the event of an attack. "An Interview with John
R. Lott, Jr." 1998. *University of Chicago Press.* http://www.press.uchicago.edu/
Misc/Chicago/493636.html.

7. At least one former player disputes the need for prominent athletes
to carry firearms. Karl Malone, former Utah Jazz star, asserts that athletes

women, often easily recognizable, and in many cases come from and occasionally return to high-crime neighborhoods. Threats such as robbery or assault to their person become real possibilities. Although the choice is personal, an athlete's decision to carry a weapon for self-defense makes sense. Indeed, when more athletes carry guns and when more thieves expect them to be armed, then perhaps all athletes will be safer.

But just because the decision to carry a firearm for self-defense is a plausible choice for people who are at risk doesn't mean every athlete's conduct with a firearm is defensible. I don't know all the facts, but it sounds like basketball star Stephen Jackson went a little wild (again), firing shots into the city air. Former NBA player Jayson Williams played with his rifle once at his home and someone ended up dead. Firearms are no joke; they demand care, responsibility, and mature behavior. Not every young person, athlete or not, should carry a firearm.

People have to make judgments about such things. Guns can be acquired (with some effort) and are easy to use. In the right hands, a firearm can thwart an attack. In the wrong hands, guns can cause problems. Determining whose hands are "right" and "wrong" is not a matter of training or expertise. It's a matter of emotional control and careful judgment. Licensure or training can't teach control and judgment. Professional athletes generally intend to be law-abiding citizens. Most do not purchase firearms in order to commit crimes. Still, some athletes will make the wrong decision or, in moments of stress, will not exhibit the control they thought they would when they made the decision to purchase. Wrong decisions with guns happen, just like many decisions prove to be wrong.

Of course, the alternative to an athlete's packing heat is to hire someone else to do it for him. I've always thought that's the func-

---

can avoid trouble by not visiting dangerous areas. Berko, Delsohn, and Rovegno. "Athletes and Guns: Armed… Dangerous?" 13 January, 2007. *ABC News Online.* http://abcnews.go.com/Sports/story?id=2792928&page=1.

tion of the "entourage" or "posse" that accompanies many athletes. Entourages often get a bad name, unjustly in my view.

Some professional athletes like to wear expensive, very noticeable jewelry: "bling." This trait is not limited to African-American athletes, of course, although some (such as Deion Sanders) appear to have brought this fashion style to public prominence.[8] These are very wealthy young people, and it is a legal and legitimate decision to express their wealth and success by appearing in public adorned with expensive jewels. It may be correct that, in certain situations, sporting valuable jewels is "asking for it," as many said with respect to the recent robbery of Sebastian Telfair's $50,000 necklace. But "he asked for it" has never been a defense to criminal liability. (It is often a defense to tort liability, which for the most part regulates unintentionally wrong conduct.) We may be foolish, but we're free to walk the most dangerous parks and streets in the city and expect to travel free from criminal theft. It's the criminals who act wrongly, not the athletes.

Athletes are not dumb. They understand that walking around with such adornments will draw the interest of thieves. Athletes might (and probably often do) remain in gated subdivisions and frequent high-end restaurants, where the risk of street crime tends

---

8. Some people, including Frank Deford, argue that athletes have gone overboard with the jewelry, cherishing these objects over the actual accomplishment of winning. The championship ring allows athletes to "literally wear victory." Deford, Frank. "Gem Dandies." 28 March 2002. *Sports Illustrated Online.* http://sportsillustrated.cnn.com/inside_game/frank_deford/news/2002/03/28/viewpoint/. Of course, professional athletes are not the only ones who express their affluence via personal possessions; it seems that displaying these status symbols is a trend. For example, many companies make their logos part of the product, such as a symbol on a shirt, initials on the side of sunglasses, and initials on the fabric of a designer bag. These symbols are easily visible to others and convey a certain message of status. With this obsession with status being more of a societal trend, is it fair to criticize professional athletes for doing the same? Are they any different from affluent actors or business people who flaunt their wealth through expensive accessories, cars, jets, giant houses, and so forth?

to be comparatively small. However, athletes whose success draws them away from the neighborhoods of their youth are sometimes criticized for ignoring their former neighbors, while those who remain visible in their former neighborhoods are praised. In many instances, these former neighborhoods are more dangerous, yet athletes are pressured to frequent them. When they do, they'll want to show evidence of their success, just like anyone wants to show success on returning to one's old haunts. Bling shows success.

Although athletes are conspicuous and wealthy (with bling) and thus subject to a heightened level of danger from thieves, they're not under serious, constant threat. For most athletes, there is no need for a professional staff of bodyguards. Hiring a bunch of pals from one's youth to hang around and look mean sounds like a good alternative to hiring a full-time security staff and carrying a firearm. A posse is more expensive than a firearm, but probably more effective in deterring attacks. Plus, it's better and cheaper than full-time professionals: one's company for the endless hours an athlete hangs around at home and on the road will consist of buddies, not silent professionals looking for threats that aren't near. When the athlete does venture out into the night, his pals (or entourage or posse) might create the image of a gang, the threat of implicit violence that some might find off-putting or even menacing. But that's the point of the entourage: a little menace and a few large men in the prime of their young adulthood probably go a long way in keeping the peace. Before condemning entourages, consider the alternatives.

Sebastian Telfair is reputedly one of the NBA stars who does have an entourage. It bears mentioning that on the night his necklace was snatched off his neck, he was out with only his fiancée and without a gun.

Banning Sports from Schools

We sometimes forget that the wide world of sports includes a lot more than organized leagues or tournaments in traditional American team games. My favorite sport as a kid? The perennial recess game: "Kill the Man With the Ball." Here are the rules: find a ball, any size. One guy gets it while everyone else chases him until he's tackled or fumbles. If tackled, he has to toss the ball away until the next player grabs it and starts his run. No winners or losers, no score, just a fun way to spend twenty minutes until class resumed.

I doubt one would witness a game of "Kill" on a school recess playground anywhere in contemporary America, or even any game close to it. I'm a little alarmed to find out that so many elementary schools have banned most playground games like tag, freeze tag, red-light/green-light, dodgeball and presumably, my favorite game too.[9] One district even banned running during recess. According to school officials, these games and activities have been banned in the interest of child well-being and safety. Of course this is bunk, and school administrators know it.

Virtually all activities carry risk. We participate in them nonetheless because of off-setting benefits. It's risky to drive a car. It's even riskier to drive fast and on crowded streets. Still, we all are willing to drive during rush hour (and drive at the speed limit) because it's worth the risk to get to work on time. For school administrators to ban tag on the grounds of its risk is to act without really giving any reason; this insults those of us who deserve and demand reasons. No activity should be banned simply because it's risky; activities should be banned because the risk exceeds the benefit. Can school administrators honestly say they've determined, in some plausible way, that the risk of simple, childhood games exceeds their benefits in terms of improved health, weight control, fun, relaxation, and revitalization?

---

9. Just for the record, according to the National Electronic Injury Surveillance System, dodge ball accounts for far fewer injuries than football, baseball or golf. Fisher, Marc. "Skittish Schools Need to Take a Recess." 24 November 2003. http://www.spokesmanreview.com/breaking/story.asp?ID=1166.

The irony is that school children are allowed to play rough, contact games, albeit under adult supervision, by participating in an organized sport. What does this accomplish? Are we to presume kids are less likely to get hurt just because an adult "coach" (just a volunteer parent, really) is standing nearby, perhaps no closer than would be the teacher assigned to recess? In my experience, coaches often push kids to play sports in a more aggressive manner than they would if left to their own devices. Yes, kids in organized sports will get to wear appropriate gear. But still, tackling another human being or charging into him as one drives for a lay-up is rough contact. (In fact, some of the gear players wear, such as a hard football helmet, tends to make the blow more severe.) Contact sports can be rough. Kids know this, which is why some of them shy away from contact sports, both at recess and in organized leagues. Yet the ban on recess sports only pushes children interested in athletic play toward organized sports, if they pursue their interest at all.

Redirecting children to adult-dominated organized sports further infantilizes these kids, retarding their development. It takes some skill to organize and maintain a fair pickup game of basketball, tag, or touch football. This is a valuable social leadership skill that our children need to develop along with their mental and physical abilities. Organized sports take opportunities for such learning away from the children. Don't get me wrong: organized sports have lots of virtues. But they cannot and should not constitute the entirety of our children's sports activities.

Some of these benighted school officials have claimed it's the fear of litigation and liability that has made them into playground bullies. Sorry, don't blame the insurance companies on this one. Schools are insured for injuries on the premises. Have insurance agents told these schools that they will not write insurance if children are allowed to run or play tag? I'd like to see some evidence. At worst, some insurer might tell a school that the rates will increase if tag is permitted. Okay, how much? Isn't some increase worth it? All school functions, all building and maintenance, all teachers and all programs cost money. Just because additional insurance costs money is not a reason not to buy it; the question is what is gained. I'd suggest that with playground recess games, much is gained.

Don't blame the lawyers either. Non-lawyers have a pronounced phobia about litigation. Even some lawyers who don't spend much time in a courtroom (instead spending their time advising school boards, apparently) often have an irrational fear of litigation. I know litigation can be expensive. But there's no avoiding litigation entirely; if you choose to run a place of public accommodation (like schools), at some point someone will sue you. Just because someone sues doesn't mean that someone will win. Let's be realistic here. Let someone sue over injuries from tag, and we'll see who wins. Over the run of cases, I'd bet on the schools.

The real reason school administrators ban tag has nothing to do with child safety, offsetting benefits, lawyers or insurance rates. It's because school administrators want to make their job easier. They don't want to deal with complaining parents who sit in their office and threaten lawsuits (when the reality is that these parents are as far away from filing a successful federal lawsuit as I am from starting in center field for the Red Sox). Rather than deal with a problem, these administrators would prefer to ban the activity and ignore the best interests of the great majority of kids. I once witnessed a kid who one day got hurt (just a bruise) during the recess game of soccer; the next day, his parents complained to the principal; the following day, soccer was banned for recess at that school, a ban that continues to this day. See? No lawyers, no insurance agent, no consideration of costs or benefits. Just ban it, because then the administrator doesn't have to deal with it.

So what should kids do during recess? Maybe mope around in the corner of the playground and try drugs?

Tim Hardaway and the Language of Rights

Tim Hardaway's remarks about his dislike for homosexuals and the popular media and NBA's reaction to it provide a lesson for us all.[10] Unfortunately, the chief lesson it illustrates is not the one most people are drawing. The common lesson is that Hardaway's comments show continuing hostility by athletes toward gays, particularly in some of the more vigorous team sports. To a lawyer interested in sports, however, the lessons are a little more elaborate.

Part of Hardaway's problem is that he believed it when someone told him that Americans enjoy a right to free speech. Maybe some high school teacher read it in a textbook and repeated it to the class. But no competent lawyer would ever so advise a client. Speech is not free, not in the eyes of the law. A person's speech can result in his paying compensatory damages for any harm his words cause. Even punitive damages or a term of imprisonment can result from one's exercise of his speech rights. All for mere words. Politicians and news commentators shed tears over the right to free speech, but really they're referring to a legal standard that they may well not understand.

Indeed, lawyers seldom use terms like "right"; it's inexact and

10. From 1990 through 2003, Tim Hardaway played for five NBA teams and was a five-time All-Star. While on a radio show after his retirement, Hardaway was asked how he would deal with a gay teammate or accept an active player's "coming out." He responded by stating that he would not want that person on his team, did not think homosexuality was right, would distance himself from a gay player, and that the player should not be allowed in the locker room at the same time as the other players. As a result, David Stern, the NBA commissioner, refused to allow Hardaway to attend the All-Star weekend festivities in Las Vegas. Stern felt it was "inappropriate for him to be representing [the NBA] given the disparity between his views and [those of the NBA]." Later, Hardaway apologized for his comments and any harm they caused. "Retired NBA Star Hardaway Says He Hates 'Gay People'." 16 February 2007. *ESPN Online.* http://sports.espn.go.com/nba/news/story?id=2766213.

not very helpful. All the "free speech" part of the First Amendment means in legal terms, which may be all it means in any terms, is "no prior restraint." In other words, what the amendment actually prohibits is the imposition of an injunction against the making of speech. (And even injunctions can be disobeyed, if one is willing to pay the price in contempt.) So that's it. All the "free speech" talk is belied by the legal reality that the sole legal effect of the First Amendment's clause is to eliminate one remedy from the menu of remedies available to a judge responding to unacceptable speech. Dry your eyes, everybody; there is no right to free speech, not one worth mentioning, not in legal terms.[11]

So the free speech protection is of very little value, legally speaking. It is, instead, ultimately a political term. Its place in the constitution and its veneration over the generations has raised "free speech" into the American collective perspective. It's a motto more than a legal term of art. That's not to say it's unimportant. The motto helps create room for toleration of each other's opinions, helps to create a culture of skeptical inquiry and intellectual honesty, and helps to send soldiers off to war with something in mind worth fighting for. Law is stingy. The right to free speech is culture and politics, not law.

The politics have changed. The cultural support for speech is disintegrating. The unspoken latitude which we allowed each other, within the ample margins of free speech, has given way to a narrowness of mind, which polices the tight borders and boundaries

---

11. Ironically, the one legal remedy a potential speaker might actually want a court to impose is the injunction, the very remedy the First Amendment precludes! The injunction stops the speaker before he puts his foot in his mouth. Wouldn't it be nice to know ahead of time if the speech one plans to make will subject oneself to punitive damages, for example, which are specifically designed to punish one so severely that he never speaks such words again? Gee, judge, couldn't you let me know ahead of time? "No," say our wise judges, putting their fingers on the First Amendment. "Go ahead and speak freely, and we'll bankrupt you or imprison you later on. It's in the Constitution."

of writings, conversations, and even thought itself. It's not a pretty sight. The call for tolerance is by those who won't tolerate dissenting, even hateful, perspectives. Tim Hardaway could spend the rest of his life building hospitals for sick children, yet his negative comments about having a hypothetical homosexual teammate will be repeated in his obituary. We live in dark times where free speech seems reduced to its bare legal requirements and no further. Soldiers won't go into battle to prevent trial judges from ordering injunctions.

Those commentators who say they disagree with Hardaway, yet defend his right to voice his opinion, confound me. If you are defending his right, why do you feel the need to say you disagree with him? Must we all stand up and be counted on this issue just because a former player, looking to sell a book, tells the world he's gay and he used to play in the NBA? If you are defending Hardaway's right to have an opinion, even his right to dislike another person because of that person's lifestyle or sexual orientation or appearance or what have you, then why don't you feel the need to stick microphones in the face of Tiger Woods or Michael Jordan or Curt Schilling and ask them their opinions on controversial political/cultural issues? What does a "right" to an opinion mean (even this extra-legal right I've described), if not the opportunity to hold and, if one wishes, give voice to an odd or even antagonistic opinion and let it be overlooked as what it is, just one man's opinion? The singer for the Dixie Chicks says she hates the President of the United States, and she wins a Grammy.[12] Tim Hardaway expresses his hatred for gays, and he'll be ostracized from the NBA for the rest of his life. Now I like our president, and I like the Dixie Chicks. How do I reconcile myself to the fact that this wonderful singer voiced an opinion I found as dis-

---

12. About three years ago in London, Natalie Maines, the lead singer of the Dixie Chicks, stated that she was ashamed that President Bush was from her home state of Texas. This comment created outrage amongst the Dixie Chick's fan base, causing their songs to drop off the charts and the radio. Maines refused to apologize, and the Dixie Chicks' latest album continues to express these controversial opinions.

agreeable as I found Hardaway's? Free speech. People will say the darnedest things sometimes.

I love how we regularly see Tiger and other stars of the sports world castigated by the media for not using their public platforms to speak out on social issues and political causes. Is the media's hubris boundless? Do they really think all these athletes, just because they seem like nice people with big smiles, agree with them on political questions? This presumptuous worldview assumes, "All nice people agree with me, and only evil people could ever think the opposite." Well, look what happens when one of these athletes, asked to comment on a political issue (here the desirability of a gay teammate) and, thinking this is America, gives voice to his genuine opinion: he hates gays. If Tiger Woods came out tomorrow and preached about saving the whales or whatever, he'd be praised for finally using his platform for public betterment. But if he said, "Please vote against gay marriage," well, I suspect we'd see a slightly different reaction.

So let's give athletes credit for knowing the score. There is no free speech, not in any practical sense, not anymore. There is certainly no free speech practiced in any form that a person like Tim Hardaway would ever enjoy.

Opinions for Sale

Last time I checked, we have a pretty large market economy in this country. We can buy or sell nearly everything, except for certain substances, sexual favors, and other prohibited items. Now comes news that the NBA's Orlando Magic ventured into the free market and bought something strange: an opinion. The team's law firm paid off a local radio talk-show commentator of some influence basically to preclude his presumed opposition to the construction of a new basketball venue. The team has acknowledged its payment, claiming it did so on the advice of counsel. I might add that it was a lot of money, around $200,000. So is there a problem with buying and selling an opinion? Lots of huffing, puffing and hand-wringing from central Florida: scandal brewing, law firm firings, Magic embarrassment, talk of legal reforms. Should we treat opinions like cocaine and ban their trafficking?

Opinions should not be on the list of banned substances. Lots of people sell their opinions, in the sense that they sell the *contents* of their opinions. Lawyers come to mind, when they represent a client. So do publicists, media representatives, lobbyists, salespeople and spokespeople of all kinds. Of course, there's a sense that when a representative of certain interests shows up at your door, you know he's being paid to give an opinion that favors that certain perspective. With politicians, we hope that the horse comes before the cart and that money follows opinions (and votes), rather than preceding it. I guess nowadays we rely on disclosure and let voters make up their own minds. Regardless, the point is that lots of people sell their opinions, so it looks like there is an American market for them.

Mandatory disclosure, proposed by some, is not the answer. Orlando's payment was merely to a commentator/activist who had a platform. A rule requiring disclosure would potentially include a lot of people. At what point does someone go from "concerned citizen" to "part-time commentator" to a regulated "political activist" subject to mandatory disclosure? Would we require people to be licensed (to trigger regulation) to offer political commentary or lead grass-roots voting campaigns?

Consumers of political opinions should assume that commentators are supported by somebody or some interests. They have to make a living, and if your product is opinions then you'd better find a buyer. It shouldn't matter if the payment arrives before the opinion is offered. Yes, it would be nice (and more seemly) if commentators made their sources of support known, much like law professors do, as a matter of professional courtesy and good manners, so that the reader can discount the speaker's opinions to the extent the reader deems appropriate. But it's not a big deal: thoughtful, informative opinions remain so no matter by whom or how much the speaker is paid.

With that said, the NBA or other leagues could preclude their teams from paying these "opinion bribes." The fact that the leagues do not have this prohibition shows that the leagues understand the importance of public support for the construction of stadia and the vital importance of stadium revenues to the financial success of professional sports. But here's the rub: more than ever in our history, governmental policy is effectively made by non-governmental actors. Radio commentators, grass-roots activists, and interest group members, when combined with modern "direct democracy" measures (such as initiatives, ballot measures, proposition voting, and state constitutional amending) together make policy while circumventing traditional governmental institutions. Notable radio personalities can have more influence over state-wide policy than certain elected officials, who are cabined in by the need to work within committee structures, bicameral legislatures, gubernatorial oversight, administrative bureaucracy, and so forth. I'm not saying private political actors should be regulated. But I do wonder how the NBA feels about the Magic's conduct.

If it succeeds, the Magic's "opinion bribe" hurts the voters. The bribe keeps one influential opinion-shaper on the sidelines, and thus keeps certain information or perspectives from the public consideration (assuming the Magic spent its money wisely). The bribe benefits the Magic and indirectly, the whole league. But it also poisons the well for the next time a professional team asks its locals for tax or bond support for a new stadium venue. It's a question of costs and benefits, but I'd think the leagues would not want teams damaging the league's reputation for their own gain.

Scandal Exposed: Helpless Babies Redshirted

In a shocking revelation, TSLP[13] has learned that certain parents, mimicking the college practice of "red-shirting" players to ex-

---

13. My blog alter ego, "The Sports Law Professor," or "TSLP." It's fun to have an alter ego and to form that "person's" fictitious personality. Un-

tend their athletic eligibility, have been red-shirting their children.[14] Yes, just like Peter Pan, certain selected American children can stay young forever, or at least for one additional year. Here's what I've learned: parents have been holding their children back at the start of the child's schooling. What they get from this plan or scheme is a child who is over-age for his grade, and who thus enjoys a mental and physical development greater than his right-age school chums. Why do parents do this? They want an advantage for their child in youth sports.

My sources? Many quiet conversations on the sidelines during numerous youth sports contests. "Gee," TSLP might wonder aloud to the proud parent screaming at the referee, "your child is just amazingly large. I've never seen a twelve-year old with facial hair!" Of course a moment's inquiry reveals the young stallion is a year or even a year and one-half older than the fearful competitors running from his shadow. How wrong is this?

Ever since college (Catholic school) I've tried to forget Kant, but man, what if everybody operated on this ethical principle, the one that says I'm going to cheat to get ahead? Yes, holding your kid back for athletic advantage is cheating. There's a reason sports are generally organized by grade: it's to make sure kids are playing against competitors roughly equal in size, musculature, and coordination.

---

like me, TSLP is cranky, bewildered, and shocked by all around him. (I, on the other hand, am a suave citizen of the world). I left in the text the playful TSLP internet banter where I thought it made some contribution to the meaning of the essay.

14. Commonly used by colleges, "redshirting" is the practice of keeping players out of games to allow them an extra year of eligibility. This practice is also common with children who are socially or physically immature compared to other children. The first year of schooling is important in a child's development, and for some kids, waiting a year before entering a child in kindergarten can provide the child with the chance to reach a higher level of development. Elson, John. "The Redshirt Solution." *Time Magazine Online.* http://www.time.com/time/magazine/article/0,9171,959029,00.html?promoid=googlep.

Of course there will be occasional and random natural variations within a single age group. But there is almost guaranteed variation when older kids are playing against younger kids, and it's all in one direction. If every parent held his student back a year then the cheating parents would have to hold their young scholar back two. One day, middle-schoolers will be able to drive themselves to practice.

I've personally witnessed a middle school basketball team where the entire starting lineup consisted of boys who should have been in the next grade. I knew this because the team roster listed their birth dates. Even a year's difference can produce obvious physical differences, especially in pre-pubescent males. How is this any different from Danny Almonte, the boy who lied about his age, throwing no-hitters against younger boys in Little League competition? Yes, unlike Little League, the schools allow parents to hold back their child. All the parent has to say is that his child needs the extra year for "social development" or what have you and it's done. Yes, of course some kids might legitimately need delay. But let's not fool ourselves: in many cases, these parents are not looking at the little apple of their eye and saying that my little darling seems somewhat slow or unusually shy or something. No, these parents are looking at their little precocious offspring and marveling at his coordination and saying, "Hey, let's hold our little LeBron back a year so there will be no question he'll dominate play!"

I know of parents (more than one set) who told me just months after their child was born that they planned to hold their child back. Quick diagnosis of developmental deficits? No. Quickly formed desire to raise a high-school sports star.[15]

---

15. Many parents make the decision to hold their children back to provide them an advantage when it comes to sports because they think that would have been beneficial to them when they were a child. In addition, some parents think this will provide their kids with a greater chance to secure a college scholarship. Haas, Rebekah. "Red Shirting." 23 February 2007. *Associated Content.* http://www.associatedcontent.com/article/152514/redshirting_examining_the_new_trend.html.

In some sports children are allowed to "play up," which means join a league consisting of older children in a higher grade. Some of these kids whose parents tell me (and everybody) that their child is playing up are the same parents who held this same kid back a grade. The story is all about how well this under-grade child is doing playing up, against the older kids (you know, the ones his age). Of course, the higher-grade league is full of other kids playing up. And the older kids who are actually in that higher grade? The best ones are in an even higher league, playing way up. So kids who play up aren't, really.

Are these parents proud when their older, bigger kids outplay younger children? Or slightly embarrassed? Redshirting is wrong, at least in this sense: schools create a rule on class assignments based on birth dates, then ignore their rule in favor of those "sports-minded" parents who are in the know and who delay their child's entry in order to gain social, academic, and athletic advantages. Parents who follow the rules are left at a disadvantage and correctly feel they've been duped. If the "real rule" is that kids with spring or summer birthdays get delayed, then schools should announce that rule so everyone's on the same page. What astonishes me is that so many of us get caught up in the grade, not the age, when assessing an athlete's precociousness. We say, "Wow, he's so good and only a freshman," when we should say, "He's good, as we would expect of a rising junior." The common assumption is that grade is commensurable with a certain age; apparently the common practice of sports-minded parents is not widely known.[16]

---

16. One reader sent me the following examples: *O. J. Mayo*—The 19-year-old high schooler, born within a week of 2nd year NBA player Andrew Bynum, received national publicity for playing varsity as a 14-year-old 7th grader. If he was in 9th grade I don't think he'd get the publicity.

Tyler Hansbrough—The North Carolina basketball sophomore was 21 and received kudos for being so good when so "young". He also won an AAU 10-and-under national championship when he was nearly 12.

John David Booty—The USC quarterback got publicity for leaving high

Schools need to set birthday regulations for grades (they have) and then enforce them (they don't, not any more). Or they should at least organize the sporting contests according to age, not grade. If that were done, and 14-year-olds couldn't compete against children still in their 12th year, then I bet suddenly little Junior wouldn't appear so developmentally delayed to mom and dad. He'd get to school on time.

---

school a year "early" to go to USC. In fact, he was 18.5 years old his junior year because he'd redshirted 5th grade to get ahead in football.

Chapter Two

Money in Sports

Thank goodness for money. Some people think that money corrupts all it touches. Most think that money has corrupted sports. They have in mind some idealized version of sports that existed, if it ever did, in some glorious yesteryear. But money isn't bad; it just represents value and has the particular propensity to translate itself into things that we want. Many things provide value, including comfort, health, fame, approval, affinity, education, and achievement. All of these values motivate human beings to obtain them simply because they are valuables; all of us pursue valuables most of the time we're awake. What's nice about money is that it allows us to pursue all of these valuables indirectly: just pile up the money and later on purchase as best you can the means of acquiring the valuables you want, in the desired quantity. Money unites us and helps translate all our varied desires for valuables into a uniform substance.

Money quantifies, and quantification simplifies. Without money, interpersonal comparisons of utility or desire become impossible. Who's to say that my immediate desire for a cheeseburger is greater or less than your desire for life-saving surgery? Of course the latter object is salient and the former trivial, but we just don't know and can't say conclusively that your desire is stronger than mine. (I really want a cheeseburger, I might mention.) But money lets us talk. If the choice were to take our taxi to a fast-food stand or to the emergency room, then the dilemma can be solved, at least well enough to move on. The cheeseburger person would likely be outbid by the ill person.[1] Reducing desires to a sum certain, a quantified bid that represents some estimate of personal desire and value, allows for more plausible comparisons of personal values. It allows two people to compete for a good along a single dimension, and allows the third person, (here, the cab driver), to consider the value of money to him as well.

Far from corrupting sports, money cleanses it. It puts all the players and other participants on the same playing field, no matter their personal tastes in valuables. Its fluid translation into whatever we want (to the extent that money can be exchanged for what we want) allows owners to accord value along a single dimension. The better player will be given more money, thus rewarding his excellence and creating incentives for others to achieve it. Money makes things clear. Rather than worry about the motivation or commitment or desire of an athlete, one can provide that incentive directly, for all to see.

Yet the very fluidity of money makes it susceptible to manipulation. The only problem with money isn't in paying it; it's in hiding it. Bring the financial relationships out in the open, and we can all assess incentives and behavioral responses and adjust accordingly. But hide the money behind a veil of double-talk and confusion, and the rest of us are left guessing. This chapter looks to take some of the guess-work out of the money issues in contemporary sports.

Should Taxpayers Receive Preferences?

More than ever the rosters of the football teams of major state universities consist of players from outside the state. On the bas-

---

1. Or maybe not. The love of a cheeseburger could be so great that the hungry person would outbid the dying one. But ordinarily we wouldn't expect that to happen; the ill person would bankrupt himself to get to the hospital, while the hungry person, with ample choices and time, can get his meal a little later, and so would likely pay comparatively little to redirect the taxi. Money allows us to put a price on things, and putting a price on things helps us compare the extent to which my desire for one good exceeds your desire for something else.

ketball side, and even more in other sports such as tennis and track, the rosters also include (sometimes predominately) students from outside the country. Should state taxpayers, the ones for whose benefit the university exists and on whose support the university relies for its continuance, have anything to say about this? Should a local athlete from among the state's taxpayers be accorded a preference, and perhaps a large one, in the allocation of precious athletic scholarships?

One perspective is that a roster dominated by out-of-state students is a good thing for the university. It enhances the geographic diversity of the student body, helps the school to advertise its national appeal and prominence, and places the athletic program in particular as competitive among top national powerhouses. Plus the team wins.

How might the state taxpayers feel about this? Some might be pleased, for the reasons mentioned above but also because they want their state team to win games and compete for national rankings. Change the description from "out-of-state" players to "out-of-country" and even ardent university boosters might hesitate. Do U.S. taxpayers want their tax-supported universities to award precious scholarships to athletes from foreign countries, instead of to the children of the taxpayers (generally speaking) who made the scholarships possible?

Is winning all that important, especially in sports other than basketball or football? Coaches clearly feel the pressure to win. Students from foreign countries can, particularly in certain sports such as basketball, track, golf and tennis, improve teams a great deal. College tennis in particular has come to be dominated by foreign-born scholarship athletes. Should we care? Is the purpose of the tennis team at the state college to win matches? Or is it to provide a place for U.S.-born college students who are very good in tennis to play tennis? It is common knowledge that foreign competition has rendered tennis scholarships significantly inaccessible to U.S.

tennis players. Should scholarships funded domestically be awarded preferentially to domestic athletes?

Foreign-born students also enhance a school's diversity, allow for claims of global standing by the university, and can be very deserving scholarship recipients, at least if "deserving" is defined to include comparative indigency, diligence, and achievement. American players might not always have the competitive, even desperate drive that athletes born in more difficult circumstances sometimes exhibit. So perhaps it's correct to say that the foreign-born athlete has earned the scholarship over the U.S.-born competitor. But that's only if the award of the scholarship is determined by "merit" in this simple sense.

That sense of merit is simple only because it assumes that the purpose of the college team is equally simple. If the purpose of the team is to win national competitions, then the scholarship should go to the best player, whatever his country or state of origin. But if the purpose of the college game is to provide young men and women an opportunity for personal growth, educational experience, individual achievement, team cooperation, and so forth — in short, all the sentimental stuff that misty-eyed coaches, athletic department faculty and administrators, and NCAA presidents refer to when they talk about the importance and virtue of the collegiate athletic experience — then the university should restrict the allocation of those scholarships to people who will actualize all that educational value. One important criterion on which state schools do in fact to allocate their beneficence when it comes to academic grants is state citizenship, limiting awards to those who are subject to state taxation and who will likely reside in the state after graduation. So which is it? What is the purpose of college sports?

If college sports are all about winning, then the goal or aim of a college team is no different than that of any professional team. Players should be paid; ideally, we should decouple the terms "student" and "athlete." The decision to force these young people to be both students and athletes simultaneously places incommensurable burdens on both roles. One of the roles gets shortchanged, and of course it's the "student" side of things that falls off. (How can a young student resist an overbearing coach? Instead, the gentler demands of the professor are put to the side.) Inevitably, the academic institution itself is corrupted. This has happened, repeatedly.

The purpose of college sport has to lie in its educational value. For this to happen, state residents should form the primary beneficiaries of state university scholarships, even athletic scholarships. (Not exclusively, of course, as there will always be a handful of deserving athletes from foreign lands.) But if some hotshot football player from Florida has a scholarship offer from a Florida school, then why should the state school in West Virginia bypass a local kid who's spent his youth dreaming of being a Mountaineer in favor of "recruiting" some reluctant Floridian to turn down his Gator offer and come to Morgantown? It's not as if the Floridian will go without the substantial educational benefit of college and college sports. But without the local preference, the West Virginian may.

What would be so wrong with this? Let's see the boys from West Virginia play football against those from other states. I wonder if a state legislature that cares more about its state youth than it does state pride could order the State U to limit some athletic scholarships to state residents. A lot of kids spend their youth practicing their games in the hope of landing an athletic scholarship. Shouldn't rewarding them be more important than fielding the best team?

Saban's Lot and the University Shell Game

Football coach Nick Saban will earn $32 million over the next eight years, not counting additional bonuses for bowl games.[2] He will

---

2. Nick Saban left the Miami Dolphins to coach the University of Alabama's Crimson Tide. He was offered an eight year package worth a guaranteed $32 million, not including an additional $700,000-$800,000 in annual bowl game bonuses. "Saban Embraces High Expectations at Al-

be paid by the University of Alabama, even though the University denies it.

Since the school denies it, exactly who is paying Nick Saban this huge sum? Most critics of the salary assume it is the University and ask why an institution devoted to education should pay what is probably the top public salary in the state to a non-educator. But according to the school, Saban will be paid not by the University, but instead by the athletic department out of the revenues his football team generates. Apparently the president of the University believes that Saban will create sufficient revenue from ticket and memorabilia sales, alumni contributions and the like that the athletic department can pay Saban his $4 million and pocket the difference, or, if there is none, still profit from the publicity and goodwill a successful football program creates.

So who pays the coach, the university or the "football program"? Is it appropriate to view University employees as paid from an entity apart from the University itself?

No. Charitable donors don't prefer to endow bathroom cleaning or sidewalk maintenance or secretarial assistance. Part of charitable giving is feeling good about the gift and being able to identify a worthy destination for the money. Hence gifts go to academic programs, faculty positions, student scholarships, and athletic programs. Schools know this and make those funding opportunities available, using tuition dollars for maintenance and the like. To claim that athletic programs are self-funded, as university websites do, may well be partially true. But the claim hardly tells the full story. What is meant by self-funded? Universities have various components. Those who make money (from tuition or ticket sales) are in a sense self-funded but are (typically) expected to contribute to the university's overhead. Overhead at an institution of higher learn-

abama." 4 January 2007. *ESPN.com.* http://sports.espn.go.com/ncf/news/story?id=2720017.

ing can be substantial, given the need for libraries, common areas, plush faculty lounges, and gymnasia, all of which are non-revenue producing (and so can't be "self-funded"). Often individual components of a university, such as a college, generate sufficient revenues to sustain themselves (were they a stand-alone school) but do not earn enough to sustain themselves and pay their allocated share of university overhead. Earnings from the university's endowment (that is, from the money donated by charitably minded philanthropists and alumni) make up the difference. Donations are sought for scholarships, buildings, and programs, and they are used as such. But from an economic perspective, it's equally true to say they're used to pay university overhead.

Once we understand the fluidity of university finances, we can see that a particular university can designate whatever components of the university it wishes as "self-funding." If it is clever, the university will designate that program most likely to appeal to donors as the program that depends entirely on the gifts of those donors, in order to present the most sympathetic object for their charitable impulse. This is not cynicism; it's just part of the big business of charitable donations. We all can give money to feed the poor, but of course some of our dollars (either directly or indirectly) pay for the advertisement that brought the plight of the poor to our attention.

From a practical perspective, it's nonsensical to justify the salary to be paid to Nick Saban on the grounds that the football program at Alabama stands apart from the University in any meaningful sense. (I think the NCAA would have a problem with a program that truly was not under the direction and control of a university.) Separating the football program is just a shell game without economic reality.

Malcolm Gladwell's *New Yorker* article on Enron[3] is one of the best non-lawyer pieces I've seen on the scandal. He describes what

---

3. Malcolm Gladwell, "Enron, Intelligence, and the Perils of Too Much Information" (*New Yorker*, Jan. 8, 2007).

lawyers have known but the public generally has not: that Enron's practice of sloughing off undesirable assets and trade positions into "special purpose entities" that were (fictitiously yet legally) separate and distinct from Enron itself was done to allow lenders to comply with legal lending requirements. In other words, all the accounting tomfoolery and fraud the Enron management concocted had nothing to do with reality. A business can move its assets all around the warehouse, but the economic reality is left unchanged. Part of the cause of the rapid collapse of Enron's stock was the failure of interested observers of Enron (investment professionals and others) to separate the fictional shell game from the economic reality. The reality was that Enron was broke, no matter how it structured its assets. The reality is that the University of Alabama will pay Nick Saban.

With that said, it may well be that Nick Saban is not overpaid once the revenue he will generate is taken into account. I doubt Saban's marginal revenue product will be that much (in other words, I doubt even a successful coach will add that much additional revenue to the athletic coffers), but that's for the University of Alabama to figure out. If the school is correct, Saban is worth it. The University will profit. But is profitability the correct criterion for university decisions? Just as Alabama may profit from Saban's contract, so another school might profit from allocating its athletic scholarships to international student athletes who might better produce winning teams. But what about the local kid whose family's taxes have contributed to supporting the university all these years? Is the answer, once again, that the athletic department stands alone, as if it were a separate, profit-making enterprise that gets to eat what it kills? Does it make any sense to say that the taxes of the local kid's family went to overhead, to pay for new toilets and replacement light bulbs, so that the kid has no claim for preference in the allocation of that scholarship?

I understand the positioning of athletic departments as "self-supported" for fundraising purposes. But let's not confuse the shell game with reality. Confusing the fundraising fiction with the reality of university responsibility for and supervision over its athletic department will lead to sloppy thinking and mistakes. It will lead us to conclude that the "owners" of a state school should have nothing to say over how the "independent" football team pays its coaches or to whom it awards its scholarships. The mechanisms for taxpayer control may not work well, and the university administration or even the legislature may be effectively captured by the athletic department and its supporters. Nonetheless, the taxpayers ultimately should feel free to exercise their dominion. They may like things just as they are. On the other hand, some taxpayers may wonder why state athletic scholarships don't often go to state citizens, or why the state locking itself into paying a football coach $4 million a year for eight years is the right thing to do, even if it is profitable. There may be a reason the state established its university as a not-for-profit institution.

Paying College Student-Athletes

It has been reported that Reggie Bush and his family may have benefited financially from Bush's status as a star college football player.[4] The news has brought out the usual cries from reformers

---

4. Reggie Bush and his family allegedly accepted nearly $280,000 in cash, rent, and gifts from various sources while playing for the University of Southern California. The specific allegations include: Agent Michael Ornstein was paying $1,500 a week to the Bush family while Bush was still at Southern Cal; Ornstein and his associate paid for hotel stays and limousine transportation for Bush's family; and clothing company New Era also provided money, paid for hotel stays and let Bush's family stay in a home rent-free. Ornstein acknowledged negotiating deals for Bush during the 2005 season but claimed he was working within NCAA rules because no deal was finalized at the time. "Report: Tapes Could Confirm Bush Received Gifts." *ESPN.com*. 25 January 2007. http://sports.espn.go.com/ncf/news/story?id =2741773. "Reggie Bush Under Scrutiny." *USA Today*. 15 September 2006. http://blogs.usatoday.com/sportsscope/2006/09/reggie_bush_und.html.

who believe college athletes deserve some fair compensation. The NCAA continues to resist, citing the amateurism of what it quaintly terms the "student athlete." I'm not sure how this debate should be resolved, but I am sure that both sides are wrong about their fundamental assumption. The truth is that college athletes are compensated, some extensively, right now.

Most top Division I student athletes in the revenue sports of football and basketball receive a full college scholarship. This is no small benefit; just ask the parent of any teenager. The full athletic scholarship includes tuition, which at higher-end schools can easily surpass $25,000 per year. An athletic scholarship also includes free lodging, often in nicely appointed athletes-only dorms, or otherwise in the university's best dorms or apartments. The athletes get free meals, typically at the "highest level" of today's college meal plans, which are a long way removed from the "mystery meat" specials of yesteryear. Free books, student fees, and the like add the little extras to the package. The total estimated cost to attend the better of the nation's colleges now adds up to over $40,000 per year. That means a college scholarship is worth about $160,000 over a college career, all tax free. That's real value for an 18-year-old whose next best job would, in most cases, start near the minimum wage.

What else do our amateur student-athletes receive? A college degree, or at least a good chance at one. Such a degree (and presumably the knowledge behind it), translates into a lifetime of superior earnings. Particularly for those athletes whose academic potential is modest, a degree from a quality university represents a significant enhancement to expected earnings. These students also receive top-level coaching and training facilities, a consequential benefit to serious athletes. Finally, again for those athletes in one of the two major college sports, football and basketball, college athletics affords them a chance at exposure and stardom. Exposure on the playing field can give athletes some measure of local or national fame, resulting in immense college fun and improved post-college job prospects. More significantly, stardom gives them a tangible chance at the athlete's biggest prize: a lucrative and glamorous post-college career in professional sports. That's a valuable lottery ticket—one so prized that thousands of youth will train countless hours pursuing the dream. Schools that feed athletes to the pros advertise this substantial job benefit to potential recruits.

Do high-schoolers labor for years and compete strenuously against each other for what amounts to unpaid servitudes, as both the NCAA and the reformers seem to believe? Of course not. Athletes see the obvious compensatory elements of college sports, even if the NCAA and the reformers cannot. An athletic scholarship? It's money. Some argue for more.

One argument in favor of paying (more) money to college student-athletes notes that players in basketball and football generate millions of dollars for their respective universities. It concludes that fairness or equity demands that they receive a substantial portion of that revenue.[5]

First, athletes do not alone generate the revenue. Many factors, including stadium design, concessions, alumni associations, and state pride, all contribute to producing sellout crowds and television contracts. With that said, the athletes are clearly the entertainers on the stage, and in other fields it is usually the on-stage performers who receive the largest compensation. But even if we ascribe the lion's share of the total revenue to the athletes, it is not always clear which players actually produce the revenue. For example,

5. Not surprisingly, Reggie Bush is one of the people who believe college athletes should be paid. He suggests that athletes should be compensated based on their performance or equally across the board, seeing as other players on the team could get jealous of a few players getting paid significantly more. Robert Brown, an economics professor from Cal State -San Marcos, has estimated Bush as a collegian was worth at least $500,000 in direct economic impact to the athletic department, and not including indirect revenue effects, such as merchandise sales. Rovell, Darren. "Bush Says Paydays Should Start in College." *ESPN.com.* 24 April 2006. http://sports.espn.go.com/ncf/news/story?id=2419723.

consider a top basketball program, like Duke University's. Duke attracts the finest players each year in part because the athletes from previous seasons created the athletic powerhouse. Basketball stars who enroll at Duke can be assured that their teammates will also be high-level players who can complement them. They can also be assured that they will play in a highly competitive league in front of a national audience. It is the Duke name and tradition, a product of the efforts of past teams, coaches and others that creates that opportunity for the next top high school athlete and assures the continuation of the revenue stream.

If, however, we were to pretend that nothing else matters and that all of this year's revenue was produced by this year's team, even then it would be difficult to say which players produced the revenue. Basketball and football are quintessential team sports, where wins are the product of the joint efforts of teammates. In technical terms, complementarity of inputs is high. A star quarterback is worth little without effective blockers and receivers who can get open; even a decent running game enhances the quarterback's performance indirectly. As a result, it is very difficult to determine a particular player's contribution. If we assume that wins are the product of a top collegiate program, it is difficult to decide how much each player, even star players, matter to the product, at the margin. How many more wins does Player X produce, as compared to his replacement?

Wins in baseball, by contrast, appear to be much less a joint product (less complementarity of inputs). Therefore, if a pro team was to hire the league's best first baseman, best second baseman, and so on, the odds are high it will have a very successful team. To put it another way, the teams with the highest payrolls in Major League Baseball usually are the best teams. (Bet on the Yankees.) In basketball, where teamwork is much more important, the size of the team's payroll is not a good predictor of win totals. (So don't bet on the Knicks, with the league's highest payroll and near-fewest wins.) When pro basketball and football teams are deciding whether or not to sign (or re-sign) a free agent, they struggle mightily to measure the value of a player, and that's despite having years of performance data and even experience in coaching the player. Imagine the difficulty of pricing the marginal product revenue of a 19-year-old college freshman.

My point is not to say that star college athletes don't matter in producing wins and revenue; of course they do. My point is that the claim that "fairness" demands that the team's revenue be distributed to the players is a bit too simple; it avoids consideration of the multiple inputs that produce revenue and also begs the question about exactly what contribution a particular player makes to that revenue. Perhaps a lock-step system that distributes some portion of the revenue to the players equally would work; that is arguably what we have right now.

What is perplexing about the debate over paying college athletes is the common assumption that if athletes were paid a competitive price for their services, their compensation would increase. Proponents of the compensation argument point to the millions of dollars earned from college sports and assume that eliminating the NCAA prohibition against paying athletes would enrich the comparatively impoverished student-athlete. Not necessarily. Let's really apply the clarity of money to college sports. Assume players were allowed to sell their services to college teams in a competitive market. Some would earn a substantial salary, for example the star athlete in a major revenue sport such as basketball. Colleges would bid against each other, and perhaps even the professional leagues, for the player's services. (Even if the player were ineligible for the NBA, he might opt for a year playing in an overseas professional league instead of college ball.) But remember, the star college athlete already in effect receives a substantial salary: in the near future he will be eligible for a professional-level income stream. If necessary, the star could (in our fictionalized free market) borrow against that income while in college, as presumably many players do already, albeit illicitly, as the bling and Escalades so often illustrate. The star can already capitalize on his income potential; the fact that the source of the income is his future professional team and not his one-year alma mater makes no financial difference.

But what about the rest of the players, whose dreams of college stardom and the subsequent pro contract do not materialize? Presently, in most cases, those players are protected from the non-renewal of their scholarship, because the rules of the NCAA and of most schools combine to limit scholarship termination to cases of academic failure, attendance problems, drug abuse and the like. As a result, as long as they adhere to team and university rules, these athletes will get to pursue their degrees and the lifetime income those degrees entail. Coaches can do little about malingerers or others whose talent they misjudged in awarding them a scholarship. (No wonder college coaches are famed for their histrionics and anger: what else can they do to players except yell?) College sidelines are full of scholarship athletes whom coaches would love to cut, but certain rules, prudence, and a desire to recruit next year's stars inhibit them.

Yet in a world in which yearly salary, not scholarships, constitutes the primary means of compensation, coaches might not be as restricted by rule to maintain pay grades. Coaches might over-promise recruits, only to cut their pay when athletic performance does not meet expectations. Certainly reputational fears would slow most college coaches from "bait-and-switch" recruiting; nonetheless, establishing a clear employer-employee relationship between the student-athlete and the school would probably render the player more vulnerable to the vagaries of at-will employment, with the college coach/sideline madman as the boss.

A scholarship package that approximates $40,000 per year in value clearly does cap certain players' earnings; at the same time, it probably over-compensates other players. Is today's lock-step system of compensation wrong (in the fundamental sense that reformers seem to claim it "wrong") because colleges profit while their athletes do not? Lots of employers and unions prefer pay grades and lock-step systems, in part because they help to insulate the employees from the caprice and vindictiveness of the boss. Judging from the inappropriate and immature behavior that is put on display by some of the coaches who roam the sidelines, a little insulation might be needed. Put another way, suppose all entering college athletes were to join to set wages: would they prefer the star system or lock step? Clearly they would want more money (who doesn't?), but the current pay rate appears sufficient to clear the market of suitors. In other words, I don't think we have any problem in our country with an insufficient number of kids trying to earn college athletic scholarships.

If one day the NCAA does allow colleges to compensate players directly, the impetus will probably come from schools who want the ability to out-bid professional teams, and not from those who say that a full college scholarship is not enough.

Give College Athletes Freedom, Not Money

College students may borrow money to pay college expenses. They can also borrow extra, if they choose, from the plethora of credit card offers with which freshman students are inundated. When students borrow, they are borrowing against future earnings. A college degree has value, hence making students a hot target for credit companies. While in college, Reggie Bush happened to have had a large and immediate future earning capacity too, only in his case as a high NFL draft pick and endorsement magnet. As mentioned, according to reports Reggie Bush received upwards of $200,000, directly and indirectly, while in college from professionals seeking his representation. If the NCAA allowed athletes to borrow against their future earnings, athletes could borrow from banks just like the rest of us, without having to turn to agents and the like.

What clouds our collective judgment about agents is our image of them. In the popular imagination, the agent is a corrupt mix of sleaze and greed. The truth is usually quite different. These people are often intelligent lawyers who make smart decisions and perform well in an extremely competitive business. They are successful people, for the most part. Now look at the college student-athlete. Again our imagination misleads us. We see on-field prowess and expertise and assume the same in all facets of life. The reality is often otherwise. They are kids, first of all. Some of them come from homes without two parents or from difficult neighborhoods. Some of them also suffer from an impoverished pre-college educational background. Even at college, they might not be surrounded by the most mature influences, at least not at the frat house.

Bringing smart, successful people (agents) into contact with college athletes can be helpful to the athlete. Moreover, if agent contact were legalized, then competition from the reputable agents would quickly drive their inferior and unethical competition from the market. Yet smart, successful people don't show up at the door for free. By denying the athlete and agent a chance to do business, the NCAA denies athletes a chance to benefit from professional assistance. (The NCAA does allow consultation with a Professional Sports Counseling panel, but that consultation is limited to discussing the athlete's professional prospects. It cannot be compared to the full benefits that can flow from an unrestricted lawyer-client relationship.)

If college athletes could be represented, what would happen? For most kids, nothing: college sports is the end of the line, and their lack of professional prospects would preclude early capitalization. Agents would not give them time nor loan them money. Stars like Reggie Bush, however, might actively consider whether it would be better to go pro or spend one more year in school; they might take part of their future earnings at an earlier age; they might even endorse products. They might also stay in school longer. If Bush is making good money as a college junior, the tug of professional money would be mitigated. A top college program playing for the national title probably provides football stars a better platform for fame and endorsements than does toiling for the pro team that drafts them. Usually those teams are losing teams, lacking the complementary players (blockers) that help make the running back look good.

Colleges don't need to pay their athletes. They need to set them free.

Free Tickets with Membership

By regulation, members of Congress may accept gifts only if the value of the gift is less than $50. At the same time, members of Congress have happily accepted free tickets to sit in luxury boxes at major sports events for years. How did they do it? How could one comply with a fifty-dollar limitation while accepting free game tickets? Our representatives figured out that the value of said tickets happened to come in at exactly $49.99. (It's a miracle!) Recently, however, careful scientific studies have hypothesized that tickets to big-time sports contests might be worth a little more than 50 bucks—maybe even a Benjamin or two.

Never one to ignore modern science, Congress has responded. Lawmakers have recently (in the case of the House of Representatives) or will soon (in the case of the Senate, the more deliberative body) prohibit themselves from receiving free tickets to sports games. What? Who would deny himself free tickets? What does this say about the mentality of our elected representatives? (I want my vote back.) This is foolishness.

Look at it this way: we don't pay our state and federal elected representatives, or even our President, very much money, at least not in terms of salary. It's about $165,000 for federal Congressmen, maybe one-third of that for state representatives; the U.S. President earns over $400,000. Now I know that's a good deal of money, but in the case of members of Congress and Senators, it has to cover, more or less, two residences (one in D.C., one in Timbuktu), plus a lot of nice clothes. It's a lot of money, but presumably, given the importance of the job and the comparison to other high-end decision-makers, it could be a lot more. (I'm assuming the skill of running the most important nation in the world is rare and therefore valuable.)

But we want good people to run for office. There are high costs associated with running for office, such as the total invasion of privacy, personal attacks, public enmity and so forth that these people have to take. (All the opprobrium that comes with higher office probably, unfortunately, draws to our public offices people who are highly insensitive to the opinions of others, which, in fact, may not be the best thing in a representative democracy.) So look at these little gifts as modest salary bonuses to help encourage non-wealthy, non-insensitive people to run for office. Wouldn't it be neat to be a congress(wo)man and watch the Washington, D.C. football squad from the soft leather of a plush luxury box? Or take off on silly fact-finding junkets to the finest tourist destinations in the world (got to keep those facts straight)? There's not much harm here, no more than when I donate to my local firefighter's fund when the neighbor comes to the door. Am I seeking favor from the firefighters? (Extinguish my house first!) No, not realistically. I'm just making a (small) gesture for the sake of civic politeness, a little token of gratitude for the public service. But at these football games, can lobbying happen, at least when the cheerleaders are resting? Sure. But it's bad manners (like talking business on the golf course: despite the belief of outsiders, the truth is that it's just not done, at least not tactfully), and truncated at best. The Senator gets more lobbying in the office, from paid lawyers. Senators take meetings with lobbyists from both sides all the time; lobbyists are not evil, they're helpful. They give the Senator information and perspectives. They're specialists informing the generalist. Lots of people lobby, and they don't have to come with game tickets.[6]

Without these little gifts, which admittedly do have value, theoretically the U.S. taxpayers will have to pay their representatives more money. (Probably not the President, as that person gets amply compensated by the multi-million dollar book deal and other post-term deals.) But for the run-of-the-mill members of Congress who get little or nothing post-term, we'll have to increase the pay. Under

---

6. But they can. Lobbyist Jack Abramoff maintained skyboxes at sports venues to entertain and started a restaurant where certain people from Congress dined for free. Drinkard, Jim. "In Congress, 'we simply have too much power.'" *USA Today.* 9 January 2006. http://www.usatoday.com/news/washington/2006-01-09-congress-scandal-analysis_x.htm.

the former system, some of this pay was provided privately by team owners and other benefactors (some nice stuff too, much of it non-taxable). Now the rest of us will have to pay for luxury boxes, assuming we don't want to, in effect, reduce the total value of the compensation package.

It should also be mentioned that the proposed regulation just says that the gift cannot have a "value" of $50 or more. What does "value" mean? I presume it means something like fair market value. But what is that in a particular case? For the Super Bowl, admittedly it's a high number, especially if the Patriots are playing. But what's the value of free tickets to see a losing baseball team play another loser in a late-season, meaningless game in a half-empty stadium? How would you like to try "reselling" those tickets? Fair market value can fluctuate wildly; for some games, even luxury box tickets might not be worth much. Is "value" the fair market price, or does "value" mean the nominal value on the face of the ticket? Luxury box tickets typically do not have a stated value. Alternatively, does "value" mean the value to the recipient? Again, there are some games I'd pay fifty bucks to see; if it's a couple of teams I don't care about, I wouldn't pay much at all. The dark secret of luxury boxes is that, sometimes, the seats aren't all that good. They can be far removed from the action and not all that much fun. It's not courtside, the best seat in all of sports.

I understand the desire to limit low-gauge Congressional payola. But lots of firms rent luxury boxes at the local stadium to be good corporate citizens, to support the local pro teams, to reward key employees and their families with fun outings, and to give some tickets away to local civic leaders and elected officials. It's just slick, rich people being nice to local politicians in plaid jackets. This general benevolence helps support pro teams. For Washington, D.C. teams, where many of the local wealthy firms are in some way dipping their beaks in the government pool, this prohibition could dampen their luxury box rentals.

Quarterbacks Are Underpaid;
Left Tackles Overpaid

Today our hearts go out to NFL quarterbacks, trying to keep the wolves at the door on their meager salaries. They are underpaid. They are the most important players on the team; we could compare linemen or defenses, but the major difference in NFL teams comes down to the play of the quarterbacks. If we had put a Bears' helmet on Peyton Manning, the Bears likely would be the 2007 Super Bowl champions. Or consider the New England Patriots: over the past few seasons the team was comprised of a bunch of mediocre offensive players, a decent, veteran defense, and one outstanding quarterback. Despite its general mediocrity, the team consistently competes for titles in the tough AFC, sells out its home games, makes tons of money from merchandise sales, and has become one of the league's most profitable franchises. All this, and Tom Brady makes about $10 million per year. How much would he be paid if he were a free agent and were compensated according to the revenue he produces?

Now, this brings me to left tackles. Michael Lewis' book *The Blind Side*[7] points out the sharp increase in pay for NFL left tackles over the past decade or so. Lewis looks for and finds a few football-related reasons for the increasing importance of and consequent demand for the extremely large, agile players who are assigned to this position. But what about the law? What has changed in the legal environment over this period that suddenly makes left tackles so important? The answer is simple: left tackles are being paid out of the quarterback's salary.

The NFL, unique among major sports leagues, features a "hard" salary cap tied to league revenues. This hard cap rather strictly limits the total compensation available to players as a whole. One con-

---

7. (Norton, 2006).

sequence of a cap is that money gets spread out more among the players. A team would have difficulty competing if most of its capped money were allocated to a few star players, leaving little to acquire better players at other positions. So competitive teams have to pay their stars less in order to pay quality non-stars more. The NFL and NFLPA (the players' union) agreed to propose the hard salary cap to the players in order to settle the antitrust battles of the early 1990's (the Freeman McNeil and Reggie White law suits, both battling vestiges of the old "Rozelle Rule" that required compensation for lost free agents).[8] The settlement was bitterly opposed by veteran players, who understood that the cap would eventually limit star-level compensation. Nevertheless, the majority of the union approved the settlement, perhaps for the same reason.

Regardless of salary differentials, quarterbacks contribute to team victory or defeat far more than any one player in any other position. NFL teams routinely rotate players in every position, even the "glamour" positions like running back and receiver, and throughout all the defensive positions. The Patriots especially seem able and willing to substitute players at all positions, and of late have notably refused to pay to acquire or retain "stars" at any position but one. Instead, the Patriots prefer to hire a roster full of quality players, not stars, producing a team with few All-Pros but with remarkable depth. There is only one star on the Patriots, and that's the quarterback. Tom Brady never comes out of the game.

---

8. In 1990, the National Football League Players Association (NFLPA) filed a lawsuit on behalf of eight football players, with Freeman McNeil as the lead plaintiff. The suit asserted that the rules restricting free agents violated the antitrust laws. In addition, the players whose contracts ended in 1989 claimed they had a right to sue because they were no longer represented by the NFL union. In 1992, a jury agreed with the players that the rule violated the antitrust laws because it was more restrictive than it had to be to achieve a competitive balance. A settlement between the team owners and the players was finally reached in 1993 when owners agreed to free agency coupled with a salary cap. "NFLPA History." *NFL Players Association.* http://www.nflpa.org/AboutUs/NFLPA_History.aspx.

But the hard NFL salary cap precludes the Patriots from paying Tom Brady according to the revenue he produces, simply because he alone produces revenue that comprises most of the team's revenue. Money comes from wins, at least in large part. The salary cap ties total player compensation to about 60% of total revenue. What percentage of credit for the Patriots' championship seasons (and merchandise sales and general popularity) would you attribute to Tom Brady? I'd put it pretty close to 60%, which happens to be the total percentage available to pay the entire team. But the Patriots cannot remain competitive if Brady were paid what he's worth. They have to pay somebody else Tom's money. So it goes to the players who are most important in complementing the quarterback, among them the left tackle protecting the quarterback's blind side. Notice how the pay scale for left tackles has undergone a meteoric rise coincident with the implementation of the salary cap.

Lewis attributes the rise in compensation for left tackles to the game and the game's rules. Left tackles are more important today than in times past for two reasons: first, pass rushers, especially linebackers on the quarterback's blind side (to his left) are faster; and second, rules changes have facilitated the passing game. I'm skeptical of the first reason; the NFL has long featured very fast rushers playing defensive end (which player the linebacker essentially replaces in the 3-4 defense in which Lewis finds his "new" fast linebackers). The second development, the rules liberalization, is as much a reason to increase the compensation of the quarterback or blitzing linebacker or pass-rushing defensive end as it is the left tackle.

Left tackles are worth more today than they were in the days before the salary cap, but they are not worth anywhere near the multiples in pay that they receive as compared to their teammates on the offensive line. They are only a little more valuable (in terms of contributing to team victories) than the right tackles, guards and center. But they are paid a lot more simply because they contribute slightly more to the production of the quarterback, and the quarterback produces most of the team's money, whether he's receiving it in compensation or not.

Want to really save money on left tackles? Hire a left-handed quarterback. The right tackle, playing on the lefty quarterback's blind side, will come much more cheaply due to less demand. I've read several commentators suggest that the "test" for Lewis' thesis on the importance of left tackles would be to find out if similar importance is given to right tackles, or to find out if left-handed quarterbacks perform less effectively because right tackles are less skilled. This is no test at all. Right tackles are just as skilled as the left tackle; they're just paid less because they don't complement the quarterback quite as much. With a lefty quarterback, a team would rationally hire a highly skilled (yet cheaper) right tackle, producing the same level of quarterback success.

Think salary caps don't redistribute income? Obviously you're not a college football coach. The NCAA has a neat little salary cap of its own: each player gets to earn pretty close to zero, not counting scholarships. So how should a college athletic department spend all that revenue? That's easy—on the man whose performance best complements and enhances that of the players: the coach. That lucky devil gets paid far in excess of any revenue he produces. Some of us in life get paid less than the value we produce (think educators). For lucky left tackles, they get more.

NBA Draft Dodging

During the 2007 NBA season, Kentucky star center Randolph Morris was an NBA free agent, available for any team to sign. Given that he's 6'10" and apparently has ability that would place him in the first round of the NBA draft, were he eligible, it would seem inevitable that some NBA team would have contacted the player to find out just how much he liked going to school. "Let's see, what shall I do tomorrow, attend my 9:10 seminar on Social Developments after the Industrial Revolution, or cash a multi-thousand dollar bonus check and pick out a number for the back of my jersey?"[9]

Did I mention free agent? Morris got to be a desirable young center unconstrained by the NBA's rookie salary scale, by which salaries for drafted players are tied to draft position. For instance, assuming Morris were to have entered the supposedly talent-rich 2007 draft, and assuming he would indeed have been a first-round pick, somewhere around the middle-to-late part of the round, Morris would receive compensation in the amount of about one million dollars each year for two years, with team options for years three and four. Not bad, but I bet in most cases a player could get more as a free agent, unconstrained by the scale (assuming the salary scale was instituted to constrict salaries, not expand them). Morris got himself into this enviable position by entering the previous NBA draft, going unselected, then returning to college.[10]

What if everyone did this? Fortunately for the NBA, not too many players could. Most players with NBA talent would probably get drafted, if only in the second round, and would be paid or cut

---

9. After the close of the college basketball season, but while the NBA season was ongoing, Morris did indeed sign a contract with a pro team: the New York Knicks, for an amount roughly equivalent to a mid-range first-round draft pick.

10. Grant Wahl, a writer for *Sports Illustrated,* examined every first-round pick in the eight drafts from 1995-2002, concluding that if a player is positive that he will be chosen in the first round and has no doubts about his capabilities, he will not benefit from staying another year in college. The average second-contract salary for sophomore athletes who go in the first round of the draft is almost exactly the same as the salary of the players who left after their junior years ($8.334 million for sophomores compared to $8.285 million for juniors). This conclusion naturally comes with a couple caveats, including: 1) It is pretty rare that a person would be 100% confident that he will be drafted in round one, and 2) it is unknown how much the 2005 switch from three to two guaranteed contract years for first round picks will affect these numbers. Wahl, Grant. "Waiting Games." *Sports Illustrated.* 22 November 2006. http://sportsillustrated.cnn.com/2006/writers/grant_wahl/11/22/the.bag/index.html.

accordingly. The player would, like Morris, have to be initially unattractive, go undrafted, and then become a late bloomer.

Still, I wonder why many draft-eligible players (19 years old plus one year removed from high school) don't register for the draft, knowing they will not get drafted, on the off-chance they grow into a first-round talent by their senior year in college. The NBA can only draft 60 players; if many college freshmen flooded the pool, most would escape the net. The players could then return to the peaceful serenity of the college campus, work on their games (and slip some studying in on the side), continually testing the NBA waters, looking for a paycheck. The college game could further its role as a farm system for the professional league.

What stops the "flood" of players is probably a coordination/collective action problem. Each player is afraid of leaving money on the table by entering the draft, going in the second round, and then being relegated to reduced salary and the threat of being cut. So each player opts out. If players could coordinate their actions, then the young pro prospect would be much more likely to enter the draft, secure in the odds that he could escape undrafted.

What's wrong with the NBA bidding against the University of Kentucky for Morris' services? The plethora of professional leagues throughout the world are always available for a player like Morris should he choose to quit college. Players who have genuine professional prospects choose to go to college because they correctly perceive it as the primary path to the NBA, the top pro league in the world. They may go for the education and enjoyment too, but certainly the historical role of college as the gateway to the NBA must form a significant part of their decision. Don't think that the NBA will always win a bidding contest; players often choose to stay in school, usually to enhance their job skills in order to increase draft status, or perhaps to graduate.[11] In Morris' case, because he may

---

11. The most recent data collected by the NCAA shows that the graduation rates for Division 1 men's basketball at 46 percent, which is up

not re-enter the draft, he will stay in school to the point where he believes he will earn the maximum compensation from entering the league. In other words, like any other player, he will balance further job training against the prospective value of the contract. Unlike other players, Morris gets to make that decision on a continual basis (not just in the off-season) and gets much better information about the terms of his initial professional contract.

What about disruption to his Kentucky team? Sure, Morris might well take this disruption into account in weighing an NBA offer. But could anyone blame the kid if he took the money? Basketball is his career, most likely, and a college degree appears of negligible value to this career. Both in and out of the sports world, many young people drop out of school; a lot of them do so because job opportunities are presented to them. Sometimes it makes sense to take the job. It might for Morris. Many colleges give student-athletes academic credit for taking classes in basketball or in other sports-related subjects, on the theory that there is much to learn about sports that is amenable to crediting. So let's consider basketball as a class: should we be upset when a kid drops a class? It's just college, right? Would we be upset if a player sat out some games because his studies needed attention? No, in fact we would praise a coach who gave his players adequate time to pursue academic interests and complete academic requirements. There's little difference if Morris dropped a class to take a job, albeit in the NBA.

---

from 43 percent reported for the previous year. Overall, it is reported that 63% of all Division 1 college athletes who started college in 1999 graduated within six years. This number is above the national graduation rate of 61 percent for the same time period. Both of these percentages are up one percent from the previous year. If transfer student athletes are accounted for, the graduation rate for Division 1 athletes increases to 77 percent. "Division 1 Student-Athletes Excel in Classroom, Exceed Student Body Graduation Rates." *NCAA Online.* 9 November 2006. http://www2.ncaa.org/portal/media_and_events/press_room/2006/november/20061109_d1_gsr_rls.html.

Criminalizing Sports Law

Jim Galante, the owner of a waste-removal company, was linked to the mob and got himself prosecuted for racketeering. The sports hook is that he also owned a popular local minor league hockey team, with his eighteen-year-old son as the GM. Nothing shocking so far. But what caught my eye is that the federal indictment for racketeering included as "predicate acts" allegations that Galante exceeded his team's salary cap in paying his hockey players. He did so by paying his players extra through do-nothing jobs for their spouses and housing allowances.

The way the federal racketeering law works, a "racketeer" is a status one attains by committing a number of "predicate acts," which are crimes as defined by state or federal law.[12] Not all crimes count, but the list is long, and includes the very flexible and amorphous federal wire and mail fraud statutes. Basically, any scheme to defraud, as long as at some point it trips across federal jurisdiction by using the mail or the telephone, is a federal crime.

Thus the indictment is terming a violation of the salary cap a federal crime. That will make GM's pay attention to salary caps.

As every lawyer knows, the jurisdictional element (the use of the phone or the mail) of the federal fraud statutes is a joke. Any

---

12. In 1970, Congress passed the Racketeer Influenced and Corrupt Organizations (RICO) ACT (Title 18, United States Code) to bring an end to organized crime. This federal law provides penalties for criminal acts performed as part of an ongoing criminal organization. Under this law, a person must commit two crimes out of a list of 35 (27 federal crimes and 8 state crimes) with similar purpose or result. Grell, Jeff. "Introduction: RICO" *RicoAct.com LLC.* http://www.ricoact.com. "Racketeer Influenced and Corrupt Organizations Act." *Wikipedia.* http://en.wikipedia.org/wiki/ Racketeer_Influenced_and_Corrupt_Organizations_Act#RICO_offenses_and_definiti ons.

useful trickery on any scale is necessarily going to involve a tele-phone or the mail. The result is that the law has always relied on the judgment of federal prosecutors not to term every act of trick-ery or deceit a federal criminal offense, instead limiting the use of federal prosecutorial power to crimes that affect important federal interests.

The rules of a salary cap do not constitute a vital federal inter-est. These are internal rules to maintain competition in sports leagues, not competition in the national market economy. The player unions and the pro leagues never thought they were nego-tiating criminal statutes when they hammered out the last collec-tive bargaining agreement. Now to be clear, the indictment here names these cap violations as predicate acts. Galante isn't being prosecuted for circumventing a league rule. But under the theory of this indictment, he could be prosecuted for violating a league rule. Did he cheat the league and impact the outcome of games? Yes.

But so does the pitcher throwing a spitball. To term a violation of a league's salary cap a federal fraud offense is to start criminal law on a dangerous path into the world of sports.

Boston Forever?

Recent sports seasons have seen the ascendance of Boston's pro-fessional sports teams. The Red Sox reign as champions, the Pa-triots have put together something of a dynasty and nearly completed a perfect season, and even the lowly Celtics, as I write, have posted the NBA's best record at the half-way mark. These things come in cycles, we're told, so Boston fans better enjoy it while they can.

True, much of life comes in waves, and certainly the three major Boston sports teams have all peaked simultaneously. But is it nec-essarily the case that this peak is a fortuity? Is it plain cyclical luck that Boston now features the nation's best squads? It's not luck. It's law. Boston's teams are among the best this year and, if the laws of sports have anything to do with it, will remain among the best, maybe forever.

The best article in the history of sports law was not written by a lawyer. Simon Rottenberg, a professor of economics, writing several years before Ronald Coase gave us his supposedly seminal paper[13] (which paper was the primary basis for Coase's Nobel award), wrote "The Baseball Players' Labor Market."[14] Basically Rottenberg's idea was that the initial assignment of property rights has no impact on resource allocation, all in reference to baseball players. To quote the paper, "It seems, indeed, to be true that a market in which freedom is limited by a reserve rule such as that which now governs the baseball labor market distributes players among teams about as a free market would." In other words, the rule of law (assigning property rights) doesn't matter; players will end up on teams that more highly value their services regardless of what particular restriction exists on the transfer of their contracts. So Rottenberg's Theorem suggests that, when figuring out which teams have the best players (and thus the most wins), we should try to figure out which teams most highly value those players. The law either is irrelevant to the distribution of players (one strong reading of Rottenberg's Theorem) or at best should grease the skids to bring about the transfer of players to their "best" teams as cheaply and costlessly as possible. Has this happened? Do we see the rules of sport helping to bring the best players to the best markets? Yes, we do. The law is complicit (happily, in my view) in assisting Boston in fielding the best sports teams.

Let's start with Rottenberg's favorite sport, major league baseball. MLB has several rules that encourage parity among teams: the worst teams draft first, the poorest teams receive revenue sharing, the highest-payroll teams pay a luxury tax. These parity rules are attempts to slow down the simple translation of wealth (enjoyed by highly

---

13. Ronald H. Coase, The Problem of Social Cost, 3 Journal of Law & Economics 1 (1960).

14. Simon Rottenberg, The Baseball Players' Labor Market, 64 Journal of Political Economy 242 (1956).

profitable teams) into on-field success. Sometimes these "parity rules" backfire, however. Losing MLB teams do get premium draft choices, thus promoting parity. Another parity rule, however, prohibits these teams from trading those choices in an attempt to ensure that these outstanding young players end up on these poorer, losing clubs. The likely effect of this restriction on trading draft picks diminishes the value of those draft choices. Poor baseball teams often have to pass on the best draftees in favor of lesser players who are willing to sign contracts for smaller amounts. Why? The high cost of the best draftees is not only comparatively expensive for poorer teams but also requires the poor teams to risk too much money on one player, an unproven young one at that. Thus by restricting the ability of these poor teams to trade or sell those high picks, MLB essentially strips away the picks' value, leaving poor teams unable or unwilling to draft the most expensive (and presumably the best) players with those top picks.

Other MLB practices also counteract the parity goal. Wealthy teams share revenue and some pay a tax, thus ostensibly promoting parity. But baseball's lack of a salary cap allows teams to increase their payroll without limit. As a result, wealthy clubs can express their wealth in player salaries without hindrance. MLB also has a league-wide television contract in which all share. Nonetheless, teams are allowed to sell television and radio broadcasts of their games locally, thus providing a huge revenue boost to teams in large, fan-crazy markets. Finally, most perplexing of all is the "pro-parity" rule that backfires enormously and implicitly encourages the best players to migrate to the wealthiest teams: the commissioner's rule, stemming from Bowie Kuhn's 1976 decision to void the sale of several Oakland A's stars to the Yankees and Red Sox, that prohibits teams from including more than a few million dollars in any player transaction. This rule keeps the poor teams down. Instead of being able to sell their young stars for cash (something like the 50 million dollars the Red Sox coughed up last season for the contract rights to star pitcher Daisuke Matsuzaka of the Japanese league) which could then be invested in established major league players, poor clubs are obliged to take back most of their trade revenue in the form of risky minor league players. The cash limitations only further impoverish the poor teams.

Let's assume the people who run MLB are not stupid. It seems pretty clear that the various rules of the game, although in part promoting parity, basically ensure that baseball hotbeds like New York and Boston will be able to capitalize on their economic advantages. These rules make it difficult for the poorer-market teams to stand in their way. Indeed, why wouldn't MLB want to have strong teams in big markets like Boston and New York? Don't all the teams profit, if indirectly, from the Yankees' big profits, both from revenue sharing and from large gates when New York is in town? Baseball would be crazy to run its league any other way.

Similar sets of rules are afoot in the NBA, thus again helping to ensure that winning teams are to be found in the best markets. The NBA has a "soft" salary cap and a steep luxury tax in place to help maintain competitive balance. Nevertheless, wealthy teams can spend over the tax threshold if they are willing to pay. Thus, exceeding the tax line provides an explicit and tacitly approved method for the wealthy teams to generate competitive advantages. (The Celtics, naturally, went well over the tax threshold in acquiring its many star players this off-season, especially with respect to James Posey, a valuable substitute player whose entire contract is "taxable" at twice its amount.) Now of course the fact that the NBA has more limits than MLB makes it harder for the wealthy teams to translate their wealth advantages into wins. (As I write, the New York Knicks continue both to profit and to lose at an astounding rate.) How is the NBA served by having a bad team in New York but a strong one in New Orleans, where no one comes?

Here's the problem with Rottenberg's Theorem: it's correct, but it does require low transaction or trade costs for players to wind up on the team that values them most. The NBA is full of transaction costs, especially the rule that unnecessarily limits trades according to the salaries of the players traded, requiring rough equivalency.

The NBA also precludes the trade of draft picks in consecutive years. These rules do not serve competitive balance; indeed, by inhibiting trades they perpetuate the status quo, making it harder for teams to escape from the cellar. Look for the NBA to iron out these transaction costs by eliminating some of these impediments to trades. We'll get a winner in New York somehow.

Even the parity-crazed NFL has its Rottenberg examples. The league notably has the most severe pro-parity rules, including a rigid, hard salary cap, even-steven revenue sharing, exclusive national contracts the proceeds of which are equally divided, and league-wide merchandising, yet still, the wealthy teams (particularly those with the best stadium deals) do have opportunities to exploit their wealth. How? Teams may get the same revenue, but they vary in their value of the franchises. The Cowboys and Patriots, for instance, have a much greater franchise value than do the Cardinals or the Rams. Robert Kraft and Jerry Jones cannot, under the strictures of the cap, offer players all that much more in salary than their competitors. But they can offer benefits that are uncapped, such as superior training facilities, stadium quality and comfort, and, most importantly, coaching acumen. Coaching salaries are uncapped, so teams can compete for players indirectly by hiring the best coaches. Owners know that, despite the requirements that they share much of their revenue, their investments will still pay off in increased franchise values. As franchise values continue to skyrocket, look for owners of the most valuable franchises to continue to acquire the most valuable players.

For a long time it's been accepted as a given in the world of sports law scholarship that league games are a joint good, and that both teams benefit financially from close competition. Fans wouldn't come to games, the argument runs, unless both teams had a roughly equal chance of winning. Boston's stunning success questions that bromide. The need for parity to generate and sustain fan interest may be overstated. By the same token, it's often been stated that the snazzy NFL represents the future of sports, with its mandated revenue sharing and hard salary cap. But these claims seem dubious. Think again of the claimed need for parity. Of all the sports, baseball would seem to be most in need of close competition. Baseball stages many games over a long season, with teams typically visiting the home team for a three- or four-game set of matches. That's a lot of baseball to sell. Yet among the major sports, baseball has the fewest parity rules. Perhaps it's MLB, the much maligned, antiquated old grandpa of modern sports, that has it about right: it has set up its rules in such a way as to make pretty sure that strong teams are fielded nearly every season in its best markets.[15] The NFL, on the other hand, with the most parity rules, may be the league least in need of parity. The Patriots just won nearly 100% of their games, while at the same time becoming the NFL's dominant television feature.

I thought we needed parity because everyone would be bored otherwise? Not so; instead of parity among teams, what may be more important is that the biggest markets have the best teams. Bostonians love sports, and will pay to watch them. Economics matters; sometimes rules don't. Look for Boston to field winners for a long, long time.

---

15. Baseball still enjoys a great deal of parity, despite the comparative lack of parity rules. Even the best baseball teams win only about sixty percent of the time. Contrast that result with football where teams winning seventy-five percent are common, or basketball, where top teams win even more often. Perhaps some level of parity is inherent in the game of baseball itself. Perhaps baseball's oft-stated axiom, that a good pitcher will beat a good hitter, rings of truth.

Chapter Three

The Violence of Sports

Violence is a central feature of many popular sports like football and hockey. Some sports, such as boxing or ultimate fighting, are even termed "blood sports" because the very object of the sport is to injure the opponent and, in some sense, to draw blood. Other sports, such as basketball or baseball, feature unplanned collisions and other moments of violence. Violence is part of many sports and forms part of their appeal to both fans and players. It can be thrilling to play dangerous games.

Normally the law allows people to play dangerous games. As long as the player consents to the game, and is more or less aware of the risks of violence, then the player may participate. If he's injured by the violence, he is without the protection of the law. With that said, sometimes the degree or nature of the sports violence lies putatively outside the scope of the player's consent. In this case, the law may intervene to provide a remedy, either in the form of civil damages or even a criminal sentence. The problem is that the law's intervention, coming at a point so close to the permissible violence of the game, may threaten to erode the violent nature of the sport. Might a linebacker hold back on his tackle if he knows that "unnecessary roughness" will lead to a criminal prosecution instead of fifteen yards of field position? Should the mighty procedures of law be employed in enforcing the arbitrary rules of a football game?

This problem brings us to the heart of the matter: what does it mean to say that an athlete (or fan) consents to undertake the risks that are inherent to a particular sport? Consider the relatively tame sport of baseball. Surely a baseball player consents to the off-chance he'll be injured by a hard-hit line drive. But does he also consent to being struck by a "beanball"? Should it matter that the pitch was intentionally, instead of inadvertently, thrown at him? At his head? To say that players or fans consent to participation only begs the question of "participation in what?" Does the decision of a court or prosecutor not to intervene with respect to a beanball mean, for the future, that when players consent to the inherent dangers of baseball they also consent to the pitcher's intentional acts of violence? Law is everywhere with respect to violence in sports, even where law chooses to refrain from intervention.

What Is a Sport?

No better question starts an inquiry into sports violence. Football is a sport; so is the discus throw. Is golf? Darts? Horse racing? (For the jockeys too?)[1] The definition of "sport" came to the fore recently when a baseball pitcher for a California junior-college team hit an opposing batter on the head, splitting his helmet and causing serious injury. Because the pitcher's teammate had been hit the previous inning, the California Supreme Court assumed the purpose of the pitch was retaliatory.[2] The defense offered by the County, which also operated the college and hosted the game, was that the batter, by choosing to play in a baseball game, "assumed the risk"

---

1. Here's one definition: "Sport is an activity that is governed by a set of rules or customs and often engaged in competitively. Used by itself, sports commonly refer to activities where the physical capabilities of the competitor are the sole or primary determiner of the outcome (winning or losing), but the term is also used to include activities such as mind sports and motor sports where mental acuity or equipment quality are major factors. Sports are used as entertainment for the player and the viewer." "Sport." 14 August 2007. *Wikipedia.* http://en.wikipedia.org/wiki/Sport.

2. Avila v. Citrus Community College District, No. S119575, 2006 WL 870947 (Cal. Apr. 6, 2006).

of being thrown at by an opposing pitcher, even if the pitch was aimed at his head in anger or intentionally. In other words, the "beanball," even when intentionally thrown, is included in the definition of "baseball."

California divides the doctrine of assumption of risk into two: primary and secondary. Under the latter, the pitcher would owe the batter a duty of care (here a duty not to negligently or intentionally injure the batter), and the question would be whether or not the batter knowingly exposed himself to the risk of the pitcher's failure to meet that duty. But under the former, "primary" assumption of risk doctrine, the pitcher owes the batter no duty of care at all. Being thrown at is just part of the game, and no matter what the pitcher intended or of what the batter had knowledge, no liability is attached.

The California Supreme Court played hard ball, applying the doctrine of primary assumption of risk to hold that, as a matter of law, a pitcher intentionally throwing at a batter is part of the game, and thus one of the risks the batter assumes when he steps into the box.[3] The interesting question is whether or not the court was right.

The court's approach to this question is what we might call "empirical," in the loose sense of the armchair empiricism of the nonspecialist. The California court wondered whether or not people in this situation (batting in a baseball game) reasonably "expect" beanball pitches. The court resorted to anecdote, reciting various instances of beanballs and statements concerning beanballs, concluding that beanballs are within the common expectation of batters. At best, this form of offhand empiricism is a poor substitute

---

3. Justice Kathryn Mickle Werdegar wrote the opinion for the 6-1 decision by the court, stating: "For better or worse, being intentionally thrown at is a fundamental and inherent risk of the sport of baseball. It is not the function of tort law to police such conduct." McKee, Mike. "Calif. Supreme Court: Ballplayer Can't Sue for Bean Ball." 10 April 2006. *Law.com.* http://www.law.com/jsp/article.jsp?id=1144414531604&rss=newswire.

for the real thing. Do batters truly expect beanballs? Should some-one sample them for their opinion? Even if someone did, a harder question would remain: what degree of a shared opinion would suffice for a court to decide that beanballs are in fact "normally expected?"

Grand empirical pronouncements based on anecdote, if based on anything at all, permeate legal decisions. It's not that judges or other lawmakers are incapable of conducting some empirical re-search. It's that courts do not actually care about the true empiri-cal answer. In other words, even if some enterprising social scientist were to present a court with convincing evidence that batters do not, to any significant degree, expect a pitcher to throw at them intentionally, I don't think the California court would change its decision; maybe the reasoning, but not the decision. Courts do not really care what actual people actually expect.

Indeed, now that this decision has been handed down as a mat-ter of law, at least in California, the intentional beanball is within the field of risks that batters assume. Legal decisions create expec-tations; they don't measure them.

Courts don't care about these empirical questions, nor should they. The purpose of legal decisions is not to describe reality; it is to prescribe it, to shape reality and offer that conception as de-scription. Maybe the California court believes it true as an empir-ical proposition that batters at the collegiate level do actually expect beanballs. If so, the court should have told us how often beanballs have to occur for the "reasonable batter" to impliedly assume the risk of getting one in the head. But courts often pose empirical ques-tions without really trying to find empirical answers. In other words, putting aside the actual answer to the question of the average bat-ter's expectations, the more plausible observation is that the Cali-fornia court chose to define "baseball" to include beanball.

Two reasons might justify this judicial practice of prescribing reality, while purporting to describe it. One is that the court may have been concerned about the introduction of tort liability to sporting activities. Tort liability for wrongful pitches would involve judges and juries assessing the unstated intentions of pitchers. It would also involve asking if the club or coach followed the proper standard of care in training the pitcher and did not negligently employ a pitcher without adequate control so as to avoid wild pitches. So the introduction of tort law would put a premium on control pitchers versus hard-throwing but comparatively wild pitchers. Perhaps it would also introduce a conflict of interest into game decisions (as coaches might put less effective but better-control pitchers on the mound, even if the team interests were otherwise, in order to avoid personal liability). In short, a mess.

Second, the court might have picked the rule it did because opposing teams can better (than courts) minimize the frequency and danger of brushback pitches. By concluding that the batter "assumed the risk" as a matter of law (primary assumption of risk), the court was effectively saying that the intentional harm done by the pitcher would result in no legal remedy. The batter would be left to self-help, a private remedy. Often courts relegate tangible and substantial harms to private remedy (which is to say no legal remedy at all). The batter's remedy is retaliation; the pay-back pitch where his teammate throws at an opposing batter. Crude, but effective. In short, the rule of no remedy makes sense if the teams can together minimize the joint costs of batting (by working together, under the implicit threat of retaliation, to take care not to unnecessarily throw at opposing batters). The alternative to teams working out their problems is to ask a jury, looking back at the event, to assess the need for retaliation on their behalf. The California court chose to leave the remedy to the players.

The NBA Brawls

Available forever through the miracle of the internet is the latest NBA fistfight. In a 2006 brawl, various members of the Knicks and Nuggets went at if for a couple of rounds. Commissioner David

Stern issued suspensions, and they were big ones.[4] Should an arrest be made? Had this fight happened in a bar, criminal prosecution might indeed be on the horizon. But it didn't. It happened in a public sports arena: punches were thrown, spectators could have been injured, and younger fans witnessed real violence. Given the public nature of the brawl, isn't the case stronger, as compared to a barroom fight, for criminal charges?

Nope. Sports are different.

Sporting contests sanction actions that would be condemned elsewhere. Tackling comes to mind. The players consent to be touched or even hurt, and that consent in effect forms the defense to what otherwise would be an intentional tort or wrong. By not outlawing football, as it has certain other sports, our country allows players to consent to being touched and grabbed in ways that cause pain. Unlike any interaction in a bar or other place, sports legally permit participants to be rough.

What follows is a trickier proposition: roughness is part of the sport, even when it violates the rules of the sport. Unnecessary roughness is a football penalty, even if intentional roughing is still a regular and expected part of an NFL game. The same could be said for illegal blocks, facemask grabs, roughing the passer, and so forth. Other sports also feature regular events that, though a transgression of the respective rules, are part of the game: the pitcher who throws at a batter, the hockey player who hits with his elbows and a loose stick, and the basketball player who defends his goal in an aggressive manner to send a message to the other team. It's out of

---

4. Seven players from the Knicks and Nuggets were suspended after a fight in the last minute of a game that ended up entering the stands at Madison Square Garden. Both teams ended up with an unprecedented fine of $500,000. Carmelo Anthony received a 15-game suspension without pay, costing $641,000. Anthony's suspension is the sixth-longest ever issued to a player for an on-court incident. Graham, Pat. "Anthony Suspended 15 Games, No Suspension for Thomas." 19 December 2006. *ESPN.com*. http://sports.espn.go.com/espn/wire?section=nba&id=2701901.

line and against the rules, yet we've all seen it, and we'll see it again the next time we tune in to a professional game.

When these "expected sports illegalities" occur, at times opposing players will retaliate in kind. We can't expect players who are al ready subject to rough (but legal) contact during the course of a game to quietly withstand this additional provocation. Response is natural; it's not too surprising or even all that unexpected. How often do fights break out in hockey? Should we look at fights as part of the game? I can remember (from the glory days of TSLP's youth) the Celtics and Lakers trading punches, and the fighting players not even getting thrown out of the game! Yet Carmelo Anthony, a big NBA star people will pay to see, gets atwenty-five-game suspension. Has the sport of basketball changed[5] or just our perception of it?

Assuming we're not about to outlaw contact sports, we should be willing to tolerate a modicum of violence. We can't have it both ways. If a person directly in front of you taunted you, as the "victim" Mardy Collins of the Knicks appeared to do to the "perpetrator" Carmelo Anthony, many of us would respond with a punch, as did Anthony. (By the way, that was not a sucker punch, either, as it has been portrayed in the press; it was the first punch. Fights have to start somehow.) True, the law condemns throwing the first punch, while simultaneously condemning "fighting words." This implicitly recognizes that the latter can lead to the former and also partially justifies the former. Today we punish Anthony for punching Collins. Soon we'll punish, to the same extent, the hard foul that started the whole thing. The punch is a plausible, if not common, result of the hard foul; the two are inseparable. The hard foul leads to the punch, which leads to the brawl. Once we start draw-

---

5. One thing did change: in 2004 an epic brawl took place at the Palace in Detroit between the Pistons and the Indiana Pacers. Much larger in magnitude compared to the Knicks-Nuggets scuffle, the league took a serious hit in the image department. Soden, Blair. "Basket Brawl Recalls NBA's Image Troubles." 17 December 2006. *ABCNEWS.com*. http://abcnews.go.com/WNT/ESPNSports/Story?id=2732918&page=2.

ing a line, the line always moves back. Why? Because when we draw lines without plausible principle, then the lines will move in search of a principle. The line will move to proscribe all conduct not sanctioned by the rules of the sport. That's a principle, so that will be the line.

But it's not a good principle. It is a mistake to draw the line at the edge of conduct permitted by the rules of the sport. Why not suspend players who attempt to injure or are recklessly aggressive with other players by throwing a baseball at them or tackling them illegally or fouling them unnecessarily? Why not, as many propose, use the rule of law and arrest these brawling players, much as we would someone who acted this way outside the arena? Here's the problem: sports depends on players who will go to the limit, tackling hard or fouling hard or pitching inside, even at the risk of exceeding the limit. Football depends on defenders going all-out to make a tackle, without worry or hesitation. Make the penalty for excessive conduct a substantial one, and players won't go near the limit.

The brawl didn't bother me much; the reaction to it does. I think part of this is the NBA's response to the non-stop publicity ESPN and its fellow outlets give to this sort of thing. Not long ago, a fight between NBA players might have been, at most, part of the highlights package. Now, a single fracas gets its own "Outside the Lines" introspective. This incessant negative publicity demands a response; our viewing of sports is itself changing sports, what social scientists term "the observer effect." The game hasn't changed since the Celtics and Lakers ruled the league; we fans have changed, and our change impacts the game.

We need to be careful lest the NBA turn into Italian soccer. Tune in some night to an Italian league game. This great sport has been (for me, at least) pretty much ruined by players looking to get their opponents in trouble, flopping around and falling to the ground in what looks like Lady Macbeth's death scene. Can we say all this playing hurt is not very manly and let it go at that? Aren't we all glad Vlade Divac has retired? Let's cowboy up, America. We want contact sports, which means we should be willing to accept the occasional fistfight that goes with it. Our penalties for fighting should be moderated; throwing the offender out of the game (or, if at the end of the game, the next one) is a time-honored response to game misconduct. It should have been enough for Anthony as well.

Blood Sports

There's no accounting for taste. Fortunately sports come in many forms, so we can all find something we like. But should some tastes in sporting contests go unsatisfied? I'm thinking of the blood sports, where human or animal punishment, or even death, is the object of the game. What brings this topic to mind is a brutally unflinching account of a bullfight, as witnessed by a young American student in Spain and dutifully recorded in my local newspaper.

I know bullfighting is limited to certain foreign locales, but Americans have their blood sports too. Cockfighting, where victory is often marked by the death of the losing bird, supposedly remains common, despite the nearly universal legal prohibition. Boxing, where the object is to score points by delivering telling punches to the body of the opponent, has left many brain-damaged fighters in its wake. Even football has, as a legitimate part of its game, the aim to inflict serious pain. What's intriguing to me is that blood sports appear to be on the increase. Just a quick tour around Youtube will show clips from "ultimate fighting" contests, animals fighting other animals, people beating the heck out of each other, just all kinds of mayhem. I guess I reveal my personal sensibilities when I say my stomach turns at some of this violence. Although this is perhaps a bit uninformed (and I'm not willing to become more informed), but ultimate fighting looks like little more than a semi-controlled schoolyard brawl, as people kick and hit each other into submission.[6]

---

6. Formed in 2001, the Ultimate Fighting Championship (UFC) is the

I can understand the arguments to ban bullfighting, cockfighting and the like: the animals are by definition unwilling participants, and their deaths are patently cruel. But what about the sports
that involve human punishment and blood? Here participants can
and do consent. Should we let them? It appears to me that the taste
that some of us have (or are developing) for blood sports will soon
produce greater excesses. Would we allow two men to consent to
fight each other until one is bleeding profusely and unable to continue? Until one is unconscious? Until one is dead? I have little
doubt that a fight promoter could find two men willing to fight to
some extreme physical result and could attract an audience to witness it.[7]

To the extent some of these activities are regulated and steps are
taken to protect participants consistent with the aim of the sport,
I would prefer that the law let people do what they want. But, despite my usual inclinations, I'd prefer stronger measures to limit
or eliminate some of these blood sports, despite the consent of the
athletes. The athletes and the audience may have a taste for blood,
but they shouldn't. It debases them and is corrosive to newcomers

---

world's leading mixed martial arts sports association. Mixed martial arts
is characterized as the use of a combination of fighting forms including jiu-
jitsu, judo, karate, boxing, kickboxing, wrestling and others to gain an
advantage over an opponent in a supervised match. UFC fighters come
from a wide variety of countries around the world, with previous combat
sports experience. Many are college educated and have dedicated their
lives to studying martial arts. "The New UFC Fact Sheet." *UFC.com.*
http://www.ufc.com/index.cfm?fa=LearnUFC.FactSheet.
    7. In 2006, it was reported that ten UFC pay-per-view events generated
more than $200 million in customer retail revenue. The fights cost ap-
proximately $39.95. Two main tactics utilized by the UFC to spur increased
popularity are: 1) a successful television show The Ultimate Fighter on
Spike TV; and 2) getting more states to sanction the fights, which draw large
crowds to the live events. Goldman, Adam. "AP Centerpiece: Ultimate
Fighting, Wrestling, Boxing Grapple for Pay-Per-View Crown." *USATO-
DAY.com.* http://www.usatoday.com/sports/2007-02-28-1382074339_x.htm.

even while it draws them to the spectacle. In many states, even viewing a cockfight is a crime.

The Ethics of Varmint Hunting

On occasion I find time to take my boys hunting for upland game birds, like pheasant and chukar partridge. We enjoy getting out in the far country under the big sky, working with the dogs and ready-ing for the shot on the flush. I often miss my target, even with my big 12-gauge pattern (bad eyes), but my boys are crack shots, and despite using small gauge shotguns, fill up their game pouches pretty quickly. We don't get to go often, but I must say our annual forays in the high country of Eastern Oregon make great memories.

Given this, you would think a simple invitation to go hunting with a friend would not generate an ethical dilemma for me. But it has. This friend has asked me to go "varmint hunting" with him on the wide public lands of Central Oregon.

A "varmint" is an animal that is not "game": in other words, people do not (commonly) eat a varmint. The animal thus serves no "purpose" for people, other than sometimes as a nuisance. The varmint may, however, serve a significant purpose on the animal food chain or in some other ecological role. Thus the term "varmint" is obviously a utilitarian construct or label that tells us as much about human eating habits and one's view of animal life as it does about the inherent worth of the animal. Which animals are varmints is also somewhat dependent on the locality. Common varmints in-clude (non-endangered) rats, chipmunks, squirrels, ground hogs, rock chucks, prairie dogs, snakes, and lizards, and even larger crea-tures like coyotes, cougars, wolves and foxes. My friend has it in mind to shoot at sage rats and chipmunks, to be specific.

I was taught to shoot only that which I planned to eat. I do eat game birds. I'm not about to eat a rat. Should I hunt them?

Obviously, I don't have a problem with hunting. I do eat meat, and by doing so I am (implicitly) concluding that it is justifiable that one animal (a chicken or cow or fish) die for the sake of the hunger of another, even if that other (me) had available to him non-meat choices to satiate his appetite. Animals dying for the sake of others strikes me (although obviously not everybody) as an ubiquitous aspect of the natural world. As intelligent creatures, we humans owe it to the animals we eat to end their life with a certain degree of mercy. (Some of the ways animals are killed at slaughterhouses, at least according to what I've read, are absolutely beyond the pale and should be abandoned in favor of more humane practices, regardless of the cost.) Taking an animal's life through gunshot (usually) imposes a quick death.

So, again speaking personally, the linking of hunting and eating makes sense. Only hunt that which you plan to eat. This is a common, perhaps even predominant, hunter perspective. But is it a correct one? The consequence of linking eating and hunting is that only people who have a taste for venison or elk meat may hunt deer or elk. In other words, if I try venison and don't like it, then I may not ethically hunt for deer. What if I'm allergic to venison, or plan to give the meat away and fail to find a recipient? Linking hunting and one's taste in meat seems odd. It also reflects a false reality, as it separates out and ignores the joy of hunting and the thrill of the chase as a reason to hunt. Under the view that eating justifies hunting, hunting is reduced to an uncommon and expensive way to put food on the table. Hunting to eat sounds like joyless work, and emphasizes one aspect of the sport that not one hunter I know will actually emphasize in any discussion of hunting. No one says something about killing enough deer or birds to feed his family; we talk about technical competence or unbending determination, not meat.

I suspect that hunting has been ethically justified by hunters as "food-provision" in order to fend off the objections of those who view hunting as an ethically indefensible sport. Indeed, hunting groups noticeably go to great lengths to describe and define the act of killing an animal as "harvesting," implicitly alluding to the food-provision benefit of the sport, with the obvious parallel to everyday meat slaughter and consumption. But although this defense may temporarily succeed in muting opposition, it's a false one and all hunters know it. Providing meat is merely a collateral benefit, at best. Hunting is not glorified farming or another way to go grocery shopping; calling hunting "harvesting" does hunting a disservice. It sells it short. Hunting is fun, and that fun occurs in the field, not when the meat is put on the table.

Hunting groups commonly bemoan the diminishing number of young hunters, and worry that our next generation will lose touch with the deep satisfaction that a hunting trip brings. Is it any wonder? What kid would want to go harvesting? All hunters know that hunting is fun regardless of whether an animal is taken or even a shot is fired. In other words, hunting is a blast even when nothing is harvested. So hunting cannot be about harvesting; it's about the stalk and the chase, the competence, the skill, and the (occasional) reward. I know of good hunters who hunt for years without once harvesting a deer. But they still love hunting.

If hunting were about harvesting and eating, there are a lot easier and cheaper ways of getting food on the table. U.S. grocery stores are packed with the most popular meats. One cannot so easily purchase true game meats, but no matter what people say, game meats are not as good as regular meats, at least not in the general case. Proof: the stores don't stock venison and quail. If one day people thought quail to be better than chicken, then the stores' provisions would change. People who have a preference for game meats over regular meats remain in the minority, obviously. Linking hunting to eating, and saying that only people who like the taste of game meats may (ethically) hunt for those respective game animals is a perfect recipe for shrinking the size of the hunting population. You're shooting yourselves in the foot, hunters. Stop saying you hunt for food. You hunt to hunt. At least I do.

I do eat what I kill, but I'd rather have a chicken than a chukar. Both are good to eat, but I can't say it's a desire to substitute chukar for chicken that impels me out with my shotgun. I can say that I'm hunting to eat and will eat what I kill, but that justification is contrived. If it's food I want, I go to the grocer.

All of which raises a problem: if hunters really don't hunt for food (food being a nice side-product of hunting, at best), then why do hunters hunt? Let's be honest, everyone: hunters hunt for pleasure. Hunting is a very full pleasure, to be sure. But inescapably one part of hunting (not the only part, maybe not the essential part, but still a significant part) is killing. If it is permissible to kill an animal for food (and I argue it is), is it permissible to kill an animal for sport? May we kill an animal for pleasure, not necessity, not even contrived necessity?

Let me try to answer my own question by first qualifying it. Hunters do not take pleasure from the killing. We take pleasure from the preparation, practice, skill, stalk and so forth, in the context of which the killing forms an inevitable, climactic part. I would analogize the kill to the photographer who captures an image of a rare animal: the photographer's satisfaction with the beautiful image would include not just an appreciation of the image itself, but a fond recollection of the effort and skill that went into capturing that image. In that sense hunters speak of successful kills as "trophies," mementos of individual achievement. Indeed, hunters take pride in their kills being accomplished as efficiently and humanely as possible, with one well-placed shot that effects a death without non-mortal wounding or suffering. Killing is not the pleasure; hunting is.

With that qualification, I won't shy away from my question. Although killing is not the pleasurable aspect of the hunt, it is part of the pleasure of the hunt, and thus fairly raises the question about killing animals for pleasure. Varmint hunting is nothing but pleasure, in the sense that no arguments about harvesting apply. Rather than justify the sport on the basis of pleasure, varmint hunters usually employ another justification: self-defense. Varmints can cause problems: they can uproot farmers' fields, kill livestock (or injure them, by digging holes in pastures), carry diseases, and decimate the populations of "desirable" wildlife (songbirds, for instance).

These arguments work for farmers and ranchers, who are justified in defending their property. But what about my invitation: to go out on the public lands, find rats and just start shooting? One could search for similar utilitarian arguments: by shooting a bunch of chipmunks, I would be helping restore or maintain the population balance that nature intended, were the natural predators of these critters (owls and the like) not so scarce. Or I could say I'm helping to diminish the population to better stretch the limited food supply for these animals. But for me to claim that position as my own suggests to me that I need to do a lot of research and thinking about the "right" number of chipmunks or sage rats that should be running around on the forest floor, and would require me to have some clear idea that the present number is too high. I'm not going to pretend to know all of that.

I could argue that I am justified in relying on the state to do that calculation for me: by its hunting regulations, states impliedly exert control over the populations of game animals and varmints. When the State of Oregon declares a perpetual open season on sage rats (as it has) the state (one hopes) has done some measurement and concluded that perpetual hunting is necessary to maintain wildlife balance in the public lands and to prevent a undesirable build-up of the nuisance rat population on the ranches and farms that border the public lands. I'll admit I'm not sure of this self-defense rationale: it works for farmers and ranchers shooting in their fields, but is a little less convincing in the context of the vast national forests of Oregon. I think I'll decline this invitation.

How to Discipline Wayward Athletes

Chris Simon of the New York Islanders earned himself the longest suspension in NHL history by viciously slashing Ryan Hollweg of the New York Rangers in the face. Simon will sit for 25 games and forfeit just over $80,000 of his $1 million salary.[8] Was Simon's suspension for the appropriate number of games? Who's to say? A lot of athletes transgress the rules and standards set by their leagues, both inside and outside the arena, and so create a problem for their respective league commissioner: how long should the suspension last?

For an answer, we can turn to the practices of judges, who are also in the business of assigning appropriate punishments for wayward citizens. Can sports commissioners learn anything from the experience of judges? In other words, let's see why Chris Simon was punished too harshly.

Assume first that Simon's conduct comprised the worst act of on-ice violence in NHL history, thus meriting the most severe sanction. Presumably that was the determination of NHL commissioner Gary Bettman. "Worst" is not an easy conclusion to make (hence the assumption). Along what dimension was Simon's slash the worst? Did he have the most malicious intent (compared to, say, Todd Bertuzzi's surprise 2004 punch to the face of Colorado forward Steve Moore (20 games))? Or should the worst be determined not by intent but by the harm caused? Hollweg ended up with a few stitches and was back in action the next game; Don Brashear, the victim of Marty McSorley's slash to the head (23 games) was knocked out of action for several weeks. Or should the worst offense be determined not by reference to the player's intention in

---

8. Chris Simon's suspension for 25 games could end up costing him more than anticipated. With his contract ending with the New York Islanders at the end of the season, Simon will be a free agent. With only about ten games to go before the end of the season, Simon will have to sit out games in the beginning of the next season to total 25. Smith, Michael David. "Chris Simon Suspended for Season, Playoffs, Maybe More." 11 March 2007. *AOL Sports.* http://sports.aol.com/fanhouse/2007/03/11/chris-simon-suspended-for-season-playoffs-maybe-more/.

committing the act of violence nor by the harm that the act produces, but rather by reference to the act itself? Thus a slash (a swing of the stick, usually with two hands) would be more severe or "worse" than a cross-check (a more common act of pushing the opponent with the stick), which in turn would be worse than a high stick (often an act of carelessness in raising the stick during a body check)? Along what dimension should the "worst" act be determined?

None of these ways of measuring the seriousness of wayward conduct seems correct. Focusing on the malicious intention of the player raises the empirical difficulty in reading the perpetrator's mind, and the philosophical difficulty of inter-personal comparisons of malice. Simon's intent seemed obvious; McSorley, who delivered the hard slash to the head of Brashear, always maintained he was swinging for the shoulder. McSorley's swing did not look that hard, not compared to Simon's. The fact that Brashear went down in a heap and hit his uncovered head on the ice accentuated the severity of the blow. However, if instead of malicious intent, the consequential harm is to be the yardstick for assessing suspensions, then a certain element of randomness and luck is introduced. Had McSorley hit Brashear's shoulder instead of his head then we'd have never heard of either one of them; same intention, same conduct, a little bad aim, and McSorley gets himself a criminal assault conviction, leading to the extension of his suspension for a season. Similarly, Simon's attack on Hollweg resulted in a small cut; from the looks of the slash, the physical damage could have been much worse. Finally, judging severity by the nature of the act is not always possible: we can't even say for sure that slashing is always worse than cross-checking, for instance. Back in 1987, Dave Brown's cross-check to the face (15 games) broke the jaw of Tomas Sandstrum.

So as I said, let's assume all this trouble away and declare that Chris Simon's conduct warrants the longest suspension in the bloody history of the fastest game in the world. Now comes the hard part: how do we measure the punishment itself? In my view, this is the trickiest question raised by sports suspensions (and by criminal

76 · THE VIOLENCE OF SPORTS

sentences too).[9] Should punishments be measured in the length of a suspension, so that a 25-game suspension is worse than a 20-game suspension? Or should the actual impact of the suspension on the player and his team be taken into account? Players under suspension usually lose salary, among other things. Does money matter? In other words, should we just pretend that Latrell Sprewell's 63-game suspension (for choking his coach) was about three times more serious than Simon's 25-game suspension? Or should the fact that Sprewell forfeited $6.4 million in salary make Simon's $80,000 forfeiture seem paltry? The difference is that, under the first measure, Sprewell was punished three times as severely as Simon; under the second, about eight times as severely. (And what can we say about baseball suspensions, which by league tradition do not involve any forfeiture of salary? For MLB players, a suspension is equivalent to a fully funded sabbatical.)

Consequences other than lost salary also matter. McSorley's slash on Brashear, which in the public eye had a racial dimension (Brashear is one of the NHL's few black players) effectively precluded McSorley from ever playing again. Tim Hardaway, suspended from his association with the NBA for impolitic comments, has likely forfeited any chance of ever capitalizing on his basketball fame.[10]

9. In the NFL, in the wake of a series of off-field incidents involving several NFL players, Commissioner Roger Goodell has released a more stringent personal conduct policy applicable to all members of the league, including coaches and officials. The new policy includes larger fines and longer suspensions, in addition to team punishments, such as stripping the team of draft choices. Kay, Joe and Michael Marot. "Goodell Strengthens NFL Personal Conduct Policy." 10 April, 2007. *ESPN.com.* http://sports.espn.go.com/espn/wire?section=nfl&id=2832064.

10. In soccer, the Union of European Football Associations (UEFA) has recently updated its disciplinary regulations to provide a harsher penalty for racism on the field, with a possible five-match ban. "Any player found to have insulted an opponent on the basis of colour, race, religion or ethnicity risks the lengthy suspension." Players are not the only ones subject to the new regulations. If supporters of a club commit a similar offense, the club will be subject to a fine. Aside from the monetary fine, the UEFA

Should all the consequences of one's conduct be considered in imposing a penalty? Or should commissioners ignore these collateral consequences and pretend one game's suspension for one player equals one game's suspension for another player, no matter how much salary is forfeited and no matter how important the player is to his team at that point in the season? Should the harm from an act include its effects on people other than the immediate victim? Which approach is right? The answer is not as easy as saying that all players must be treated equally; it only begs the question of what consequences are included when we assess equality.

Back in the day, the salaries of professional athletes clustered around the median. Today, especially in those sports without hard salary caps, salaries among players differ quite a bit, with big stars capturing the lion's share of the salary pool. Similarly, star athletes typically earn lots of income from off-field endorsements and other engagements. So star players lose a lot more when they get suspended. If we want punishments to be roughly equal, then stars should be suspended for fewer games than scrubs, even when they engage in the same conduct—at least in theory.

Better yet, commissioners should not resort to suspensions in disciplining players.[11] The collateral consequences from a suspen-

---

will have "the option of closing stadia, deducting points, or in the most extreme cases, imposing disqualification." The harsher penalties have come about as a result of more stringent guidelines imposed by Fédéracion Internationale de Football Association (FIFA). According to FIFA, any national association that does not impose the new racism rules could risk suspension. "UEFA Increase Racism Punishments for Players." 31 July 2006. *ESPN.com.* http://soccernet.espn.go.com/news/story?id= 374735&cc =5901.

11. There has been criticism of the NBA concerning the bench suspension rule, which basically means that if a player gets up off the bench during an altercation, that player is automatically given a one-game suspension. Specifically this rule was highlighted during the recent playoffs when two players from the Phoenix Suns were suspended. Making this outcome more controversial was that the two players lost were integral to the team, and their absence undoubtedly contributed to the Suns losing

sion (to a player's salary and endorsement income, to his post-career earnings, to his team and its fans, and so forth) are too tricky to determine in any plausible way. Rather than ignoring such obvious collateral effects (as league commissioners implicitly do now), commissioners should replace suspensions with fines as much as possible. Fines are easily comparable across athletes: a $100,000 fine is twice as punitive as a $50,000 fine, and that's true for all players on all teams. Fines are nice in other respects too: they make money for the league, do not hurt the player's team or its fans, and can be just as punitive as a suspension. And don't think that rich athletes won't care about a fine: they appear to care about suspensions, and a suspension's major and direct consequence to the athlete is the coincident loss of income. (By the way, Latrell Sprewell's $6.4 million "fine," so to speak, may have been the largest monetary penalty in human history for an assault. Sprewell would have been much better off had he been prosecuted criminally.)

So Chris Simon was over-punished because in effect he pays a fine, along with his suspension, that is substantially larger than that paid by any of the other NHL miscreants, simply because Simon's salary (at least in absolute terms; I don't know about its comparison to the league average) is higher than theirs. I'm not condoning Simon's conduct, but I do think his suspension penalty should have been moderated in light of the rather pronounced collateral effects Simon will suffer to his income and his income potential.

---

the playoff series. "Stern, Owners Satisfied with Current Bench Suspension Rules." 7 June, 2007. *ESPN.com.* http://sports.espn.go.com/nba/playoffs2007/news/story?id=2897178.

The Proper Punishment for
Albert Haynesworth

The defensive lineman for the Tennessee Titans, Albert Haynesworth, kicked center Andre Gurode of the Dallas Cowboys in the head, causing a cut that required thirty stitches to close. Some commentators called for Haynesworth's arrest; others for a lifetime banishment. In any event, they think that the five-game suspension imposed by the NFL was not enough. In my view, it was plenty.

First, the five games are without pay. Since NFL players are paid by the game, Haynesworth forfeits about one-third of his yearly salary. That's a lot for any of us, especially for a highly-compensated professional athlete. In Haynesworth's case, he stands to lose about $190,000. If he had been arrested and convicted, his criminal fine would have been comparatively meager, if one were imposed at all.

Second, Haynesworth will suffer this sizable financial penalty without the benefit of a hearing or other adjudication. Sure, he's guilty; we all saw it on television.

But trials can reveal a fuller story. Was Haynesworth provoked? Was he retaliating? Was the force he used more than he intended, thus somewhat mitigating the seriousness of his conduct? Realize that it was Gurode's thirty stitches that caught everyone's attention. But what if the kick had merely glanced off Gurode? Would we care as much then? Remember, Gurode said he was ready to go back in the game had he been needed, thus suggesting a trial might have revealed better information about the seriousness of the injury.

Third, if convicted of a crime Haynesworth would probably be guilty of simple assault. Many professional athletes appear to have done worse, such as the Boston Celtics' Tony Allen, who at the time of the Haynesworth incident, awaited trial with respect to more serious conduct.[12] Yet no one's called for Allen to be banned from the

---

12. Tony Allen was accused of fracturing a man's left eye socket in an

NBA without a trial; indeed, he's in camp working on his jump shot right now. Let's not overreact to Haynesworth's conduct just because it happened on the field of play.

Fourth, let's remember that even penalties have to be marginal, increasing with the seriousness of the conduct. If the NFL were to impose a lifetime ban on Haynesworth for this conduct, as some commentators have advocated, what additional penalties remain to be imposed in the more serious case? Incentives matter, but this doesn't mean that penalties must be larger to be effective. Instead, it means that penalties have to be graduated in order to encourage wrongdoers to commit marginally less injurious crimes. Put another way, if Haynesworth will lose his livelihood by kicking Gurode, why stop at kicking him just once? He might as well go back and finish the job.

Finally, I'm more than a little uncomfortable with the distinctly modern practice of occupational disbarment as a remedy for undesirable or illegal conduct. Pay scales differ, which means the magnitude of disbarment penalties differs too. Haynesworth's loss of five weeks of pay would constitute a much larger penalty for him than for a middle-class worker, thus meaning that otherwise identical offenders would be given unequal punishments. The magnitude of the disbarment penalty also depends on at what point in the career the disbarment is imposed; a worker at the end of his career would suffer a far smaller penalty than a young person. In short, disbarment as a remedy is uneven and clumsy, at least as compared to the imposition of a fine.

Haynesworth will pay a large fine, and that seems like enough.

---

altercation outside of a restaurant in Chicago. The fight also resulted in one man being shot in the left arm and side, an event for which Allen was not a suspect. Ultimately, the judge found Allen not guilty of the charges. "Allen Found Not Guilty by Judge." 25 April, 2007. *ESPN.com.* http://sports.espn.go.com/nba/news/story?id=2848099.

The Fine Line

This may be the hardest question in law, yet it's one that is seldom discussed in a law school classroom. Albert Haynesworth's assault on the football field has brought the question into public discussion. The question is whether or not Haynesworth should have been criminally prosecuted.

In the previous essay, I argued that Haynesworth's NFL-imposed punishment sufficed, for NFL purposes. But certainly Haynesworth's conduct transgressed more than just the NFL's narrow interests in creating and selling football contests. Haynesworth's reprehensible conduct, like that of any criminal, also transgressed the interests of the wider community in peaceful compliance with its laws. Should the local government have responded to Haynesworth's action with a criminal prosecution?

I think not. Let's make the following assumptions: one, that Haynesworth's non-compensated suspension will cost him a lot of money, somewhere in the neighborhood of $190,000; two, that Haynesworth will work again in the NFL and will make professional-level money; three, that he will wear a "scarlet letter" for the rest of his career, and as a result, his professional earnings and his post-career earnings will be something less than they would have been had the Gurode incident not occurred. How much less is anyone's guess, though likely not a lot in this case because Haynesworth appears to have a propensity to rash acts of violence and so would not have left the game with much goodwill. Let's also assume that Haynesworth may well have to pay Gurode some money in settlement, perhaps even be compelled to do so in response to a civil lawsuit and that, without Gurode's cooperation, criminal charges will never be brought.[13]

---

13. In the end, Andre Gurode, the Dallas Cowboys center who was the recipient of Haynesworth's assaultive actions, decided not to press any criminal charges. The possibility of a lawsuit has not been completely

We might think of Haynesworth's loss of income as a fine. A fine can be just as punitive as a term of incarceration. This is a complicated point, but to put it quickly, would you take $190,000 to spend some time in prison? Any time, if only a day or week or month? If so, then you've just agreed that, at some price, you would exchange prison for money. The only question left is settling on the price.

A criminal conviction also carries a stigma that itself is a punishment, and that stigma can diminish income and social standing. Yet the stigmatic effect of a conviction varies; in some communities, a conviction is a big deal, while it is not in others. For a professional athlete, although undesirable to be sure, a criminal conviction is not uncommon, and many players enjoy long and lucrative careers despite their criminal records. Adding a conviction to Haynesworth's shame and embarrassment would probably not add much.

The harm that results from an incident goes a long way to determine the appropriateness of the sanction and whether or not criminal prosecution is merited. One hundred people can speed down a road, yet only the one unlucky motorist whose car strikes a pedestrian would be charged with a crime. So even though Haynesworth's kick could have injured Gurode much more seriously, by the same token it might have missed him altogether, sparing Haynesworth's conduct more than passing notice. So when we punish Haynesworth, we shouldn't punish on the basis of what might have happened, only what did.

One supposed test for criminality is if the conduct has public ramifications, in that it victimizes more people than the immediate victim. I've never put much stock in this test; every violent act against the person makes everyone else feel a bit less secure. But

---

ruled out. "Gurode Won't Press Charges." 5 October 2006. *ESPN.com.* http://sports.espn.go.com/nfl/news/story?id=2614453.

Haynesworth's act does not threaten the rest of us in the least; it took place in a very contained environment surrounded by security. It did diminish our enjoyment of the game, but the game is just entertainment. I just don't buy the view that what Haynesworth did will lead to flag football kids kicking each other. Maybe I'm too dismissive of this appeal to public sentiment and volatility, but this appeal covers everything. Even bad stuff that doesn't happen on TV is later put on TV. We see it all, so much so that, really, were any of us truly traumatized by what Haynesworth did? Yes, we express outrage to each other because we're expected to, but honestly, was the public truly a victim here?

With that said, Haynesworth's act was a public act, and thus it would not be "unfair" to make an example of him. We could say the same lots of times when athletes go too far, which they do from time to time. These are not necessarily violent men. They are ordinary men playing violent games, crashing into other men at full strength. Inevitably tempers will flare and players will act out, even rashly. There is a reason prosecutors, who are asked to make this difficult decision about criminal prosecution, have historically looked away when athletes commit crimes against each other during games. If they didn't, then we'd ask all athletes to do something very difficult, to act with utmost violence one moment and be well-mannered gentlemen the next. Athletes can do it, of course, and most have, in very difficult circumstances. But this expectation is still a very high one, one much greater than the rest of us carry, and so we shouldn't be surprised if sometimes these athletes fail. I played college hockey and yes, got in a few fights. I swung my fist, but luckily no one got hurt (bad aim). But someone could have. There but for the grace of God go I.

Chapter Four

Sports Books

I dislike book reviews as a rule. They spend most of their paragraphs summarizing the book's basic information or plot, follow that with a little criticism, and end the piece with a quick moral lesson, either about the book's theme or about the book's effectiveness in developing that theme. What I want to see in a book review is the extent to which the book stimulated the reviewer's thinking. I want the book review to argue with the book's thesis, or take the thesis in new directions. Even if I differ with the review, the fact that the book generated a strong intellectual reaction recommends the book in a way that mere description and accolades could not.

A big part of my job as a university professor is to read books and other materials relevant to my area of work. Sports law is a nice combination as it melds my two passions. But it also poses a problem. There are many, many books on the various subjects of law and equally many on the various subjects of sports, but precious few that deal with the intersection. In most areas of legal study, a fairly well-developed reading list of books and academic articles supplies researchers with an essential introduction to the most important schools of thought. For the few of us that make sports law our focus, no canon exists. We have to create our own reading lists. Indeed, the paucity of good books and academic articles that fall precisely into the narrow niche of sports law also means that we have to create our own books. We will, in time.

Other academic disciplines such as economics, sociology, and anthropology, have a rich literature applying their tools of analysis to sports and the sports industry. Legal academics have lagged.

Part of the reason for this dearth is the old bromide about sports law, that "there is no such thing as sports law." This view reflects a misapprehension about the proper subject of sports law. Traditionally, most legal scholars interested in sports law have come to sports from other areas of inquiry, such as labor law or antitrust law or intellectual property law; their sports law scholarship has generally consisted of application of the analysis and doctrines of that (familiar) area of law to sports subjects. Hence, when reading an article about the antitrust implications of sports franchise relocation, for instance, one is really reading about antitrust jurisprudence, not sports law jurisprudence. Antitrust law supplies the verb, so to speak, while the object of the verb happens to be sports franchises. Little about the unique aspect of sports matters much to the discussion. As a result, legal scholars happening across some traditional sports law scholarship would see an article nearly indistinguishable, in terms of cases and doctrines, from most other antitrust articles. There is no sports law, came the conclusion, any more than there is "the law of the horse."

We are beginning to see the development of a jurisprudence of sports law. The starting point for this development is the recognition of the rules of sport as a separate set of rules distinct from those of other industries or other legal subjects. When sports franchises relocate and lawsuits are brought, the federal antitrust statutes are implicated, and a book that discusses that franchise relocation necessarily becomes a book about antitrust law. But everyday sports are chock-full of rules that have the force of law, at least the force of law immanent to the game. A baseball hit over the fence in fair territory is a home run; that's a rule of baseball. This simple rule has all the attributes of what scholars term private law: it is privately devised and agreed to, and it is enforceable, both privately (through the umpire and, if necessary, league officials) and publicly, should the home run present some issue (perhaps about ownership of the ball) to a judicial tribunal. Lots of our private rules, such as the particular terms of a contract, share the same attributes, with private enforcement provided by a retained arbitrator or public enforcement through a judicial tribunal. There is no particular shortcoming of the rules of sport that renders them unsuitable for legal categorization and analysis; rather, what has been lacking is the attention of those scholars who claim sports law as their field.

Part of the effort to establish sports law as a separate legal field is to collect books on sports topics from other disciplines, or even from the popular press, that might provide useful comments on the law of sports, to elucidate that comment, and to see where a particular thesis or line of thinking might take us. Undoubtedly this project is ambitious, and likely over time none of these books (or mine) will make the cut. But we have to start somewhere. So here are some books that I thought made some impact on sports law, if only because they took the subject of sports seriously—and some are books that I read just for fun.

How Soccer Explains the World (Franklin Foer)

Most of my written comments about any book I read are going to be favorable. Although I read a lot, I'm also picky. I'll give nearly any book 100 pages and then decide if the book is worth finishing. I'm merciless, putting down best-sellers not worth further investment. One of the differences between my book notes and a book review is that the person doing the latter (for pay) probably feels constrained to finish even a bad book just to tell you it's bad.

Foer provides an entertaining and readable story that basically places soccer (futbol) in the middle of regional, national, religious, cultural, and socio-economic tensions all over the world, even in the U.S. Of course the magnitude of the fans' perspectives and class seems overstated and stereotyped, but it's almost impossible to tell a cultural-tension story in a few hundred double-spaced pages[1]

---

1. Yes, it's double-spaced; lots of "air" between the lines. Why are so many books like that today? Even the New Yorker has noticeably short-

without making some fairly quick generalizations. If you're looking for endless qualifiers, careful documentation, and footnotes, this book is not for you. Think of it as airport reading but with some pretty thoughtful commentary.

As wonderful a read as this book is, on one level it doesn't quite work. Foer writes with charm about soccer[2] and about specific rivalries, team histories, and fan characteristics. He neatly ties much of this narrative into a legal/cultural/political/economic story. However, the next level of abstraction is where the trouble begins. He tries to tie the whole narrative together into a tale of "globalization" versus its opposite, which I guess would be parochialism or sectarianism or nationalism or the like. He also ends up throwing the terms "liberal" and "conservative" into the mix. Here the superim-

---

ened up the feature pieces. Is America dumbing down, or are we being dumbed-down by smart people like Foer who refuse to write fuller treatments? I suspect a heavy-handed editor or officious publisher in the background on something like this. But still, I think Foer had it within his obvious erudition and research to write a much fuller account. (Of course, then I wouldn't have read it.)

2. Here's what I like about soccer: every player is important (so no worries about whose kid gets to play quarterback), lots of running, premium on teamwork, marginal advantages combining to pay off in ultimate, long-term gains (in the form of goals, for instance), and few stoppages in play. Here's what I find distasteful about soccer: can't use the hands (hard to call a sport ideal when our most useful and coordinated appendages go to waste), flopping around for calls, penalty kicks from about ten feet in front of the goal as a result of a perceived "push" in one team's box (the whole game can be decided right here), and headers. I hate headers. I played some soccer in school and we had a drill where a coach would throw a ball at your head and you had to practice heading the ball into the goal. Wet, cold New England afternoons. Look out. I saw my teammates take a few of these practice headers and stagger around, probably concussed. For TSLP? Amazingly, I always missed, every single time, for two full seasons, despite my very best efforts to slam my forehead into a heavy ball thrown directly at it. I knew then that I might need to make a living with whatever brains survived into adulthood.

position of a story line threatens to obliterate the facts of the story. Although he seems ambivalent about the virtues of globalization, Foer is a self-proclaimed liberal. Not a big deal by itself, but here's the problem: he just can't bring himself to say that "liberal," in domestic contemporary political terms, includes notions like leftist, socialist, communist, and so forth. At least in this sense, "liberal" more correctly indicates or describes the comparative position of the socialist than would the term "conservative." Not for Foer. Every movement that yearns for freedom and goodness and morality is "liberal;" every oppressive force that seeks to dampen or delay such yearning is "conservative." Thus for Foer "conservatives" take the shape of authoritarian military dictators, socialists, communists, and theocrats. Foer might claim that when he says "liberal" he means classical liberal, but that's clearly not the sense in which he employs the term. By liberal he means Democrat. I appreciate people who are passionate about their politics. I worry for those who confuse their politics with all things good and reasonable.

Nonetheless, it is so good to read a book like this that takes sports seriously. Tell someone you're reading a book about sports and he thinks of ghost-written hagiographical trash with nice action pictures. Many sports books fit that bill, of course. But anyone who thinks sports today exists for young boys to dream of playing-field glory hasn't been paying attention. Maybe we are all kids, maybe we are dumbed down, but today's sports are big, big business, capturing the attention of huge segments of the adult population. By capturing that attention, sports have become a sieve through which much of contemporary culture is filtered, through which so much conversation and thought and even knowledge itself is processed. The only discipline or interest that matches sports as a common cultural filter is law. Is sports law irrelevant? It's the center. Visit any European museum that features late gothic or early Christian art; it is obvious the extent to which those societies understood themselves in relation to the Christian narrative. For better or worse (okay, worse), today's narrative is sports and law, maybe both. We need more books like Foer's to help us understand ourselves.

The Blind Side (Michael Lewis)

I'm going to have a lot of negative comments to make about a book I liked a lot — one that has been praised universally, as far as I can tell. On the bright side, the book is engaging, well-written, and thought-provoking. What more could you want from a book? Let's see.

The thesis is straightforward. Lawrence Taylor and other big, fast blitzing linebackers who came to the NFL in the mid-1980's became disruptive to the passing game. At the same time, various rule changes involving the coverage of wide receivers put a premium on successful passing attacks. The combination of fast linebackers trying to disrupt the increasingly important passing game led to the need for especially quick offensive linemen to play left tackle (on the right-hand quarterback's "blind side") to protect the quarterback. And that's it. Nice angle, enough for the typical *Sports Illustrated* feature piece that goes toward the back of the magazine, but no more. So how does Lewis make a book out of this small story? And what's wrong with making a small story into a big book?

The book spends a lot of time in breathless praise of Lawrence Taylor. Praise is fine, but continual glowing tributes get tiresome. They also seem overstated. The NFL has always had big and fast athletes; in the past, a player of Taylor's size and speed would play defensive end. In the 3-4 defense in which Taylor played, the linebacker is essentially substituted for the defensive end. I know Taylor was an exceptional athlete and would have excelled in any era, but the fact that he played linebacker instead of end should not matter much; it's somewhat arbitrary where he played and how his position is labeled, contingent on the coach's preference.[3]

---

3. On the same point, why, in baseball for instance, when discussing all-time greats, will commentators typically assess the player's offensive production in terms of his defensive position? Ryne Sandberg was a great-hitting second baseman, they'll say, comparing his numbers to other sec-

The bulk of the book involves the upbringing and eventual high school stardom of Michael Oher, a very large young man with very quick feet; in short, a prototype for the rare athlete that fits the NFL's current model for left tackles. And it's quite a story: how a young boy from an unimaginably destitute and (virtually) parentless childhood is more or less adopted by a wealthy nuclear family, sent off to private school and propelled on his way to college stardom and presumably NFL riches. The problem is that the story about Oher's childhood and recruitment does not appear to tie into the NFL's stipulations for left tackles; an athlete of Oher's great size and speed would have been desired by college football recruiters in any era. So the Oher story doesn't really fit the rest of the book. But it is a compelling story. Oher presumably will play left tackle one day in the NFL (although who knows? What if Belichick puts him on the right side?), and it does fill out the book.

However, by forcing the Oher story into the NFL-rules-changes-Lawrence-Taylor-blind-side story, I think Lewis misses the real story about Michael Oher. What's interesting about Oher is not that one day he may play professional left tackle; what's interesting is the incredible extent to which the people and institutions that surround this young athlete will go to make sure that his NFL career happens. It's a joke, really, and one that Lewis reports largely without comment. Oher may be a gifted football player, but by every measure he is singularly unqualified for the academic hurdles an NFL

---

ond basemen. By the same token, Brooks Robinson, a fine fielding third-baseman, was a weak-hitting one. Why put it in these terms? Sandberg could have played third or first or left-field just as ably, and indeed might have been assigned to one of those positions had his team needed him there (see Alex Rodriguez playing third or Nomar Garciaparra at first). Brooks Robinson might have been just as adept in left or at second base. Would Sandberg be less of a hitter had he spent his career at third base? Is he more of a hitter because he played second? Why should his defensive position, or Robinson's, matter when assessing his offensive numbers? Sure, some coaches like small, quick players in the middle infield, but let's not forget that lumbering Cal Ripken spent over a decade playing shortstop.

career implicitly imposes. It's not entirely the kid's fault (although part of it is), but this young man pretty much evades any semblance of an education right up to high school. Yet today he's enrolled in a four-year college program. How did this happen?

For all intents and purposes, one has to go to college to play in the NFL. This is a mistake, one that no other sport imposes. God doesn't give out both brains and brawn to everybody. Some people aren't meant to do time in college. Making all pro football prospects go to college corrodes institutions.[4] For example, Oher got

———————

4. For instance, in the wake of the Duke lacrosse scandal, Duke's faculty formulated a "plan" that would entail the assignment of a "faculty associate" to tag along with Duke's sports teams to practices and games and most things in between. Putting aside the practicalities of faculty inertia (I could see a faculty member taking this assignment if it meant seats next to the bench at Duke basketball games. But travel around with the cross-country or rowing teams?), what seems troublesome to me is the aim of the program: to improve communication between the academic parts of the university and the athletic teams, with the faculty associate as a liaison. Since when are athletics assumed not to be academic? To me, everything the university does, or rather everything it should do, is academic. I know, things have gotten a bit out of hand in sports, as student-athletes are in many cases quasi-professional nomads who merely don the university colors for a period of time, with little expectation of real education or graduation. But many programs in the modern university are equally out of hand. At some universities, majors in certain specialized departments, such as music, art, pre-medicine, and many newfangled majors that look like occupational trades, complete a few desultory "general coursework" requirements and that's the entirety of the young specialist's non-vocational education. How would musician-students and their instructors feel if the university assigned them a faculty associate to help them communicate with their "academic" colleagues? Admittedly college sports has some problems with the academic side of things. But so do many college specialties. Only because sports appears weekly on the national television does the hyper-specialization of the student-athlete seem such an unusual problem. It's not. Many of today's "hyphenated students" need a faculty associate. Let's just call these associates "professors" and have them hold classes that these students must attend.

through high school with what can only be described as intense, continual and personal tutoring, special attention, begging, pleading, and so forth. One has to read between the lines (Lewis didn't) and wonder just how much his tutor, for instance, helped Michael learn, or learned for him, if you catch my drift. By all appearances, at least as Lewis describes it, Michael does not seem capable of performing well academically. What was the big rush? Why not take this undereducated kid and start him over in a lower grade? Why was it so important that Oher matriculate? Not much draft interest in a 25-year-old player, that's why. Oher had to get to college "on time" to maximize his professional riches.

Oher's grade point average, in combination with his board scores, were well below the NCAA minimum for student-athletes. So how does Michael get his grades up? How does he change F's and D's (in completed courses) to A's? Don't ask Michael: he gets A's in subjects that he can't even name. He made those F's into A's by completing (with his tutor's help) some on-line courses that Brigham Young University offers (according to the book). These courses lasted all of one single week each! Yet they changed, in the eyes of the NCAA, semesters of F's into A's. BYU, a reputable institution, should be ashamed of itself, as should the NCAA. I'll refrain from putting any blame on Sean and Leigh Anne Tuohy (Michael's adoptive parents), and Michael Oher himself, only because the young man appears singularly well-suited for pro ball, and it's not their fault the path to the NFL goes through college. But still, I hope no one was proud of himself for changing those earned grades.[5]

---

5. The NCAA seems fixated on graduation rates. It recently announced that graduation rates for scholarship athletes have gone up again this year, and are now approaching eighty percent, even outpacing non-athletes. Does anyone realize that graduation rates are manipulable? Offer easy enough credits and any university will graduate more students. Can I offer evidence that credits are today comparatively easier to obtain? I just did. Graduation rates are up. Res ipsa loquitur. The NCAA should review the academic rigor of some of the courses populated by today's student-athlete. Universities and coaches wanting to field winning sports teams, yet

I could go on; read the book and you'll see. The real story of *The Blind Side* is the blind eye we turn toward the means by which we "educate" these young athletes. As good as the book is, I wish Lewis had seen the field a bit better.

Game of Shadows: Barry Bonds, BALCO, and the Steroids Scandal that Rocked Professional Sports (Mark Fainaru-Wada and Lance Williams)

The latest bestseller! Wait, it's been out for over two years. Sorry, but it takes me a while to get to all the books I'd like to read. Part of the delay is due to the fact that this is not the kind of sports book I usually like to read, so I put it off. I would divide sports books into four categories, in no particular order.

Category 1: The sports autobiography, often ghostwritten, which I never found interesting, except when I was a kid. They can be fine, as long as the reader totally suspends disbelief and absolutely adores the player. (As a kid, I read every book on Bobby Orr.) Hagiography.

---

brag about high graduation rates, have every incentive to coddle and ca-jole their distracted young stars through to graduation. Easy courses, spe-cial tutors, flexible deadlines, friendly professors made aware of grade requirements, early enrollment to ensure seats in the easiest classes, and more. It's not that hard to graduate a student. The incentive is obvious. Yet the NCAA, the popular media and everybody else ignore this obvious incentive and repeat the propaganda about graduation rates without hes-itation or qualification. University presidents must giggle at our ingenu-ousness. It is a profound mistake to think of graduation as the aim of a college education. Education is the aim. College degrees are laudable (and financially valuable) because they reflect educational accomplishment and completion. Take away the education and the degree is not worth the paper on which it's printed.

Category 2: The next category I'd call sports biographies, written with or without the subject's permission and usually by a researcher/journalist. These can be very good. (I just finished Kenny Moore's excellent biography on Bill Bowerman, legendary Oregon track coach and, by the way, one of Nike's founders.[6]) But even though I'll read one or two of these every year, biographies are simply not to my taste. Some people find the life stories of others endlessly fascinating, but for me, most lives look pretty much the same. I don't care to learn about Lebron James' childhood, wherever it took place. I don't even care about what he does once he walks off the court. Athletes aren't celebrities to me. I enjoy watching the games, but that's it.

Category 3: These are reporter's books, and I'd put *Game of Shadows* in this group. Investigative books, behind-the-scenes books, follow-a-team-for-a-season books, and so on. These can get pretty tedious, especially when the book ends up reading a lot like a series of newspaper accounts of the previous day's action. These books better have a big payoff in terms of insight or inside information if I'm going to wade through all the game recaps. They rarely do. John Feinstein's tedious *A Good Walk Spoiled* may have ruined this category for me forever. I was thinking of buying Jack McCallum's book on a season spent with the Phoenix Suns, but I'm afraid to be disappointed again. But I do like how the Suns play basketball, and Steve Nash is a passing genius. By the way, I'd also put inside accounts written by players in this category (George Plimpton's *Paper Lion*, Phil Jackson's and Charley Rosen's *More Than a Game*, etc.).

Category 4: Here we are, the category where I do most of my sports book reading. I think of books in this category as offering "perspectives" on sports, such as where a game is going (*Moneyball*) or why it has evolved (*The Blind Side*) or how it should be understood (*The Wages of Wins*) or to what it bears significance in a

---

6. Kenny Moore, Bowerman and the Men of Oregon: The Story of Oregon's Legendary Coach and Nike's Co-founder (2006).

broader sense (*How Soccer Explains the World*). I find books in this
category stimulating. Often they're written by academics on a bus-
man's holiday, so I guess it's no surprise I like them.[7]

About the book, first, really, the authors should be in jail. There
are some pretty significant reasons that grand jury testimony must
be kept secret. The writers had a source leaking that information to
them, and it appears to me that the source didn't just provide a few
generalities. The writers appeared to have had significant access to the
testimony of several witnesses, including Bonds, Giambi, and San-
tiago. The reporters can argue all they want about journalistic priv-
ilege, but they were breaking the law when they elicited this
information, and from the sound of things, they knew it. Maybe it's
ironic that the reporters go to prison while Bonds goes to the outfield;
on the other hand, maybe the reporters' wrong was more serious.[8]

Some questions trouble me about the ban on performance-

---

7. Category 5 should be called Category Simmons: Since Bill Simmons,
ESPN's "Sports Guy," writes columns, and since he's put together some of
those in his book (title too long to type in), and since I read it, and since
it's about sports, I guess I have to put his book somewhere. In my view Simmons is re-creating sports writing, probably ruining it forever. If you
haven't read his writings (you should), think Hunter S. Thompson covering a Red Sox game, from his sofa, and substitute coffee for cocaine.
Simmons' writing is fun, slashing and veering wildly from complaints
about his dog, wife, and friends, to thoughtful paragraphs on what makes
a competent baseball pitcher an ace. Now everybody's starting to write in
his style, talking as much about one's personal reaction to what's happening on the field as about what is actually happening on the field. Simmons' articles are the journalistic equivalent to philosophical idealism, the
view that says that everything we know is in our heads only. Simmons
doesn't really write about sports, he writes about Simmons, and it just so
happens that the Simmons he writes about is the Simmons who watches
and writes about sports, and a few other subjects. So he gets his own category. As much as I admire his work, for the sake of the nation, let's hope
he remains this category's exclusive inhabitant.

8. It's incorrect to say that the reporters were "convicted" and were
"sentenced" to eighteen months' imprisonment. There has been no crime.
There has been stubbornness and defiance. The reporters were ordered to

enhancing drugs. First, in most sports, when players are tested for performance-enhancers, they're also tested for other drugs (marijuana) which do nothing to enhance athletic performance, and in fact hurt it. (Golf may be an exception here, I'm told; being high on marijuana might help even out that putting stroke. Are PGA tour pros smoking weed before putting on their plaid slacks? Now that would be a Category 3 book I'd read.) Next, the ban doesn't make a lot of sense, given that all kinds of non-pharmaceutical substances can enhance performance: are they any different in principle? Are genetically engineered enhancements (the coming thing) any different? Given that all of us differ genetically anyway, if an athlete's very genetic makeup can be altered, in what sense is this enhancement non-natural? We can be born weak and yet lift weights to make us strong, so why can't we undergo gene therapy to accomplish the same alteration? Finally, baseball's ban does drive drug use underground. This is the big story of *Game of Shadows*.

On this last point, the book's lasting image (much like the revelations I hear were in Jose Canseco's book,[9] a Category 3 book too, by the way) was the vivid account of the relevant portion of the life of Barry Bonds. Not his life as a superstar baseball player, but his life as a druggie. Really, this account reads a lot like other stories of drug use: the shady characters, clandestine meetings, covert

---

reveal the source of the grand jury leak. They said they would refuse the court's order and told the world they would go to jail to keep their promise to their source. In short, the reporters publicly rubbed their defiance in the judge's nose, leaving him little choice but to employ one of the strongest powers of the trial judge: civil contempt. Because the contempt is civil in nature, and not criminal, the reporters hold the keys to their cell. The very day they decide to answer the prosecutor's questions is the day their jail stay will end (as indeed it did end the very day prior to the first scheduled day of prison, when the source identified himself). The problem is the promise the reporters made to their source. Their claim is that they promised confidentiality. That's a great idea, but very few of us can legally maintain confidentiality in the face of a grand jury subpoena.

9. Jose Canseco, *Juiced: Wild Times, Rampant Roids, Smash Hits, and How Baseball Got Big*. www.amazon.com.

deliveries, secret injections in the bathroom, and so on. Not a pretty sight (especially when the boys share a bathroom stall to inject each other in the buttocks). The health risks to steroids are debatable and controllable (hey, most of these substances, as well as human growth hormone, are prescribed every day). But here's a bunch of ballplayers, track stars, and football linebackers getting health advice and, for all purposes, medical direction from this lab-owner who was a charlatan, community college dropout, huckster and salesman whose medical training results from the frightening methodology called trial and error. How much better would it be if Bonds and his ilk could be administered drugs in a sterile environment under a physician's supervision?

Don't read this book if you like your sports superstars unblemished. This account of the steroids scandal looks at just one little corner of it, just one lab servicing a few athletes. Undoubtedly there are many, many more. The one quibble I have with the book is with its subtitle; it refers to the steroid scandal that "rocked" sports. Wrong tense. The steroid era is just beginning. Look for a lot more shadow games before it ends.

Seven Seconds or Less: My Season on the Bench with the Runnin' and Gunnin' Phoenix Suns (Jack McCallum)

As mentioned above, all sports books come in one of four categories, and *Seven Seconds* is not in the category I prefer to read. But after I expressed an interest in this book, it arrived at my office doorstep. You've got to love freebies. I'll read (a little) of almost anything stuck in front of me, for at least 100 pages. Since that was about half the book (and a quick 100 at that) I went ahead and finished it. Not to imply I'm slumming. This book was pretty fun, and there's nothing wrong with a quick, light read to relax away the evening hours. Just in case your books don't arrive gratis, here are a few thoughts to consider in spending your book budget.

Just how many times can the "F" swear be used in a conversation/book/film until we're totally inured to its scatological effect? Do people really use this swear so often? Have American schools (I'm referring to the recess part) diminished so much that kids know no other swears or other terms to express emphasis? I mean, what the f***? Anyway, McCallum fills his book with F bombs. The Suns' coaches use them, the players use them, so many people were using them I didn't know who was f'ing who. I suppose this is the (cheap) way a writer infuses his book with gritty realism, allowing the reader to hear the unfiltered frankness of talk in certain walks of life. I also suppose this is the language of youth, and that such language allows middle-aged coaches to appear youthful (albeit probably pathetically) to the young people they work with everyday. The coaches at least should be mature enough to find some other adjective.

So on the one hand the book shares the gritty realism of frank locker-room talk. On the other hand is the utter banality of what most people quoted in the book had to say. Minus approximately 1,000 swears, almost everything the people said could have been reproduced in a newspaper without major repercussions. Where was the real frank talk, not the swearing, but the "everyone hates that guy" or "he can't coach" revelations? One of two things must have happened.

The first is compromise. McCallum asked for and received a season-long insider's access to the Suns, hanging around at practices, in the locker room, and on road trips. The book discloses nothing in the way of censorship, so I'll take it that McCallum could relay everything he witnessed of interest. If not an explicit agreement, was there an unspoken contract to refrain from yielding company secrets? Or did the writer's own sense of propriety or desire to be invited back filter his book? If so, where was that sense of propriety when he was typing all those expletives? If so, where was the limitation on reportage or conflict of interest disclosed? If player privacy was to be protected, the reader should have been told (maybe even on the book jacket).

The alternative explanation is more dismal: maybe the players don't have anything much to say other than the banalities one reads in the newspaper, except with a swear or two added in. Should players or coaches express much publicly in the way other than a banality, they risk trouble, even big trouble. So players learn, quickly, to express platitudes, to compliment teammates and opponents, to say nothing even slightly derogatory about their coaches or general managers. To quote the poet Rasheed Wallace, "It was a great game. Both teams played hard." If what these players learn to say is a bunch of banalities, pretty soon they're thinking in banalities. Maybe they don't have much else to say, no opinions to express other than the post-game clichés that find their way into the morning stories.

It would be better if they had opinions, even repercussion-free opinions. I recently watched the football movie *Any Given Sunday* and the star, a young, headstrong black quarterback, went on some interview show and proceeded to issue a series of interesting opinions on the state of the game and the particular role of the black athlete and black quarterback within it. His comments were debatable, and I found myself moved to debate them. Wouldn't it be nice if our real athletes similarly shared their opinions with us, assuming they were encouraged to cultivate them? I think someone like Rasheed Wallace, who strikes me as thoughtful and engaging, might have something to say.

One fact needs to be made clear. As the book title suggests, the writer spent the season on the bench with the Suns: he was allowed to join the coaching staff. Thus, like any coach, his access to the stars of the game was limited to a certain extent. From what I could detect, he saw the players during practice and games and during certain interactions while traveling. I would assume players would generally be on their best behavior around the coaches, especially on a team like the Suns where the head coach (Mike D'Antoni) functions also as the team's personnel manager, empowered to make trades and set salaries. As a result of this season "on the bench," the focus of the book is the coaches, particularly the assistants. They seemed interesting enough, but their role on the team is limited to advice-giving to millionaire players and the head coach. Second bananas, yet they're the ones with whom McCallum hung out. I'm not blaming McCallum (he hangs with a better crowd than I do), but still, it is a limitation and should be made evident.

The book was well done overall, a story well-told by a well-known *Sports Illustrated* writer. But here's my beef. I read the book (free or not) for one reason: I wanted to know how they do it. How do the Suns teach NBA players to play the up-tempo running offense for which the Suns have rightly become famous? So many teams promise their fans a running team (I'm a Boston fan, still waiting for the vaunted Celtics fast break to start); yet the Suns, almost uniquely among NBA teams, run a real up-tempo offense. I'm not just talking about shots early in the shot clock, which a number of teams accomplish. I'm talking about old-school fast breaks, with the ball seldom hitting the floor, where lay-ups and dunks result off of made baskets, where (in a modern twist) open lane penetrators kick out to waiting wing shooters, where the team is just fun to watch. The Suns are about the only team (besides the Celtics or Blazers, my two losing favorites) that I'll scan the channels looking to find.

So how do D'Antoni and his staff inculcate this amazing offense? How does he take rookies, free agents and players off of other teams' rosters and teach them the Suns style? McCallum even poses the question: is Steve Nash great because D'Antoni and the Suns are great, or are the Suns great because they have Steve Nash? But what's the answer? The book doesn't offer an answer. Couldn't McCallum have spent his season on the bench getting to the bottom of the central question of our time, NBA-version? Yet about all we hear from D'Antoni is pre-game "let's go" speeches and repeated exhortations to his players to run. Is that it?[10] Surely there's more to

10. Could the Celtics win as many as the Suns if only Tommy Heinsohn returned to the bench? (Inside joke for Celtics fans.)

the Suns special offense than "everybody run, spread out and make incredible passes to each other."

McCallum was with the team from pre-season camp to the very end. What's the insight? How does D'Antoni teach the offense? Realize that most NBA players were stars in high school and college, where they probably dribbled and shot the ball more than anyone else on the team (think Kobe Bryant or Paul Pierce). How does the Suns coach get these ball hogs to play so unselfishly? What is his special theory of offense that has produced such a remarkable and aesthetically pleasing approach to the game? How does a coach engineer an offense that will produce an open shot for a good shooter in a mere seven seconds? You would think a year on the bench would have suggested an answer.

Sorry to seem ungrateful. Thanks for the book.

Sports Illustrated Swimsuit Issue 2007

Let's be absolutely clear about this: I did not read the *Swimsuit Issue*, not one word, so no one give me grief on this. I only looked at the pictures.

Before I saddle up my high horse and get on it, I should fess up and say this annual *Sports Illustrated* edition made the freeze of the New England winters of my youth much more bearable. Back in the day, when sexual innuendo and scantily-clad bodies were not something that showed up on commercials during baseball games, to see a woman wearing a bikini, especially the beautiful women who found their way into *SI*, was a pretty inspiring event. My pals and I would pass the issue around, and photos today that aren't worth much more than a glance would, in those days, elicit a genuine "wow." Men my age can remember where they were when that shot of Cheryl Tiegs in a fishnet bathing suit came out. It sounds so quaint now, but back in the day, the very idea of an annual pictorial of women in bikinis (or fishnets) was actually quite a note-worthy, controversial, and even revolutionary event.

Until a few other nascent sports magazines started doing the same thing many years later (and before the internet), *SI* had the field to itself, much as it had serious sports journalism to itself. The only equivalent event I could hypothesize for today would be (if there were no internet) to subscribe to some high-brow literary magazine, and then once a year *Playboy* comes in the mail. We boys couldn't believe we could get away with this, with our parents no less renewing our subscription as an annual Christmas present. Needless to say, we watched the late January mail deliveries pretty closely.

Now I'll be honest in saying that, in the many years since TSLP's legendary youth, I've barely given the annual issue more than a glance. It's not that pictures of beautiful women wearing the barest of bathing suits don't interest me, it's just that I can hardly take my morning turn through my regular websites or watch evening sports on television without being exposed to lots of women dressed to hit the beach. I open *SI*'s web page everyday, and every day a new image of one of *SI*'s bikini models jumps out at me from the side-bar. I seldom give her more than a glance, if I see her at all. Maybe I'm reflecting my age, and a younger man might find every new image of another and another and yet another bikini-clad model to be endlessly fascinating. I suspect, however, it's all now rather boring for most of us. Even bathing-suit beauty has a saturation point, and I reached it years ago.

So it was with a bit of nostalgic curiosity that I decided to page through this year's *SI Swimsuit Issue*. I was shocked. My stomach turned. I wept for our country and our future. It wasn't the models or the bikinis; it was an advertisement. I grasped the thick 2007 swimsuit issue in my hands, let it fall open, and there before me was a two-page picture of an entirely nude Burt Reynolds, circa 1975, with his forearm carefully placed to hide the most private part of his private parts. Just Burt, nothing else. Probably some company name somewhere; I didn't study the page to find it. Does *SI* have any idea how that photo made me and presumably millions of other American males feel? There we were, opening *SI*'s famous swimsuit issue, eagerly ready to assess the 2007 version of Cheryl Tiegs, and the magazine falls open to a naked man, so hirsute I'd call his body hair a pelt, just sitting there grinning at us. Sorry to play the heterosexual card here, but heterosexual men (at least this one) do not look at other men as an object of beauty, and have no desire to look upon naked men in any context. Yet Burt the Bear was the nudest person in the entire magazine (at least the swimsuit models kept on their bikini bottoms). It's hard to describe a more disheartening moment of confusion when a man, expecting to ogle nearly naked women, sees an entirely naked man. *SI* should be ashamed of itself, publishing such images.

After I got up off the floor, I was able to look through the rest of the magazine at the pictures of the models. Again, perhaps I'm just revealing my age, but I found the experience on the whole somewhat boring. I flipped rapidly through to the end. After the Cheryl Tiegs picture, there's really nothing more that a fairly reputable magazine can do. The photos at this point are only a couple of inches of material (or a small movement of a hand) away from a flat-out *Playboy* pictorial. There's nowhere else for *SI* to go. Literally. So it's obvious that the magazine is trying some twists (body paint) and turns (celebrity models, like Beyonce) to keep the interest going. It's a dying franchise, I would think, although I'm told this issue is *SI*'s annual sales leader. It might sell, but it's boring. And (Burt Reynolds aside) it was difficult at times to discern which of the photos were *SI*'s and which were advertisements. The ads were just as racy as the rest of the magazine. The fact that those same ads presumably appear in other *SI* issues or other magazines speaks volumes about the degree to which our common, everyday experience has caught up to the former infamy of this annual swimsuit edition.

One small joy of the *SI* experience back in the day was the apparent glut of letters *SI* would receive (many of which were published) of the "cancel my subscription, I have children at home" variety. TSLP has children at home too. I will admit I more or less hide the annual swimsuit issue until a safe place can be found for it deep within the recycle receptacle. (One year it disappeared, only to reappear months later in the closet of my youngest. At least he has good taste.) Even as a kid I thought the letter-writers were overreacting to more or less harmless fun, but then again, I always made sure my mom never got near the issue. Now that I'm a parent, and the photos are racier than ever, I don't feel too protective in keeping the swimsuit edition away from the boys, but I don't feel I have to cancel the magazine either. I suspect, and I'm not happy about this, that my children are as inured to sexualized images of nearly naked models as am I. Thank you, television commercial producers.

Looking back (figuratively speaking), nearly all the photos of yesteryear consisted of models actually wearing a bikini that plausibly could have served as beachwear, even on the breezy New England coasts where we took our annual week at the shore. The 2007 bikinis by comparison do not strike me as very practical stock. Seldom did the models even bother putting on the tops, instead relying on a hand or lock of hair to keep *SI* from requiring a brown-paper wrapper. But without a top, and with the slimmest of bikini bottoms, little of the actual bikini was visible. What's the use of putting a woman in a tiny white bikini bottom and then making mention that the bikini was designed by some guy in Italy? Okay, I guess there's a use, but certainly not for the swimsuit. The swimsuit issue is not very useful as a purchasing catalog.

So I promise (Mrs. TSLP) that I won't look again at the *SI Annual Swimsuit Issue*, at least not for another ten years or so. I wonder what could possibly change. I can't see where else the magazine could go, short of the Burt Reynolds direction. The women can't wear less, the bikinis can't be smaller, and the paint can't be slopped on anywhere else. Really, what's next other than the ground already inhabited by *Playboy* and the world of pornography? We'll see.

I can't wait for the 2017 issue to find out.

The Wages of Wins: Taking Measure of the Many Myths in Modern Sport (David J. Berri, Martin B. Schmidt, and Stacey L. Brook)

Much of *The Wages of Wins* appeared as articles in various economics journals, including the prestigious *American Economic Review*. The articles were adapted for a lay audience. (Thanks, authors.) This means the footnotes were truncated, equations omitted, and subjects and verbs added (only half-kidding on the last point; academic writing can be abstruse). So the book is entirely readable yet not overly dumbed-down for us dummies, which is an economics term for non-economists.

Buy this book. Really, it's a good read and makes a big contribution to all kinds of sports debates. The book will definitely offer some conclusions you'll disagree with, even strongly, but it will make you think again about the common wisdom you once readily accepted. Lots of wild and crazy propositions here, all meticulously supported by arguments and digestible data. Perfect for starting those bar room sports arguments.

Part of the book was indispensable. The authors dispel the "myth" that the wealthiest teams in baseball have automatic advantages in fielding winning teams. They also use regression calculations to suggest Allen Iverson is not the star player he's cracked up to be; basically he gets his lofty scoring numbers by using up opportunities to score that might have gone to teammates. They show that scoring averages of NBA players are overvalued by the adoring public and by owners at salary time. Even the "fan drawing power" of the NBA star is called into question. You get the idea: lots of economic iconoclasm served up jargon-free. Think *Freakonomics*, except that you care about the topics.

Part of the book I could have done without. The subtitle promises to dispel myths, yet a chapter or so is devoted to proposing a numerical measure for NFL quarterback performance. Umm, authors, there are already a host of quantitative measures of NFL quarterback performance; it's hard to keep them all straight. The NFL even employs one of its own. So the battle over whether or not quarterback performance can be captured with some plausibility in numerical data has long been over. The accountants have won. The authors argue that their measure of performance is better because, as the result of regressions, the measure is more closely tied to game outcomes. I'm convinced. But I wouldn't quite think that the authors' improved technology should be thought of as myth-busting.

My test for a book about sports is roughly this: do I feel more intelligent having read the book? (Some sports books are so bad that, on completion I feel like I need a shower.) This book is a good one. It's wonderful when people with giant pulsating brains like the authors of *The Wages of Wins* point their throbbing cerebral cortices at sports issues. Sports are big business and, in this scattered age of internet fragmentation, they are an important cultural circumstance. Our games are more than games, and we need to treat sports with the care they require.

Running the Table: The Legend of Kid Delicious, the Last Great American Pool Hustler (L. Jon Wertheim)

So what's wrong with this picture? A young man, just a kid really, has trouble with traditional schooling and suffers from severe mood swings, chronic obesity and depression. But he finds he has a skill, an extraordinary talent, to shoot pool at a professional level. His talent breeds interest and lifts him out of his suffering and gives him cause to live. Building on local success, he travels the countryside playing pool against all comers, earning money that allows him to support himself, while making friends and learning strategies to deal with his mental illnesses. He even earns a memorable moniker, "Kid Delicious."

Success story, right? Troubled young American overcomes obstacles to attain self-sufficiency. The problem is that, thanks to the widespread American prohibition on gambling, Kid Delicious' climb out of the doldrums involved a long string of criminal actions. Betting on a contest, even one in which one is a participant, remains illegal. Why?

I'd characterize this title as a safari book, or Category Three, for those of you carefully scoring according to my overall breakdown of all sports books. The classic of this genre is the reporter who follows a team up-close for a season, or maybe even "participates" in some minimal way, as did George Plimpton famously in Paper Lion or Jack McCallum more recently. Author Jon Wertheim's narrative encompasses several years. Wertheim obviously did not follow this young man around, and instead had to reconstruct events through witness interviews and the like. The author's literal and chronological distance from his subject and the events of that subject's life is the strength of this book. It's also the problem. What makes the story interesting is less the chronology of events and more the ambiance of the pool room, the mechanics of the hustle, and the colorful and at times pathetic cast of characters that pass through the Kid's life. Wertheim's distance makes him relate this aspect in historical, matter-of-fact terms that don't adequately convey the tension in the smoke-filled pool hall. The market is ripe for a pool player with Wertheim's sensitivity and eye for detail to write the true insider account.

Tension in the pool hall is immense. Imagine shooting pool for all your savings and as your sole source of income. As is your desperate opponent. Side-bets galore, all in cash, the implicit threat of cheating and subsequent violence always just one wrong word away from the table action. We're not talking high-living athletes on guaranteed contracts trying to decide which Bentley they'll motor over to the stadium; these pool players make tomorrow's rent today. What reckless daring, what a strong constitution, what courage. Like most people, I'd love to play professional sports. Also like most people, I could never put my entire life's savings on the line in any bet where my opponent stood a significant chance of winning. To me it is a weird personality strength/defect that allows (mostly) men to have that huge preference for risk. And it's fascinating for the rest of us to watch these wild swings in fortune that depend on the tumbling of a billiard ball.

Often we lament the sad lifestyle of the problem gambler, and equate this particular addiction with drug or alcohol abuse. Yet is it correct to lump these addictions together? We have to recognize the contribution our laws make to the impoverishment of the "problem gambler." These are people who have a unique skill: they have an apparently bottomless tolerance for risk. In a world in which large bets were legal, people who are willing to take big risks would make money from their unique risk preference. Anyone who has played poker knows that a player who is willing to risk his whole stack, even on a slim advantage, can win pots others would lose. Not only does the widespread legal prohibition on gambling preclude risk-takers from profiting from their comparative advantage, it also (conveniently) protects the rest of us from losing money. Gambling is illegal, generally speaking, and so for these risk-takers to make money from their skill they are driven underground, to the dingy and dangerous late-night cash games far from official eyes.

Some gamblers can make money legally. The law allows speculation in the stock market, in so-called derivative instruments, and in certain commodities futures. Some of these investments are nothing more than a bet. Some derivatives, for example, allow speculators to wager on fluctuations in the value of foreign currencies and movements in indexes: it is doubtful that many investors who make these bets know what they are doing.[11] Access to the legal markets for large bets is limited to the comparatively few. Obviously some risk-taker living out of the trunk of his car is not going to to be speculating on the rise of the Mexican peso. Why not allow betting markets for the middle class? We can go to Las

---

11. See Frank Partnoy, FIASCO: The Inside Story of a Wall Street Trader (1999).

Vegas or Atlantic City and bet hundreds of dollars on the turn of a card or the fall of a roulette ball; why not allow pool sharks to bet on their practiced skill?

What's remarkable is how well this underground economy runs itself. Pool sharks new to the game hit the road, traveling from town to town, on the lookout for competitors who are willing to lay thousands of dollars on the line playing against traveling players of unknown acumen. The shark will try to hide his talent, setting up the opponent for the big score, and then leave town (in a hurry) after the victory. Word travels fast, and the shark's ability to get games diminishes as his notoriety spreads. Eventually the shark's run is complete, and he's left to turn to professional pool, with its meager payouts, and to occasional high-stakes matches against players of equal skill. Gone is the easy money from overmatched suckers. Gone is the nice income. Why shouldn't suckers be allowed to lose their money? It's just like the stock market: one sells, another buys; someone made the wrong bet. The loser learns to be a winner, or finds something else to do.

The pool hustlers will play and wager despite the legal prohibition on gambling. It's the rest of us, the suckers, who fear the law and withdraw, relegating the sharks to the back roads and dank halls in search of a game. The prohibition limits the market to the few, the committed, the addicts. It drives the unaddicted, the easy marks and clueless suckers, out of the game. Our protection of the addicts makes them play against other addicts, shark against shark. Even very good players will struggle when the competition gets this stiff. The law doesn't protect against problem gamblers. It protects the rest of us, and relegates pool sharks to a hard life on the road.

Chapter Five

The Consequences of Law

If one were to go back and read legal scholarship from as few as fifty years ago, one would be struck by its unspoken suppositions. Judicial decisions or legislative enactments were analyzed according to an undisclosed normative criterion; was this particular rule "fair" in some sense? Of course; what is "fair" is in the eyes of the beholder, and people on both sides of a dispute think their position is eminently fair. Without an ability to discuss a rule much beyond assertions of fairness, legal scholarship in the main was descriptive, discussing how the law of one jurisdiction differed from that of another, or refining categorizations of rules. It was a useful scholarship, especially for legal practitioners, but to describe it as engaging in "legal analysis" was misleading.

The unspoken embarrassment of legal analysts today is that there remains no such thing as legal analysis. Modern legal scholarship does engage in "analysis," or more accurately, one of a number of available analyses. But these forms of understanding are not unique to law; legal scholars have imported these heuristics wholesale from other disciplines, including economics, psychology, sociology, anthropology, semiotics, and philosophy. Of these importations, the economics model has provided the most fruitful platform to critique legal rules. The "economic analysis of law" studies the behavioral consequences of legal rules: how will people's behavior change in response to a new rule, and will that change further or frustrate the purpose of the rule's designers? The persuasive power of the economic critique has been so pervasive that today all legal scholars, even those who would reject the economic approach, must consider the likely behavioral consequences of the rules of law they prefer. Like it or not, legal scholars are all economists.

Despite the infiltration of economics into legal studies, seldom have the rules of sport been subject to a similar appraisal. This neglect is surprising. Sports provides a rich and visible laboratory, and new rules are implemented all the time. Moreover, players and coaches take an active interest in adapting their behaviors to accomplish their ends, and so will test, push against and circumvent rules whenever possible. In short, sports is ripe for the modern focus on the consequences of rules.

Legislating Fairness on the Playing Field

Gregg Easterbrook, known as the "Tuesday Morning Quarterback" on the ESPN website, is probably the best sports columnist on the web. He's always fun and is usually right. But TMQ is quite wrong about his recurring criticisms of football teams that run up the score. He has proposed that teams with large leads run the football up the middle, put in the scrubs, and kneel on all "extra point" attempts, all in an effort to prevent lopsided final scores.

Easterbrook's perspective reflects the growing consensus that lopsided football games are a problem and something needs to be done about it.[1] Some people have, actually legislating fairness on the playing field. The state of Connecticut's high school football asso-

---

1. In response to the TMQ article on running up the score, a high school football official wrote in to say that he and his colleagues legislate "fairness" on the field themselves. The official described a signal that the referees use. They punch their fists together, which indicates that the winning team is running up the score. From this point on, the officials will "find" penalties, most often "holding," because it is "the easiest to sell." The official admitted that the referees do not use this tactic often, but had a game recently where a team ahead by five touchdowns faked a punt and would have scored again, had it not been for a holding call made by one of the officials. Easterbrook, Gregg. "TMQ Nation Fires Back." 1 Novem-

ciation will suspend for one game any coach whose team wins by more than fifty points. Other states are sure to follow.

Are we really sure there's an epidemic of lopsided football contests, as Easterbrook presumes? It is a classic (and recurring) legislative mistake: a few salient and recent catastrophes occur, and suddenly everyone thinks we have a problem that requires a legal solution. Modern mass media, the internet age, and the resulting reduced costs of information have made all kinds of bad behavior appear to be more prevalent; I can learn of a lopsided football score from Mississippi almost as easily as one from the local high school. Indeed, TMQ's habit of publicizing such games in his national column may help create the perception that he argues to be fact.

I seriously doubt that we do have an epidemic of lopsided football contests. There is a strong corrective to running up the score: revenge. Coaches move around; teams wax and wane in strength. Payback can happen. Indeed, the occasional lopsided scores we see may be paybacks for previous slights. Prohibiting purposeful lopsided scoring may strangely lessen deterrence of the same by letting previous wrongdoing go unpunished.

Lopsided scoring can also be avenged more immediately. Losing players who feel they are being treated unfairly don't usually like it. In football, revenge is possible on every play. I played schoolboy hockey, another contact sport. In the closing minutes of a heavily one-sided contest, let's just say if one were on the losing side, one wanted to be on the ice to get some immediate opportunities to feel better. If one were ahead, tell the coach you're tired and stay on the bench in order to stay out of harm's way. Coaches knew. Those last minutes of blowout games could be brutal. I'm not recommending this of course, but boys will be boys. Trust me; you never wanted your coach to try to run up a score.

Let's pretend I'm wrong and that lopsided scores are indeed more

ber 2006. *ESPN.com.* http://sports.espn.go.com/espn/page2/story?page=easterbrook/061101.

common today than they were in some past golden age of competitive football games (maybe around the time TMQ was a child). In other words, let's assume that the deterrents to rubbing it in to a beaten opponent I've mentioned above have failed. Do we need to solve this problem with some sort of rule or legislative act? My take is this: the object of all games is to score. Every play in football, even a running play, if perfectly blocked and run with skill, can result in a touchdown. What else can you tell the offensive players? Miss their blocks (and get the running back nailed)? Run out of bounds (and stop the clock, only prolonging the game)? Take a knee? If any of these seems attractive, why not just send the kids home?

The defense has some complicity here too. I was watching the Patriots dismantle the Vikings on Monday Night Football the other night, and the Patriots continued throwing even with a very large lead. Was Belichick a bad sport, trying to run up the score? No. The Vikings were still stacking their defense at the line to stop the (expected) clock-killing runs up the middle. (In fact a Vikings defender after the game expressed his surprise at the Patriots' tactic and said the Vikes were geared to stop the expected run.) Why pound a running back into such a vortex, where he's sure to be tagged by one of Minnesota's huge linemen? If the Pats have some sort of ethical obligation (as TMQ would argue) and should, when ahead by 30, just run up the middle, then don't the Vikings have an equivalent duty not to tackle the runner too hard? Shouldn't the Vikes clear out some of their linebackers so that the running back can advance a few yards (TMQ doesn't say how many yards is the ethical amount) and then fall safely to the ground? Or do TMQ and the rulers of Connecticut football believe (and require) running backs to lower their heads and run into the teeth of a defense that knows exactly where they'll be going? After all, the defense will know of the ethical restrictions on offenses too. Would you like to be that running back, heading straight into an overloaded run defense that features large, powerful young men who are angry as can be about getting beat? Would TMQ take that ball?

The solution is to keep playing football. If at any point the score is so lopsided that the game is essentially over, then just turn off the scoreboard and stop keeping score. In Connecticut, where folks don't want anyone beat by more than 50 points, just turn off the scoreboard when the margin is 50, that way no one will ever lose by even one point more. It's silly to try to engineer the final score while pretending to continue regular competitive play.

Trust me, the players won't mind turning off the scoreboard. When I was a kid, I played lots of pickup games in all sports and we competed as hard as we could. Yet often we'd lose track of the score and had to make one up as the time for play drew near its end. Or we simply ended the game without ever knowing the final score. No one cared. We played to play. Sometimes I suspect that the exact final scores of games are more interesting and important to parents, school administrators, and sportswriters like TMQ than they are to the players. But we do it all for the kids, right?

Fourth Down Debate

A nice debate is forming in the sports world over the paucity of NFL coaches "going for it" on fourth down. It all started with a paper by economist David Romer that argued that NFL coaches do not maximize their team's chances of winning.[2] Instead of attempting to gain a first down (or a touchdown) on fourth down, they opt for a punt or field goal attempt. So, duly informed by Romer's analysis, how have NFL coaches responded? By punting even more. Boo.

Michael Lewis of *Moneyball* fame has the latest word, writing in the pages of *ESPN The Magazine*[3] that the reason that coaches decline to opt for the winning strategy is that they don't want to appear reckless to their fellow coaches, who regard the punt as sound strategy and who will likely hire them into their next job. Coaches might become more emboldened to take "job risks" (by going for

---

2. David Romer, "Do Firms Maximize? Evidence from Professional Football," (UC Berkeley, July 2005).

3. Michael Lewis, *ESPN The Magazine* (Dec. 18, 2006).

it on fourth down) once they gain tenure. (I would also think one could see a similar story with college coaches.)

But still the question nags: Why are football coaches neglecting a proven and relatively simple winning strategy? Is it fear of blame and ridicule, as Tuesday Morning Quarterback has argued, should the "unusual" strategy backfire? Is it peer pressure from the coaching ranks, as Michael Lewis suggests? No and no.

Romer's paper is clever and enlightening, but I did have a problem with his using third-down data to estimate the outcome on fourth down, were an offense to go for it. Romer had no choice but to use third-down data simply because fourth down non-kicks are so rare. But one problem with using third down to provide information about fourth down is that the defense on third down as a practical matter has to prepare for a wider range of offensive plays; on fourth down and short yardage, in contrast, an offense will tend to be more limited in its play selection, eschewing high-risk plays. For instance, a coach is very unlikely to put the quarterback in the shotgun on fourth down, although this formation is common on third down. Defensive formations lack the variability of offensive formations, and thus the effectiveness of the defense will not be diminished due to down and distance. As a result, the average yards gained on third down might be higher than they would be on fourth down because the offense on third down can take advantage of the variability of play calls and the implicit requirement that the defense prepare for that variability. In sum, defense, on fourth and short, should just blitz into the backfield.

Romer acknowledges this problem with his use of third downs, but argues that it is unlikely that the defense has an advantage on fourth downs that it lacks on third downs. (He states that it "seems unlikely that the defense has substantially more scope than the offense to affect the distribution of outcomes.") I think it is likely. Offenses in short yardage situations will have to show the defense a formation that, at least to a small extent, threatens a pass; however, in reality the defense knows that the play will nearly always be a run, most probably one up the middle, or perhaps a short pass. Defense, on fourth and short, blitz.

For a comparison, we all see how difficult it can be for an offense to score a running touchdown when the line of scrimmage is just a few feet from the goal line. Many times in those situations we see defensive linemen and linebackers advancing into the offensive backfield to stop the ball-carrier. Why is the defense often so effective in making these goal-line stands? Why don't the linemen penetrate into the offensive backfield on every play? Defenses are effective because in a goal-line situation the defense "knows" what is coming. Options are reduced due to the small size of the field the defense must cover and due to the offense's reluctance to attempt a risky pass. The "goal-line-stand" defensive advantage is replicated whenever a team goes for it on fourth down and short yardage. In effect, fourth and short yardage becomes a "small field," no matter where the play originates. The defense has an advantage on fourth downs that it lacks on third down. Romer's use of the third-down data will lead him to overestimate the likelihood of success of going for it on fourth down.

The other problem with third-down data is that third down, although pressurized, requires less of the offensive players than does fourth down. Third down is important; a failure will typically lead to a punt. But fourth down is crucial; failure might lead to extraordinary field position for the opposing team. Players get more nervous. Offense is harder than defense (that's why all the "skill position" players are on the offensive side of the ball). Nervousness can show itself in errant passes, fumbled handoffs, or dropped passes.

Romer did analyze available fourth-down outcomes and found no significant difference between third and fourth downs. So probably I'm wrong. But he admits the fourth-down sample size is small. So maybe I have a point.

It could be that NFL coaches have some intuitive feel for the problem of using third down results to predict fourth down outcomes. The downs may differ in some fundamental way that impacts the likelihood of making a first down. I'm not saying Romer's analysis is wrong; it's probably not. But I am saying that NFL coaches may be responding intelligently to Romer's analysis by rejecting it on the grounds of inconclusiveness or dubiousness in regards to the use of third downs. When in doubt, punt.

Running Up the Score, Again

Now Lincoln University's basketball team ekes out a 201-78 win over Ohio State-Marion (I'm assuming that's not the Ohio State that Greg Oden was attending at the time). That's good, because I had Lincoln giving 100 points. Anyway, perhaps needless to say, the final score earned the attention of the news media and others who search the daily scores for signs of "unsportsmanlike conduct." Some complained personally to the winning coach, an ex-Marine who was reduced to tears by the helpful feedback of these folks hell-bent on making sure sports players are nice to each other. The media outrage was led by Mr. Tuesday Morning Quarterback himself, Gregg Easterbrook of ESPN. Easterbrook has made it a running theme of his column to identify and condemn instances of these lopsided travesties that threaten "the integrity of the sport."

It bears noting that these were college teams, and the leading scorer for the victor is 28 years old. Not children going home crying. From the sound of the news accounts, the losers thought little of their loss, and were surprised by the public reaction. If the "victims" weren't upset, why should we be? No social impact here; this was just a basketball game.

Lincoln's 201 point total set an all-time Division III scoring record and a record for three-point goals. If Easterbrook has his way, I guess all current scoring records are permanent. What coach wants to risk setting a record and seeing his name ridiculed by the Worldwide Leader in Sports?

How does a basketball team avoid lopsided victories? It's not easy. The coach can call off the press (apparently Lincoln's coach did this, but not soon enough), pass the ball around on offense, walk the ball up (again, done by this coach, but perhaps not soon enough). Even with such tactics, the game itself rewards superior players: that's the point of it. Should a player shoot to miss? Not take open shots, even from three-point distance? Not take the ball away from an opposing player even when he dribbles right in front of you? Let him score? At some point, and we're close, the teams might as well go home. Calling off the press and passing the ball around is customary for teams winning big. But it's no fun playing ball if you can't play defense or take open shots when they present themselves. As the coach said, when the game got lopsided he put all his scrubs into the game and used the game for instruction and practice. Should we complain if his team practiced perfectly? Losing by over 100 points is a painful loss. But not as painful as having your opponent forego open shots or play no defense in order to avoid the lopsided victory. The first is a deserved loss; the latter is an insult, and says to the loser that the loser doesn't really belong on the court with the winner. The first treats the loser as an equal; the latter treats the loser as a child.

Can we really stare at the final score of a game and condemn the coach for unsportsmanlike behavior? We weren't at these games. Maybe the losing team had no discipline and refused to play defense. Maybe the losing team took plenty of good shots, but just missed them. Maybe the losing team, also using the lopsided game for practice, was trying to push the ball to practice up-tempo basketball. Lots of explanations could account for a lopsided final score, all of them consistent with good sportsmanship and fair play. In the Lincoln game, the losing team had but six players, and apparently did not play in the same division as Lincoln. If you set up a lopsided prize fight, someone's going to get killed. Perhaps the tournament organizers need to share some responsibility.

With that said, the winning coach shouldn't have been pressing in the second half. So he's guilty, but only of bad judgment. Usually these mistakes are corrected during the game, as one coach has a word with the other. In my experience, when the issue is brought to their attention, coaches will call off the press. Coaches are busy coaching their players, trying to get them to play their positions correctly; in a blowout they are not as aware of the score as fans or others might be. The losing coach (who somehow was a player-coach in this game) has a responsibility too. My point is, let's not make more of this slight than needed. Easterbrook goes way too far in terming the coach's conduct "bottom-of-the-barrel," "without class," and "bad sportsmanship." This is pretty personal. Easterbrook complains often of parents who take sports too seriously. Maybe that's what is happening with his comments.

The best solution, as I've said before, is to turn off the scoreboard and run the clock. Perhaps that solution, a standard happenstance in youth leagues, would not work in a college game. Why not? Because we want to know the final score, in part to determine all-time scoring records and the like. We can't have it both ways. Either the final score matters or it doesn't. If it matters, then we give teams inducements to run it up and set those records, and we shouldn't complain when they do. If the score doesn't matter, then the losing team can concede the game, turn the scoreboard off, and just enjoy playing basketball.

Pitch Counts and the Preference for Rules

It's July, and as every parent of a Little Leaguer knows, it's time for the annual Little League "All Stars" tournament. Yes, it's more than a little presumptuous to think that a ten-year-old boy, like the tiny TSLP Junior, can properly be called an all-star at anything, other than getting into mischief at school. And yet each summer the happy TSLP clan looks forward to another round of our boys against your boys, double elimination for all the marbles.

A new set of rules is in play for this year. Little League has instituted a strict pitch count for pitchers. The rule limits pitchers to 75 or 85 pitches per game, depending on the player's age. It also requires two days of rest for pitchers who throw more than 45 pitches in a game, one day of rest for 21 to 45 pitches, but no rest requirement for a pitcher throwing fewer than 21 pitches.

Now it's hard to look at a couple of games played in my little corner of the country and determine that we have a national crisis, but hard tasks never worry me. We have a national crisis! These pitch rules are a problem.

Let's start with the premise that pitchers need to be limited in their pitching. I'll grant the premise, but with some skepticism. During the summer, I work a lot in my home office, which customarily gives me a good look at my son's play habits. On most days, he is on the run the whole day. When he and his fellow baseball-loving friends get together, some version of baseball erupts, usually in the form of my son playing catch with one of his friends. No coaches, no rules, just these kids throwing the ball, pretty hard most of the time, and usually at the limit of their distance, back and forth. They don't stretch their arms beforehand[4] (and I'm not about to run out there and insist these kids in sandals and bathing suits run through a warm-up stretching routine) and they spend at least one-half of their throws trying to curve the ball. Like kids in my day, these boys crave knowledge about how to throw the exotic pitches they see the pros make on television. (And they find that knowledge; the internet has ended all hopes of keeping such adult images from the young.)[5] They just throw, hundreds of times, without limita-

---

4. By the way, is it really necessary that young boys stretch before baseball games? Not sure if my kid is typical, but he spends the entire summer day on the run. Does anyone out there have his kid stretch before the kid rides off on his bike, or plays with the dog, or plays wiffle ball in the front yard with his pals? Then why when this same kid puts on the uniform and arrives at the ball field that evening does he now have to perform all this stretching that looks designed for 40-year-olds? Kids are limber by definition.

5. Is it really all that bad, as we often read, for a young boy to throw a curveball? I've read the research linking curveballs with arm injuries, but I'm not convinced. Watch kids play catch. About all they do is throw

tion. Is Little League worried about kids throwing baseballs with no one counting? Should I sit near the window and count my son's throws, racing out to stop him before he throws number 76, or insist on two days of rest if he throws more than 45?[6]

---

curveballs, or any other pitch that might put a little shake into the ball. They throw knucklers, screwballs, knuckle curves, curves, sliders, cut fastballs, you name it. (Of course, in reality all these pitches are "gravity balls," whose slow sinking to the earth results from the distortion of space-time, so that as the ball travels through space it also travels through time. But try convincing a stubborn boy on this point.) So when a game comes and the same kid puts a spin on the ball and the spin (or perhaps the theory of general relativity) results in the ball sinking to the earth, is the player attempting something he hasn't done countless times before?

Also, research shows that a baseball with spin cannot actually curve unless it is traveling pretty fast (something like sixty miles per hour, a speed very few Little Leaguers will ever reach). So very few LL pitchers actually curve a ball; what we see when a ball appears to break is probably an optical illusion. Gravity moves the ball.

With that said, I've been watching some of the Little League and Cal Ripken playoffs on television. I also watched the team on which my son played finish third in the state. And my conclusion is that EVERY youth pitcher is throwing curve balls. The kid on television just threw about seven in a row. I'm not so much worried about arm injuries (although I wouldn't want my kid throwing like that) as I am the future of pitching. Curve balls can get most batters out until about high school. What these curve-balling kids are losing is the ability to command and get people out with the fastball. I think the kids who end up pitching at the higher levels will not be the ones who are dominating at the youth league level.

6. My child likes to arrive early at the ball field (did I mention he likes baseball?) and as soon as he arrives, he wants to play catch. Again he'll throw it hard and long. He does stop when he's tired, but minutes later he'll be back at it. Watch any LL team warm up and the players will easily throw the ball fifty times each over the course of the pre-game hour. Plus add in the 5-8 warm-up pitches a pitcher makes between innings. If the rule is that a child my son's age should be limited to 75 pitches in a calendar day, well, on most game days, between the play at home and pre-game warm-ups, he'll exceed that number before he delivers his first pitch. Again, I would assume my son is not unique in his love of throwing. Perhaps an in-game pitch is a little more physically stressful than a warm-up throw, but not by much. These kids throw way more than 75 times.

So, even though I'm granting the premise that a pitcher's pitches ought to be limited, it's a bit of a sketchy premise, given all the throwing kids do on their own. But here's the question: if the pitches are to be limited, should that limit be created by a rule or a standard?[7] Lawyers and lawmakers struggle with this choice all the time. A rule is a fixed point; a standard is a less specific, less descriptive range of outcomes beyond which one should not go. Seventy-five pitches as a limit is a rule; "pitch until not unduly tired" is a standard. Rules take away discretion; standards rely on it. Now to be sure, a rule and a standard may be seen as two points along a continuum. LL's former rule, which limited pitchers by innings, not pitch counts, operated more in the way of a standard because the stress on a pitcher varied by inning; a pitcher throwing two innings may work a lot harder than one throwing four. Thus, a coach might reasonably allow a pitcher to throw his maximum innings, if they were easy, or limit him short of the maximum if not.

One big problem with rules is also their virtue: they allow for no discretion. Some boys, especially when working easy innings with plenty of rest in between, are physically able without apparent difficulty to exceed the maxima LL has set; they can also come back for more pitching a day or two later. Other boys, especially those with poor throwing motions, may struggle even to reach the limits. Now all of us have heard, if perhaps only through the newspapers, of coaches leaving young pitchers in the game for excessive lengths, or of the increased incidence of arm surgeries among the comparatively young. Rules suggest we don't trust our coaches. Maybe we shouldn't, since many of them are dads who bring little in the way of expertise to their volunteer roles. But still, any adult can tell when a pitcher is tired out, and when a pitcher is done, it's time to take him out. But a kid will often tell us too. Pitchers who

---

7. I'm not saying young pitchers should throw without limitation. Instead, I'm questioning the effectiveness of pitch count limits, as opposed to relying on coaching discretion to supply the limit to pitching. Little League has relied on the latter for the first 75 years of its existence.

are tired will have trouble repeating their motion and will lose velocity and get wild.

But that's not the real problem. It's this: by eliminating discretion in decision-making (even about the right time to change pitchers), rules generate incentives to take advantage—what lawyers term unforeseen or adverse collateral consequences. The pitch count rules, for instance, have coaches remove perfectly effective pitchers after just 20 pitches, even in the middle of counts, so that the pitchers will be eligible the next day. Is it healthier for a boy to throw 20 pitches every day instead of 40 with a day of rest? Jonathan Papelbon, the star young reliever for the Boston Red Sox, claimed after his rookie season that his frequent appearances as a short reliever were hard on his shoulder and that a move to the starting rotation would be better for his health. Is it wise to use a 10-year-old daily? Unmistakably this is happening, as the rules implicitly encourage it. I've also repeatedly seen coaches call out the "remaining" allowable pitches to their pitcher, exhorting full effort on the last few pitches. A pitcher not subject to pitch limits might naturally adjust his efforts to coast through certain weaker hitters and to be sure to save some strength for later innings. With the pitch count, the pitcher will go all out at the end, hoping to finish with a strikeout. What sense is there to encourage a boy at his maximum pitch limit to throw the last few with greatest effort?

On the other side of the ball I'm also witnessing offensive coaches instructing batters to take pitches in order to run up pitch counts to drive effective pitchers out of the game. The third-base coach for my son's team told me he has at times given the "take" sign on a three balls and one strike count (a hitter's count) to add to the opposing pitcher's total pitch count. Watching the games, I have every reason to conclude other coaches are doing the same. The pitch count has become an offensive weapon. Batters will learn to take strikes instead of to hit the ball.

One beneficial effect of the pitch count rules is to encourage teams to use more players at pitcher, albeit as a bunch of short relievers. But if Little League really wanted to extend pitching staffs it would allow tournaments to schedule teams for more than a single game per day. By limiting pitchers to one game per day, coaches would have little choice but to use pitchers for more than the 20-pitch "short relief" role. The problem is of course that, despite what the parents think, not every kid can pitch.[8] It's not easy to stand on the mound in a pressurized baseball contest with runners on base and a full count, while stands full of parents and other fans hang on one's every move. A coach is lucky to field a team with three or four serviceable pitchers. Not too many would be happy to manage a "walk-a-thon" featuring each team's sixth-best pitcher. Not too many parents would enjoy that either. Little League needs to recognize that the reality of the situation is that few players can pitch effectively, while keeping the games competitive and completed before nightfall.

Rules are a problem in law because they lend themselves to easy manipulation, and thus engender lots of socially undesirable consequences. They do have a place, but it's comparatively rare that lawmakers can be so sure that a certain rule is the "right" one. For a rule to be "right," it must permit no exceptions; in other words, all conduct on the wrong side of the rule should constitute a behavior we want to prohibit. That's why lawmakers and courts and the like favor standards and prescribe words that signify standards ("reasonable," "substantial," and "good faith"). Standards allow for flexibility and judgment, and flexibility and judgment form bulwarks against manipulation and unwanted collateral consequences. LL's

---

8. All-stars teams usually have quite a few players with pitching experience, and certainly teams at that level could go deeper into the roster for pitchers. For a regular season team, however, finding even four solid pitchers is good. In order to not walk every batter (assuming batters swing at strikes, which is a discipline more and more batters are able to exercise each season), a player, to be a pitcher, needs to throw six out of every ten pitches for strikes. That's not easy, especially when the pitch needs also to be at or near the maximum velocity the pitcher can reasonably muster.

pitch count rules seem to invite manipulation, and do so without, at least in my mind, generating clear offsetting benefits.

The Laws We Don't Teach (and Golf's FedEx Cup)

I've been trying to digest golf's new FedEx Cup, a season-long PGA competition for players to earn points. The top 144 point-earners will get to participate in a four-week playoff, with each play-off awarding more points, until the top 30 get to play in the "season-ending" Tour Championship in September. The winner takes home $10 million. Lots more details, but those are the basics.

Golf is a "natural" game. For most sports, scoring values are contrived and even the mechanics of the game appear arbitrary. (Why is a football touchdown worth six points, instead of five or seven, or a basketball goal worth two or three? Why does baseball have four bases in a square instead of five in a pentagon or three in an isosceles triangle?) But for golf, scoring is intuitive and obvious: one stroke counted per stroke attempt, lowest score wins. Par is not relevant to scoring; it is a yardstick for one's score, but in a competition the lowest score wins regardless of its relation to par.

Why mess with golf's scoring? Why mess with golf? Some rules seem so natural and obvious that they don't need to be taught. We have some of those in law too.

The Law of Averages: We don't cover this one in law school but maybe we should. Golf's majors are consistently outstanding events because the combination of their importance, the difficulty of the courses, and the preparation of the players nearly always bring the world's finest to the fore. The top of the final scoreboard at the Masters usually so testifies. But now, a season-long competition for points? Be prepared for a nail-biting contest between journey-men grinders, at least in most years. The FedEx people will be very lucky if it's Phil and Tiger shooting it out on the back nine. Odds are, they won't, and this could happen year after year, on average.

The Law of Large Numbers: Under the FedEx scoring system, the winner of a golf tournament gets 4,500 points, with the remainder of the 25,000 points each tournament is "worth" being distributed to the remaining top 70 finishers. Majors are worth 4,950 points to the winner; low-end tournaments count less than half as much. The FedEx final tourneys are worth something like 9,000 points to the winners. Fans will love this, assuming those fans are CPAs.

Why use such large, non-intuitive numbers? (Why not award millions of points, while we're at it?) Seriously, why not use the money list? The fact that tournaments vary in their prize money should be taken into account; higher prize money draws a more competitive field.

Golf is the ultimate cross-over sport for non-traditional viewers. Compared to the endless complications of a football game, very few rules come into play in golf. A player commonly goes an entire tournament without once needing to summon a rules official for interpretation or assistance. One stroke counts for one stroke. Seldom does a need to ask (or answer) questions arise. Large, arbitrary numbers as promised by the FedEx Cup auger just the opposite. All you golf fans watching from home better study up on the FedEx rules—you might need to explain them more than a few times. When you're watching the U.S. Open, will anyone care about the points? Will any player?

The Rule of Thumb: Here is another rule that's not covered in the modern curriculum, and probably for good reason. We can think of this rule as a generalization that might help solve problems quickly and easily without resort to more precise calculation. Here's the "rule of thumb" problem with the FedEx Cup: it's aimed at the wrong target. The purpose of a season-long competition that culminates in a tournament is to crown a champion. If Tiger takes two majors next year, and Vijay or Phil dominate the money list, will any respectable golf fan say that the best golfer for the season was Mike Weir or Stewart Cink or Steve Stricker or whoever comes out on top of the FedEx points total? People debate the best teams in sports that crown champions because we've all accepted the premise (and developed the interest) in identifying the year's best team. But in golf? Who was the best golfer in some random year? Few care. And no one except the winner will care who wins the FedEx Cup. We care about who wins particular tournaments.

Murphy's Law: This law should definitely form a major part of a legal education. Note this fact about the FedEx Cup: the winner of the $10 million will be the player who has the most points at the end of the last tournament. This player will not necessarily be the player who actually wins the last tournament. This could be a nightmare: some journeyman pro finishing fifteenth in the Tour Championship, his day ending early on Sunday, jumping around wildly on the last green, posing for pictures and giving interviews. All the while, the "real" tournament, the so-called "Tour Championship" with a paltry million going to the winner, goes on in the background. One of the two events will be overshadowed, and I'm guessing it will be the FedEx Cup, especially if the second-place point-earner stands far back in the tournament competition.

A $10 million prize awarded in the middle of a Sunday golf telecast? It sounds like some lucky kid made the half-court shot at halftime.

College Football's BCS Tournament

In the wake of Boise State's thrill-ride finish to its undefeated season,[9] many in the popular press are calling for the NCAA to im-

---

9. Boise State had an undefeated season, with the Fiesta Bowl capping off an already extraordinary year for the team. The Broncos were the underdog going up against Oklahoma. Not only did Boise State hang with the Sooners, they ended up playing one of the greatest college bowl games

plement a playoff for the college football season in order to be certain to crown the true national champion. Under the current formula for BCS (Bowl Championship Series) games, the contest that pits the top-ranked BCS teams is designated the "national championship game." Implementing a more elaborate playoff series wouldn't be too hard, conceptually at least; just push some bowl dates around, pick an even number of teams, set them in brackets, and begin. Or the NCAA could just tack on one additional game (for 2006, Florida vs. Boise State) to determine the champion.

All of these approaches would suffice to crown a winner. But would the winner of the tournament be any more the "true champion" than the team that wins today's BCS championship game? Of course not. There's no way to determine a college football champion. So give it up.

The current BCS uses a complex formula to rank teams. The formula includes a heavy dose of opinion polling, computer rankings, comparisons of schedule strength and game outcomes. The fact that opinions and estimates of schedule strength are expressed numerically shouldn't fool us: there's a ton of subjectivity built into

---

ever. With seven seconds left in the game, the Broncos tied up the game with a fifty-yard hook-and-lateral trick play. In overtime, the Broncos converted on fourth down running a halfback pass from a player who had not thrown a pass all year. As if that wasn't amazing enough, the Broncos went for two to win the game. With a faked pass, the QB snuck the ball behind his back and handed it off to the running back who ran around the left end to score (also known as the "Statue of Liberty," a play that has not been seen in college football since somewhere around the Fielding H. Yost days at Michigan). As if the story was not amazing enough, the undefeated team was lead by former offensive coordinator, Chris Peterson, in his first year as head coach, and the unbelievable play-calling was done by the first year offensive coordinator, Bryan Harsin, age 30. Forde, Pat. "Boise State-OU Destroyed Press Box Professionalism." 7 June, 2007. *ESPN.com.* http://sports.espn.go.com/espn/columns/story?columnist=forde_pat&id=2893905&sport-Cat=ncf.

the rankings. Even computer-generated ranks have necessary subjective elements in their design. Subjectivity is inevitable; anyone who has ever put a few nickels on a football game knows just how little even experienced observers can tell about the strength of a football team. "Upsets" happen all the time; one explanation for the frequency of upsets is that we really cannot tell before the fact which team is the better team, or how much better. So imagine the difficulty of putting a couple of dozen plausible candidates into a rank order. Now imagine that rank order being meaningful (especially financially) and we can see what the BCS is up against.

But assume perfect information and perfect analysis. (Those BCS people are wicked smart.) What are they measuring? What does it mean to be the "best" team? Even a significantly better team won't be able to beat the next-best team all the time. Assume Team A would beat Team B eight out of ten times: Team A is decidedly better. Yet when the teams actually face each other (if they do), the game could be one of those two in ten where Team B prevails. So, if the job of the BCS is determine which of these two teams would beat the other more often, then the actual game outcome should be rather irrelevant to the question. If Team A is substantially better than Team B, then even if Team B wins the actual contest (as it might, twice in ten games), Team A is still the better team and should be ranked higher. In other words, should rankings be determined "on paper?" The actual outcomes of games will only tend to mislead us as to which team is the better. (That's why I seldom watch college football; I don't want to be distracted in determining which team is best.)

Most would say that the "best" is determined by who wins on the field, not on paper, and therefore game outcomes must determine rankings. Luckily, college football is pretty widespread and the leading teams don't play each other too often. If they did, then we'd have a mess. Team A beats B, B beats C, then C beats A. So we have to go back to eyeballing the teams and deciding that Team B, although it lost to A, is actually better than A. In other words, we're back to deciding rankings on paper, so to speak. With that said, at this point everyone's pretty convinced that, were the NCAA to

add just one more game, at the close of last season Florida should
have played Boise State to more accurately determine the champion. But assume Boise State had lost to Oklahoma and was out of
the picture. Arguably, the next best team in America after Florida
would be Ohio State, which is ranked second. Should Florida and
Ohio State play again, even though Florida beat Ohio State once
already? What if Ohio State wins, as well it might in a game between these two strong teams? Now we have a problem.

Strangely, college football rankings are made easier by the fact that
the top teams are spread out among the six BCS conferences, a few
others, and Notre Dame. The result is the top teams don't play each
other enough to determine which team is best (assuming that we can
tell which team is best by the outcome of the games). If they played
often, they'd beat each other willy-nilly and we'd never sort it out.
So opinions count, a lot. One problem with opinions is that they
are in part the consequence of one's view at the outset. We form
opinions, defend them and are slow to abandon them. So, to a certain extent, the rankings at the end are a product of the rankings at
the beginning. For example, in 2004, Oklahoma, USC, and Auburn
all finished the season undefeated. Oklahoma and USC were ranked
high in the preseason; Auburn started in the teens. So Oklahoma and
USC got to play for the national title while Auburn got to watch.
(Why do we rank preseason? This only exacerbates the problem.)

Let's assume we can push past all these problems of definition,
subjectivity and the rest and actually rank the teams. If the rankings are accurate, what would a tournament resolve? Surely no one
believes the winner of the NCAA college basketball tournament is
truly the best team in the nation. It's called "March Madness" for
a reason. Any team, even the best team, will lose some percentage
of its games to inferior opponents. The brevity of the contest and
the element of luck ensure it. In fact, the odds are probably against
the best basketball team winning the tournament.[10] Why would a

10. As consumers of sports entertainment, we have to realize that post-
season tournaments or playoffs are not designed to determine the best

single-elimination tournament in football be any more likely to identify the nation's best team? Footballs are oblong and take funny bounces. I think luck has more to do with determining (close) football contests than any other of the big American sports. And scoring is hard in football; as a result, lots of football games are close, ending with a margin of victory of less than a single score. Close games allow for more upsets.

My point is that college football is inherently resistant to the

---

teams. They're designed to entertain us and make money. This is not a bad thing, of course. But we shouldn't be duped into thinking that the playoff system some league designed to maximize fan interest also, by wonderful coincidence, just so happens to identify the best team. That is not the purpose of the playoffs. If we genuinely wanted to identify the best team we'd have the teams play in a balanced schedule and then crown the team that won the most games. The larger the set of games the better. Very old school, much less interesting if some team ran away with it, but superior, if the goal is to identify the best team.

Some sports leagues care very little about any plausible claim to crowning the best team. NCAA basketball, for instance, with its single-elimination tournament, produces champions almost capriciously. The NFL tournament is similar: virtually the only significance of the regular NFL season is to eliminate the weaker teams and decide the location for playoff games. In baseball, no way the Cardinals were the best team in baseball this past season; they would not have made the playoffs in virtually any other National League division and certainly not in the American League. One could make a plausible argument that the Cardinals were the weakest team in the entire playoffs. Yet we celebrate them as champions because they won the tournament. I understand that we all have tacitly agreed to pretend the tournament winner is the league's champion because that's the way the league has organized itself. But really, just a few plays here and there can determine the outcome of a short series, even seven games.

The best team in baseball, Season 2006? The dread New York Yankees. Good pitching, decent defense, unbelievable offensive lineup. Now, to use the stock sports argument, since the Cardinals won and the Yankees didn't, the Yankees should emulate the Cardinals in order to improve their team. Yankees: weaken your lineup, trade for mediocre pitching, shed any decent backup players, and then you'll be ready to compete for the title.

kind of organization and structure that the BCS beefers want to impose. We don't know what we mean by "the best team," nor how to go about measuring it even if we did. And beyond that, we don't really have a mechanism plausibly available to determine the champion. People may want a championship tournament, as soon will the NCAA, I presume. A tournament may be justified for entertainment's sake or to make more money. But let's not say we need one to determine which team is the best in the land.

Against the Infield Fly Rule

It should not come as a surprise to reveal that the sport of baseball has long been the darling of the legal academy. Maybe it's because the sport is played in the summer, when classrooms are empty and the professor can find room in his "schedule" to watch a game or two. Whatever the reason, clearly baseball, more than all other sports put together, has found a home in the legal literature. And no rule of baseball has attracted more attention and adulation from law professors than the Infield Fly Rule (IFR). Let me summarize the position of these scholars succinctly: they love it. The IFR is a bit complex (compared to most sports rules), counterintuitive, has a strange history, presents an unessential appendage to the otherwise necessary rules of the game, and, most important of all, it's a rule that mitigates the competitiveness of the game, as I'll explain below. Perfect: a complex, strange and unnecessary rule that reduces competitive behavior! No wonder legal scholars love it. Serious legal articles have discussed the IFR as it pertains to baseball law, sports law, federal taxation and criminal sentencing. In short, the IFR gets a lot of flattering attention.

Now that TSLP has made tenure, it is safe for me to say this publicly: I hate the Infield Fly Rule.

Some rules in baseball are necessary, such as the rules defining "out," "fair ball," "strike," and so forth. A baseball game could not take place without such elementary concepts defined. But without the IFR, the game could go on. To refresh your memory, here's an explanation of the rule from Wikipedia:

> The infield fly rule applies when there are fewer than two outs, and there are runners on first and second base, or on first, second and third base. In these situations, if a fair fly ball is hit that, in the umpire's judgment, is catchable by an infielder with ordinary effort, the batter is out regardless of whether the ball is actually caught in flight.

As every baseball fan knows, the purpose of the rule is to prevent the infielder from allowing the batted ball to fall to the ground in order to make a double-play on two of the baserunners. The implicit assumption is that the runners could not reach their next base before being forced out. The rule prevents this "gamesmanship" and was brought into being in response to some sharp practice going on back in the formative years of the sport. But, if the rule were eliminated, baseball would go on, albeit with the occasional "unsporting" double play. In other words, we could still play baseball; the IFR is not an "essential" rule endemic to the game.

I don't think the rule prevents anything that needs prevention. If the IFR were abolished, baserunners would modify their behavior accordingly. Runners on first and second, one out, the batter hits a pop-up directly to the shortstop. Today, with the IFR, the runners jog back to their bases and resume checking the stands for attractive fans. The batter is called out and the runners won't even think of advancing (although they may, if the pop is dropped or after tagging up). But with no IFR, baserunners would get off the base, maybe a third of the way on the pop-up, in order to prevent the purposeful drop and double play. But the shortstop could (maybe) complete the double-play by catching the ball and throwing quickly to second or first. But the shortstop could most likely never complete the double play by allowing the ball to drop and then throwing to third with the relay to second base. The baserunner who was on first would get to second base before the throw. (And the batter will have reached first base too.) The point is, the IFR was cre-ated (actually it evolved from the old "trapped ball" rule) to prevent players from missing the pop-up on purpose to get a double play: that is, it was thought unsporting or ungentlemanly for a fielder to miss on purpose to gain an advantage. But if the IFR were abol-ished (and runners went down the baseline on pop-ups), the only way a fielder could get an advantage would be to catch the ball and then double the runner off the base (if he could; some pop-ups would be too hard to catch to make a quick throw feasible). The point is, the fielder would benefit only by fielding the ball to the best of his ability. This is baseball, not gamesmanship.

The aim of the IFR is to temper competitive, cunning play by elim-inating one strategem that the rules of baseball (without the IFR) would permit. We might honestly wonder why a double play on an infield pop-up is considered unwelcome gamesmanship. Cer-tainly a fielder, with runners on base, can glove a ground ball and turn two; indeed, this defensive play was prevalent even from the game's founding, and was thus well-known to the drafter of the rules (Alexander Cartwright, founder of the New York Knicker-bockers). A batter who, with runners on base, hits a hard grounder to an infielder will often be part of a double play; so too will a bat-ter who hits a line drive right at a first baseman with a runner on first. All of these double plays are "unfair" in some sense, since a well-struck ball results in two outs. In both cases, good fielding is rewarded; so too would smart fielding be rewarded were there no IFR to pre-clude a double play on a pop-up.

I like cunning, strategic plays. I loved it when some college foot-ball coaches this past season deduced that college football's new (and since abandoned) rule on the clock running during kickoffs allowed them to run out the clock on a tight game. (In the game, Wisconsin outsmarted Penn State, with Joe Pa throwing a fit.) I loved it when Tiger had a 400-lb. boulder declared a "loose im-pediment" and had six men roll it out of the way; I cheered when Bill Belichick ordered his team to take an intentional safety by hik-ing the ball out of bounds rather than punt the ball from the end zone. Why not use the rules to one's advantage? Why not allow teams to compete mentally as well as physically?

The reason is not nice. A football player can grab and so forth, even against the rules, because he can get away with it and it's all "part of the game." But let one athlete gain advantage by use of his brains rather than brawn and suddenly it's not good sportsmanship. Watch carefully: whenever some announcer or commentator decries a legal athletic act as "unsporting," you can be sure that the castigated athlete was using his head. It's as if these ex-jocks turned announcers resented being outsmarted in the classrooms of their youth and see the sports field as a place where cunning has no place, where the nerdy guy who can figure out angles and exceptions is a "cheat" and not a good sport and, implicitly, cannot use his comparative advantage (brains) against his brawnier competitors. Years ago I wrote columns for a lawyer newspaper. Shortly after the golfer Jean Vande Velde basically blew the British Open, I wrote in a semiserious tone (a very unusual tone for me to take) that Vande Velde could have won the Open had he manipulated the rules to his advantage (if he only had a lawyer, I mused).[11] Well, I got back about 50 emails on the piece, maybe two or so saying nice job. The other 48 basically accused me of arguing in favor of bad sportsmanship. Even a USGA rules honcho wrote me just to call me a bad sport. No one said I was wrong in my interpretation of the rules, or commented on my suggestion that the rules needed to be changed lest some future competitor figure out what I had. What? Was Vande Velde just to lose the Open rather than apply a clear rule to his benefit? This rule of golf (the lost ball definition) is just as much a rule as the one defining "stroke," "hole," etc. Are some rules meant to be enforced and some not? Which ones? Could someone please tell the nerdy people so we don't run around acting unsportingly and risk angry emails from muckety-mucks?

I just don't believe there's a "spirit of the game." There's the game,

---

11. This column is reproduced in Chapter Nine.

it has rules, a beginning and an end, a final score, and that's it. Where do these people get the spirit from, anyway? Why is it "proper sportsmanship" to re-place an embedded ball but not good sportsmanship to declare an unembedded boulder a loose impediment? Both are permitted by the rules of golf. Sure, the rule on the latter issue is titled "loose impediment" (and so connotes loose pebbles), but if the definition includes large boulders, as it did, then the rule is that large, unembedded boulders can be moved, even if it takes a team of weightlifters to do it. That's the rule. There is no "spirit" apart from that rule. What the "spirit" people mean is that there are some outcomes to certain applications or consequences of rules that they did not think of, and so when they find out that someone else has thought of an application they did not, they charge unfairness or sharp practice or poor sportsmanship. Was Bret Bielema (Wisconsin's head football coach) a bad sport in refusing to kick off to Penn State at the close of the first half, denying Penn State a last chance to score? I would bet Joe Paterno thought so. But that's not why he was so angry. Joe Pa was mad because he was outsmarted.

So I break ranks with my fellow law professors. The Infield Fly Rule is designed to thwart sharp practice, to keep players from winning by using their heads. Far from celebrating the Infield Fly Rule, people who make their living teaching others to use their brains should despise it. I know I do, but then again, I guess I'm not a good sport.

The Problem with NFL Player Agents

The NFL Players Association recently found itself in front of a Congressional committee over its suspension of agent Carl Poston. Poston is the agent who mishandled linebacker Lavar Arrington's contract with the Washington Redskins, leading to the apparent forfeiture of a six-million dollar bonus. Poston's was a problem of ineptitude, not honesty. But the latter has been an issue too. The

NFLPA also had a problem with agent Tank Black, who when last heard from was being sentenced to five years federal time for swindling money from his player-clients. Why does the NFLPA seem to have so much trouble with (certain of) its agents? Why do the agents for Major League Baseball players seem so effective and ethical, by comparison? What can be done?

Pay the NFLPA agents more money, that's what.

Let's start with baseball. Lots of pages have been devoted to weepy tributes to America's pastime. Baseball, it is said, hearkens back to our pastoral history, to the uniquely American sense of open fields and grassy, flat spaces.[12] Unlike the time-regulated sports of basketball or football, baseball with its potentially limitless contests brings to mind the endless summer afternoon. But baseball is uniquely American in another way: with very few formal limitations, its players can hire virtually anybody to serve as an agent in negotiating a contract. (Although the MLBPA does require agents to be certified, certification requirements are minimal.) In addition, the agents are free to charge players what the market will bear for their services. You get it: a free market.

As a result of this free market in baseball agents, we have some very wealthy player agents, most notably Scott Boras, who routinely grants media interviews from his mansion overlooking the Pacific. But the presence and success of Boras sets a bar for other baseball agents, and the bar is a high one. Boras serves his clients with vigor, relying on modern statistical analysis, thorough preparation and glossy presentation to sell his players to bidding teams. If I were a professional baseball player looking to maximize my earnings from a short career, Boras would certainly be tops on my list of preferred agents. Other baseball agents, if they want to com-

---

12. Michael Mandelbaum, *The Meaning of Sports: Why Americans Watch Baseball, Football and Basketball and What They See When They Do* (2005).

pete with Boras and make Boras-style money, have to deliver representation of equal or superior competence.

Now let's check out the NFLPA. Like most unions, the NFLPA claims to be the exclusive bargaining agent for NFL players. Although that claim is not problematic in itself, the problem is that, unlike its baseball counterparts, the NFLPA doesn't trust the free market. It doesn't allow its players to select their own representatives (at least not as easily: the NFLPA has a pretty serious certification process, with obligatory continuing education obligations). More importantly, it doesn't allow the players and their selected agents to agree to a price for the agent's services. Instead, agent compensation is capped at three percent of the contract value, or even less, in certain circumstances.

Should it surprise us if a talented, industrious and effective sports agent, looking to profit from his work, opts to represent baseball players instead of football players? Why should the NFLPA set a price that it knows will tend to drive the best agents to other sports?

How do NFL agents compete for players? In baseball, Boras and his ilk show the players their organizational competence and marketing acumen, the manner by which Scott Boras famously wooed a young Alex Rodriguez. In football, of course some of the same goes on. But football agents must operate closer to the margin, making the kind of bells and whistles Boras has on hand marginally less affordable. A uniform price ceiling prevents a player from paying more for better representation. Players can't pay for the best even if they want to. All of which leaves player agents selling players on less important goods, such as friendship or relationships or what have you. Is it any wonder football players are notably famous for picking agents on the basis of a perceived compatibility (such as friendship or shared backgrounds) that probably has little payoff in terms of contract value? On what other basis can football agents compete? How can player agents say they're the best if they don't charge (and maintain) a fee that would tell players they are the best?

The NFLPA's limitation on the number of agents and its ceiling on the prices agents may charge has another problematic consequence: it leads to ethics problems. Limiting the profit an agent may collect from a single player means that the agent, to make money, has to spread himself thin. Lots of clients; volume sales; quantity over quality. At the same time, players compete for a finite number of roster positions. Effectively diminishing the number of agents means more agents will represent more than one player who might be suitable for a particular job opening. In addition, because the NFLPA rules promote volume sales, the necessity for those agents who survive in the industry is to take on as many clients as feasible, not just to make money, but also to be perceived as an important or effective representative. Most agents can't devote tons of resources and time to representing a small handful of players: there's not enough money in it. So agents have to become prominent to attract clients and survive; prominence is ensured by a long client list.

The 3% compensation limitation causes another problem: for some would-be agents, a guaranteed three percent of a lucrative NFL contract might be overpayment. These substandard agents might try to sell their inferior goods for more than they're worth: the NFLPA stipulated maximum in effect sets an artificial price for all representations. Indeed, it is not uncommon in the NFL for player agents to represent rookies for free, as a loss leader for subsequent representation when the stipulated rookie deal expires. One could see this practice and think that the player agents are nice people. One could also see this as predatory pricing aimed to try to up the barriers to entry for those agents selling lemons (and to keep out all agents, as again survival in the NFL depends in part on volume). Maybe this predation works. Or maybe the lemon-sellers re-target their enticements to players at the end of their rookie contracts instead of at the beginning. The fixed agent fee makes it difficult for players to assess the quality of agents: the best predictor of quality (a higher price) is precluded. Fixed fees draw to the NFL exactly those agents who will want to take advantage of the players' comparative inability to distinguish the good from the bad.

I understand the NFLPA's motivation: it wants to save its players as much money as possible. Indeed, the PA may look to the plethora of credentialed agents and think its system and compensation limits are sufficiently generous to attract numerous agents and ensure adequate contract bargaining representation to its players. But this belief assumes one fact, erroneously: it assumes that the players, not the owners, are the ones paying the agents, and that the percentage agent fees come from the player. Not so, at least not probably. Assume the NFLPA is "successful" in generating wages above market wages (else, why have a union?). Some players are more important than others; starting football players are for the most part rather unique athletes; perhaps the reserves are more interchangeable. Put another way, the supply of star players is clearly inelastic (hard to find a substitute). Where teams cannot find a substitute, then the bulk of the agent's fee will be borne by the team (since the player has more negotiating leverage); the opposite is the case where demand is elastic, as would be the case for comparatively fungible special-team players. The result of all this is that teams, not players, bear most of the cost of paying agents precisely in those cases where the NFLPA would probably fear the agent's compensation would be unconscionably high: with star players drawing large contracts. Only where players earn compensation at or just above the mandated minimum wage are agents effectively paid out of the pockets of players. (Interestingly, it is here, with respect to minimum wage players, that the Major League Baseball PA prohibits agents from collecting a fee; a similar restriction could protect journeymen NFL players as well.)

But to the free market the NFLPA will not turn. Instead, in the wake of recent scandals and Congressional oversight, the football union will likely adopt more certification and continuing education requirements and more limits on the ability of players to contract freely with agents. Further regulation will only create additional costs to entry, exacerbating the NFLPA's problem. The NFLPA should try to draw the best agents to professional football, not push them away.

Chapter Six

Gambling

It is the job of the legal academic to question rules of law, especially those that are in the form of a prohibition. Most human conduct produces some benefits, both for the person performing the behavior and usually for others as well.[1] As a result, when a government or an organization decides to prohibit some activity, it is essentially concluding that the benefits the conduct might produce are, in all circumstances, exceeded by the costs of the behavior. Prohibitory rules are expensive. Not only are any offsetting benefits lost, but the costs of creating and enforcing the prohibition must be added to the equation. This is not to say that no prohibitions are worth it; rather, it is the unique job of the legal academic to help elucidate those costs, compare them to the benefits lost, and let the chips fall where they may. If the better conclusion appears to be that the prohibition should be reconsidered and perhaps terminated, then as a matter of conscience the academic is duty-bound to make that conclusion clear.

All of this is a backhand way of admitting that I've never quite understood the antipathy of organized sports leagues toward gambling. Like most problems, perhaps my troubles can be traced to a childhood in New England, home of one of the nation's first state lotteries, and where weekly bingo games, pinochle at the house,

---

1. Some conduct, such as crimes against the person, are so harmful that any putative offsetting benefits are ignored in establishing a prohibition. Conduct that is termed a crime has by definition little or no socially valuable uses.

and all kinds of casual gambling were an everyday part of life. I grew up playing golf, and most times we had a dollar on the game. So I never developed the reflexive phobia about bets that appears to be the common reaction. To me, bets enhance the competitiveness of the players and the importance of the game, instead of threaten it.

One could argue that gambling is no more connected to "sports law" than illegal drug trafficking is to authorized medicinal prescriptions. But gambling and sports have much in common. In tournament-style sports such as golf or tennis, players are accustomed to getting paid on the basis of outcomes, a result tantamount to a winning wager. Moreover, sports gambling, as a counterpart to casino-style games, remains a fixed point in American social behavior. The various accoutrements to gambling, such as point spreads and odds, permeate sports discussions. Along with betting on game outcomes, fans sate their appetite for gambling on sports through fantasy leagues with points geared to individual statistics and team performances.

In the midst of the apparent ubiquity of sports gambling, for the major American professional leagues to enforce bans on betting by its players, coaches and other employees strikes me as a rule that needs some justification. Perhaps that justification is wanting, as the following essays suggest. We start with a piece that takes an off-handed look at the world that might have been.

The Beauty of Bets

Betting and sports go together so well that they should be legally joined. Professional athletes should be allowed—read: strongly encouraged—to bet on their games. Currently, all pro sports leagues forbid player gambling on games. The leagues fear that the players might try to win bets, not games, and that those who are good at games but bad at bets might be corrupted by bookmakers. Allowing athletes to gamble could pose problems—if only in keeping track of all those bets. I've played golf with a guy who, in the middle of a round, bet me on whether a flying bird would land in a tree. But all choices are comparative. How much better is the modern salary system at promoting team play and maximum player effort?

The biggest problem in pro team sports today is not the rampant drugs, groupies, and lawlessness; it's that compensation is distributed by individual player contracts, not by team victories. Player incentives do not correspond to team goals. Team play requires sacrifice and sublimation of ego. Do players on salary drives sacrifice personal accomplishment for the team? Maybe sometimes, but their financial incentives point the other way. Now compare this to a game in which player earnings come from bets, such as a weekend golf foursome. The primary bet a golfer makes is the team wager. A golfer might bet $25 and hope to double up. For pro athletes with entourages to support, maybe $25,000 per man, winner-take-all, for a half-million-dollar team bet per game is more realistic. That kind of cash would align monetary incentives perfectly with team goals. Indeed, team play wouldn't be thought of as a "sacrifice" at all. Those weekend golfers do all they can legally to help their teammates, and everybody on the winning team takes his money whether he made the winning putt or just helped line it up.

Side bets might further add to the excitement. Players could wager against certain opponents on scoring totals, for instance. But these bets would never be contrary to the team interest, because if they were, the player would be betting against his own stake in the team bet. That's why golfers' side wagers are always consistent with the game bet, and indeed most commonly increase the leverage of the main bet. Miracle shots from the sand or close tee shots on par threes not only win the side cash, they make team victory more likely. Even the occasional instance of a golfer aiming an approach shot at the bunker to try to win the ubiquitous "sandy" bet (which pays off for pars from the sand) is done where victory is lost and only miracle shots can salvage some value. So maybe a pro would try to augment his personal statistics at team expense when the game was essentially won or lost. But wouldn't that be a good thing? If the Rockets lead the Celtics by 30 late in the third quarter, wouldn't a $5,000 side bet on a scoring duel between Tracy McGrady and Paul Pierce make an otherwise meaningless final quarter worth watching? T-Mac and The Truth staying in the game, going head-to-head, their teammates (for a cut) double-teaming on defense to help ensure side-bet victory. No more garbage time.

But would all teams willingly wager? Golf has the handicap system, which allows mismatched players to make plausible bets. How would other sports address talent differentials? The answer, again, is to allow gambling—lots of it. All pro sports leagues desire team parity. It's a joint good that ensures competitive games. To achieve it, the leagues use various mechanisms such as draft order, with the worst team going first (thus creating tangible incentives to lose games—in other words, the absolutely stupidest league rule in the world), waiver claims, salary caps, weighted schedules, and so forth. Abolish all that. Just let teams bid on players in a free market, allocating percentages of the team bet as inducements. Teams all want to sign great players, but they'll also want to make sure that their opponents are just as good as they are. Too many good players on one team will render opponents unwilling to make large bets, thus lessening the action. It will also mean too many players demanding a bigger share of the pot. The best players will want to be distributed throughout the league to better command their large percentages. Teams will trade to keep the wagers substantial and the loot spread around.

Limitless, persistent gambling will also end the tiresome cult of the manager. In today's pro sports, with their antiquated salary practices, managers constantly have to coax spoiled athletes with million-dollar contracts to please take that Band-Aid off their little toe and get in the damn game. Managers with this kind of persuasive talent can be expensive. And note this: Even though the team's chances of victory are hurt by the shirker, few other players intercede, preferring to let the manager try to correct wayward teammates. Why should they care? Their contract isn't affected. But under a regime in which compensation is tied to bets, any player who shirks will cost his teammates big money. On their own, players will rein in the delinquents, pass the ball to the better shooters, and even take themselves out of the game if a superior player is ready on the bench. Most teams, acting sensibly, will fire their manager, relying on bookmakers and other professional gamblers to oversee the requisite pre-game wagering. Managers, freed from the confines of sports, could then become full-time psychotherapists—their true calling.

What about the common fear that pathetic athletic losers will throw games to earn huge bribes from their shady bookmaking friends? This is unlikely to happen. A player taking the opponent's side would be betting against his own $25,000 contribution to the team wager. And if the player declined to bet on his own team, would his teammates trust him? Not betting would be correctly understood as disloyalty, as a decision to allocate less than one's best efforts to winning. The non-bettor would find himself riding the bench, thereby diminishing his chances of corrupting the game. So any bribe to throw a game would have to be generous enough to make up for the player's team-bet loss.

In addition, the push to keep games competitive will ensure that players change sides often enough to worry about a reputation for disloyalty. A player caught throwing a game would be forever mistrusted. Thus the prospect of a one-time windfall from a thrown game would have to be weighed against the long-term diminution in betting gains. It would be rare that a player's entire career winnings could be capitalized in one "shut-down" bet. Of course, it could happen. Again, the choice is comparative. Under current compensation practices, athletes can still throw a game. Indeed, the fact that they lack immediate financial incentives to win games makes forfeiture of loyalty more marginally profitable.[2]

---

2. But what about rookies you wonder? Where would they get the large sums needed to place lucrative wagers on upcoming games? From winning their bets in college, of course. Only winning collegiate athletes, as

Here are 11 (my lucky number) applications of our new rule permitting bets:

1) Not only should Pete Rose be in the Hall of Fame, he should immediately be made commissioner of Major League Baseball to spearhead the league's transition to all-betting player compensation.

2) Even under the current compensation scheme, players should never be disciplined for betting in favor of their own teams. Such bets only further align player interests with team goals. In fact, if I were a general manager, I would immediately trade away any player who didn't show a heartfelt interest in taking on some heavy action.

3) Risk-averse players (a.k.a. non-bettors) should also be traded before they completely ruin team morale. In a short period of time, all the risk-averse players will likely congregate on the same team, which will likely purchase insurance against betting losses, enabling these babies to make modest bets and still play pro sports.

4) After firing all the managers, fire all the general managers, too. Most owners are self-made millionaires who have placed bets all their lives. They can negotiate team wagers and trade players to equalize talent levels themselves.

5) No more point spreads. Just track the player wagers to find out what Tom Brady really thinks the Patriots' chances are against the Jets.

6) Pay off the bets immediately after the game. I want to see the losing team handing over large wads of cash and the winners dancing around waving Benjamins at the crowd.

7) Demand absolutely huge television contracts, payable in weekly installments, which will basically double the payoff on everyone's bet. Las Vegas has bonus payoffs all the

---

proved by their large bankrolls, should be allowed to play pro sports anyway.

time, and they're real crowd-pleasers. We're talking win-ner-take-all football every week of the season. What a re-ality show! The networks would bankrupt themselves to get the rights.

8) Hire at least fifteen extra referees for every game. Like I said, winner-take-all football. Beef up venue security, equip law enforcement personnel with anti-riot gear, check Amber alert systems, and double hospital staffs.

9) End the prohibition on performance-enhancing drugs. I've never been quite convinced by live rat tests, anyway. Some-one has to establish the lethal-dose levels, so why not hugely compensated volunteers? Of course, that has nothing to do with gambling.

10) Consider applying the beauty of bets to other contests of paramount interest, like global conflicts (the United States should put North Korea "all in" immediately), border en-forcement (take the illegal aliens over the Border Patrol, no matter what odds you get), and Miss Universe pageants (bet on the Earthling; it's fixed, trust me).

11) Demand Pete Rose run for national elected office. The man is ahead of his time.

Prediction Exchanges and Gambling on Sports

On the odd chance that you're not a billionaire and thus can't buy a sports franchise, you might wonder how you can purchase a pro-prietary interest in your favorite sports team. The easiest way would be to purchase some stock, if you're a fan of one of the few teams that offers it, such as the Green Bay Packers or the Boston Celtics. Alternatively, because some teams are owned by publicly traded corporations, investors interested in these teams could purchase the parent's stock: Time Warner owns the Atlanta Braves, last I checked.

Assuming no stock is for sale, the investor could try a wager on his team as a means of participating on the team's upside potential. Wait, one small problem there; sports gambling is illegal in nearly every state. In addition, the federal Wire Wager Act (affecting businesses that offer sports gambling)[3] and the new federal Unlawful Internet Gambling Enforcement Act (UIGEA) (affecting banks and credit companies that fund internet gambling sites)[4] inhibit gambling pursuits over the internet.[5] So what's the eager sports investor to do?

---

3. For years there have been failed attempts to prohibit internet gambling. Previous legislation did not fully address advances in modern technology and also did not cover all forms of gambling. McCullagh, Declan, and Anne Broache. "Lax Standards for Feds in Data Breach Vote." 25 May 2006. CNETnews.com. http://news.com.com/Lax+standards+for+feds+in+data+breach+vote/2100-1028_3-6077199.html.

4. In October 2006, Congress passed a bill outlawing credit card and money transfer companies from accepting payments to gambling Web sites. The act requires banks and other financial institutions to identify and block any transaction to unlawful gambling websites. While American banks will comply, other non-U.S. based banks may not. In addition, many smaller non-U.S. gambling sites that are not publicly traded companies may continue to take bets from customers in the United States. Olson, Parmy. "Online Bets are Off." 2 October 2006. Forbes.com. http://www.forbes.com/business/2006/10/02/internet-gambling-offshore-tech-ebiz-cx_po_1002gambling.html. This Act is discussed below in "The Biggest Game of All."

5. There is and has been a long-standing and significant controversy over whether or not the federal wire act prohibits on-line gambling. It's pretty clear (to me) that it prohibits sports books and the like. The big question is whether or not the act prohibits games that mix chance and skill, namely poker. The new federal statute, by causing problems for illegal gambling sites, clearly raises the question over whether or not poker constitutes illegal gambling, at least under federal law. One would think the million-dollar businesses offering internet poker might be a little curious about the answer. Instead, in the wake of the new act, most of the major poker sites have ceased accepting all bets from U.S. residents; other sites have stubbornly or foolishly pledged to continue on (look out: big risk of abetting liability). Why face this Hobson's choice (the choice classically il-

Some interesting websites have been launched in recent years, such as Tradesports[6] and Ticket Reserve.[7] They allow people interested in sports to make investments in the success of their sports teams. But are these investments legally indistinguishable from illegal gambling?

Sports bets are not all that different from sports investments. Both increase in value when the team wins. An equity investor (such as a team owner) profits from a winning team in the form of enhanced ticket demand, merchandise sales, broadcast viewership, and eventually franchise value itself. The bettor also profits from team

---

lustrated in Ex Parte Young)? Why shut down and forego millions of dollars of business, if it turns out poker is not illegal gambling? On the other hand, why continue business, only to run the risk of criminal liability?

Poker people, you have another option: sue the attorney general or some other federal bigshot in federal court for a declaratory judgment. There is a federal statute that permits precisely this cause of action. Certainly, with web sites shutting down left and right, you can demonstrate a sufficient case or controversy to merit federal declaratory jurisdiction. A judge will tell you whether or not the act refers to your operation. If it does, then shutting down is an option. If it doesn't, then plug your servers back in and recommence raking. Why rely on a lawyer's opinion, which after all is just a prediction of how a court would likely rule? Get your legal advice from the horse's mouth. With a declaratory judgment, you'll know the winner of the contest ahead of time, every gambler's dream.

6. Tradesports allows individuals to participate in a virtual and transparent "exchange" on various events, including financial, sporting, current events, entertainment and more. Individuals trade directly with other individuals. A small transaction fee is charged per lot traded. The events include those that are long-term (i.e. who will win the March Madness tournament) and short term (i.e. will the Dow close up today). "About Tradesports." TradeSports.com http://www.tradesports.com/aav2/aboutUs.jsp.

7. Ticket Reserve is a site that basically allows people to purchase options to buy tickets to various events ahead of time. These options can be sold at a later time for a profit. For example, tickets originally purchased to the Super Bowl have sold for more than double their original price when loyal fans look to Ticket Reserve to make last-minute purchases. Mohl, Bruce. "Big-Game Options Yield Rich Profits." 23 January 2007. TicketReserve.com. http://www.ticketreserve.com/news.html?ugid=&contentId=700028990.

victory, albeit more immediately and in the form of a cash payout. Certainly there are meaningful distinctions between ownership and betting. The team owner lends skill to the job, and so can contribute to the likelihood of his team's success and the resulting increase the value of his investment. The bettor is merely passive, and so the outcome of his investment is out of his control. (Of course, owners with minority interests can also be passive and their investments highly risky.) The team owner's investment also has an economic substance to it that wagers appear to lack; along with betting on the team's fortunes, the owner produces sporting contests for spectator enjoyment.

So what is an illegal sports gamble, as opposed to a legal sports investment? Federal and state statutes typically avoid trying to distinguish the two (thanks a lot). The statutes that do attempt a definition either do so by the broadest of terms (gambling involves "games that involve chance in the outcome") or by referring to particular casino-style games, such as roulette. The recent UIGEA clarifies nothing by defining "gambling" to include risking something of value on the outcome of a game subject to chance. Any investment in a game involves some degree of chance, maybe even a lot of it, even where the investor is personally involved. The problem with the law's flexibility in distinguishing a potentially illegal sports gamble from a legal sports investment is that few of the available sports investments fall clearly on either side of the line.[8]

Ticket Reserve and Tradesports are instances of the growing internet phenomenon of so-called "prediction exchange." What's that?

---

8. To take the comparison further, one could say the gambler's outcome does not depend entirely on chance, but in part is the product of knowledge about the team, just as the limited owner's profitability is the product of informed decision-making. Knowledge by either the bettor or the investor is optional; one could just make a choice and get lucky. Nevertheless, the role of both is quite passive but can be improved through diligence.

I predict one event will happen ("the Red Sox will win") and my counterparty predicts the other ("the Red Sox will lose"), and we each make a stated investment in our prediction from a pre-funded trading account, with the correct predictor winning both investments. How can such an exchange not be an illegal sports gamble? Most likely, websites that offer direct exchanges in the outcome of particular games seem directly comparable to traditional sports gambling, and thus are most susceptible to an unfavorable characterization under American law. A website like Tradesports, although it calls itself a "betting exchange," looks like a gambling site. (By pure coincidence, the site's not located in the U.S.)

But some prediction exchanges do have an underlying economic purpose and thus possess a significant feature of an investment. Ticket Reserve sells futures contracts ("fan forwards") in game tickets. Say an investor thinks the Red Sox will play in this season's World Series (trust me, they will). The investor can purchase an option to buy a World Series ticket that is contingent on the Red Sox participating in the Series. (Structurally it's a put option; as the investor/option buyer must exercise the option, that is, purchase the ticket, if the Sox win the American League pennant.) If the Sox get in, the investor gets to purchase the ticket for the face value plus whatever premium he paid for the option. The investor could also sell the ticket (or the option at any time) to another Red Sox fan, assuming there is one who would be willing to pay a price substantially in excess of the premium plus face value, thus giving the investor a profit. In this instance, the investor could use the forward contract to speculate, taking a position financially similar to a bet on Tradesports that the Red Sox will win the American League.

All kinds of equity investments, including stocks or derivatives, can be used for speculation. However, what a prediction exchange about the value of World Series tickets offers is a large measure of economic substance; the investor could use the exchange to hedge the risk of the cost of Series' tickets, allowing the investor to view the game at a reasonable cost. The investor limits his downside risk to the cost of the option premium. Other factors beyond the team's success, such as the quality and location of the opponent and the wealth of its fans, will also affect World Series' ticket prices.

Ticket reselling appears to be gaining acceptance; the NBA recently contracted with Ticketmaster to be the official ticket reseller of the NBA. Season ticket holders, along with team owners, take a long position in the team's winning, betting that the team will be in contention and therefore play valuable late-season games. Ticket reselling allows ticket holders to recover at least some of their ticket costs should they lose their bet. The investor in a prediction exchange like Ticket Reserve takes the same position as the season-ticket purchaser, except that the investor takes that position with respect to fewer games.

Prediction exchanges have value apart from their primary hedging and betting functions. They also provide information about the beliefs and preferences of large numbers of people. Indeed, one academic group has received permission from the Commodity Futures Trading Commission to create a prediction exchange just to study the predictive value of its data.[9] Even Tradesports has provided useful data for academic research.

So to me it looks like Ticket Reserve is not operating a gambling site, but is offering an economically substantial means for fans to make intelligent investments to hedge the risk of future ticket prices. At least I think so. By the way, Ticket Reserve is located in Chicago. Talk about a gamble.

A Defense of Pete Rose

After years of prevarications, baseball great Pete Rose finally admitted in his latest book[10] that he bet on baseball games while a

---

9. Iowa Electronic Markets. http://www.biz.uiowa.edu/iem/.

manager for the Cincinnati Reds. The gist of the book's argument about Rose's gambling is that his violation of baseball's Rule 21 is no more serious than the drug and spouse abuse of many current and former players. Yet they didn't get banished from the game and from the Hall of Fame, so why should Rose?

Pete's argument is both convincing and irrelevant. It is irrelevant because no law and no reason require logic in the remedies imposed by governing authorities. For example, it may well be the case under federal criminal law that property crimes are as serious as drug crimes, and thus should result in similar penalties. But federal criminal law suggests the opposite view, and the bottom line is that legislatures, in specifying appropriate penalties for crimes, are pretty much free to rank offenses at their discretion. Same with Major League Baseball. Moreover, its status as a voluntary private association only further insulates its rules from legal review. If baseball wants to say that placing a bet on a game is worse than beating one's wife, then it's worse; baseball can impose light sanctions for the latter and lifetime banishment for the former.

As a matter of logic (assuming it matters), then Pete's position seems persuasive. Gambling on sports, even betting on the game in which one is participating, is not inherently wrong, in my view. If it is wrong, it's not as wrong as purposely striking one's comparatively defenseless spouse. Wagers and investments appear nearly indistinguishable. All investments involve risk, to varying degrees. Rose's bets on the Reds to win were not much different from a team owner's purchase of the club; the owner's profits and the franchise value will both increase commensurate with the team's success on the field.

A "bet" is hard to define. Perhaps it stretches meaning too far to say that Rose was taking on "single-game-equity" positions. People make bets on all kinds of equity and derivative financial in-

---

10. Pete Rose and Rick Hill, *My Prison Without Bars*. (Rodale, 2004).

struments. With the advent of legalized ticket resellers (scalpers) and websites that create futures markets in game tickets (like Ticket Reserve), investors can also take long positions in the success of sports teams. There should be no significant legal difference between over-the-counter derivative instruments and a forward contract on Red Sox World Series tickets. Really, is betting by athletes on their own games all that bad? Golfers do it all the time. Is betting on games in which one doesn't play all that wrong?

So I'm not troubled about Rose betting on his team to win. But, some might wonder, might Rose bet to lose, and then throw the game, using incompetent rookie pitchers and ordering intentional walks? Not likely. No bookie's going to take that action, and believe me bookies know who's making the bet. Plus, if Rose were found out, he would receive certain banishment and the enduring enmity of his fellow athletes. So I believe him when he said he bet on his team to win. A manager or player who bets on his team to win bets consistently with his team's interests, and so his bet is harmless to the team's goals, or perhaps even enhances the manager's interest in striving to win. Bets just underscore the incentive we want participants to have.

It's a seldom-discussed, dirty little secret of professional sports that players and managers don't always want to win. League commissioners and team owners fret about competitive integrity and players talk about giving 110%, but really that's just sloppy speech, if not actually misleading. Teams do not want to win all the time. A manager will rationally use his pitching staff differently in Game Seven of the World Series than he will in some early season getaway game against a non-division opponent. In the World Series game, the manager will empty his bullpen, using even highly paid starting pitchers in relief. In the early season game, the manager will err on the side of caution, using only rested pitchers accustomed to bullpen work. Even player exertions vary, as players will smartly avoid risking injury in non-significant games lest the season be lost. Of course players try to win and everyone talks about "competitive integrity," but that phrase does not mean that players and managers will try their hardest to win. It means that they will try to win given the relative importance of the game to the team's long-term interests in a successful season and even seasons. Owners want managers and players to play to win only to this limited extent. No one really wants players giving 110%.

So here's the problem: Rose's bets may have made him try too hard to win. If Pete had, say, $10,000 on the Reds to win some early season game, he might have treated the game like it was a World Series game, inserting stars nursing small injuries into the lineup, warming up his best pitchers, and so forth, even at the risk to the team's season. Pete Rose, in other words, may have been trying too hard to win the "bet" games, where everybody else was putting out an effort more appropriate to the game's relative importance. (It would be interesting to correlate Rose's bets and his managerial decisions, to see if indeed he tended to go with his best relief pitchers and so forth in these games.) Now this would not be a problem if Rose bet, as his book says he did, on all of the Reds' games, and did so in roughly equal amounts; his betting income from the Reds' next games would give Rose a reservation value in making sure he didn't overtax his team to win today's bet at the expense of tomorrow's.

But John Dowd, the lawyer who investigated Rose's betting on behalf of MLB, said upon hearing of Rose's admission that in fact Rose did not bet on the Reds when his less competent pitchers were starting.[11] This looks like a problem. By betting on some games and not others, Rose does give himself the incentive to manage games differently; it also tells his betting accomplices that Rose will

---

11. The official report from John Dowd states that "no evidence was discovered that Rose bet against the Cincinnati Reds." However, Dowd later claimed his investigation was close to showing that in fact Rose bet against the Reds, but time constraints prevented this aspect of the investigation from fully developing. "Report: Dowd says Rose 'Probably' Bet against Team." 12 December 2006. ESPN.com. http://espn.go.com/mlb/news/2002/1212/1475769.html.

likely manage those games differently, and to structure their bets accordingly (take the opponent). Thus, the competitive integrity of the games is compromised; Rose would care about some games too much and about others too little.

But this is not too much of a problem. First, who cares if the bookies get signals from Rose's betting patterns? They might just as easily get signals from a player's drug habits. Why should MLB care about the integrity of the illegal sports betting market? Let the counterparties lose their bets and learn not to deal with insiders. Second, if Rose did indeed have an interest in winning some games more than others, is that really all that different from what managers do anyway? Managers can't try to win all the games, or they'd overtax their rosters. Managers have to pick some games, perhaps against tough pitchers, to rest some of the star hitters, or perhaps, to use a series against a weak opponent to pitch some reserves. Doesn't a manager signal to bookies and the rest of us that he's not trying too hard to win when he puts his slugger on the bench and inserts some rookie into the starting lineup? If Rose or any other manager decides to go all out to win two games out of a three-game series, what's the problem if Rose put his money on those two? Would anyone rationally put it on any other games?

Rose's question is a good one. Why should wife-beaters and druggies gain admission to the Hall of Fame, a purely honorary event, and not Pete Rose? Does a bet on his own team to win a game more seriously compromise (compromise in the sense of enhancing) the competitive integrity of the team's performance than does a center fielder pumped up on anabolic steroids or a first baseman swinging for the fences in his contract year? All three have incentives to excel and have taken action in conformity with those incentives: one made a bet, one took a needle, one plays selfishly. Which one's conduct is most in line with team goals and is most consistent with fair play and good sportsmanship? I'd argue the bettor. The drug user cheats the game and gains unfair advantage over his competitors; the home-run hitter pursues his financial incentives at the possible expense of the team's situational needs.

The bettor? At worst he'll try too hard to win. Not too bad of a teammate.

Notably, Pete Rose lied about his betting. Why did he lie? Lots of reasons. To confess the truth in his case, given his massive gambling losses, would be tantamount to admitting to an addiction; never something easy to do, especially not with the whole world watching. To confess the truth also would subject Rose to baseball's irrational lifetime ban and group Rose's name with the "Black Sox" who threw the World Series. What Rose did is so far from throwing the World Series that it's just about the exact opposite. Do these concerns justify the lie? Of course not, but they do help explain it. We don't expect people accused of crimes to confess, and in fact we allow them to refuse to testify at all. Rose didn't have the luxury of refusing to answer questions, yet like an accused criminal, Rose faced serious and immediate sanctions for a concession of guilt. Rose couldn't take the Fifth; what else could he have done except to deny and to maintain his denial, year after year? He made baseball prove its case, and only after it did was Rose willing to concede to the truth. Could his concession have come more quickly? Yes. But, in the "court of public opinion," the only way to put the prosecutor to his case is to lie.

Professional golfers gamble. They play for money, albeit on most tours for someone else's money. Whatever the source, it's still a pile of money, and whether a player makes or misses a putt on the eighteenth green can mean hundreds of thousands of dollars. Players who win hold up large checks. So let's stop pretending money and winning payoffs corrupt professional sports. The term "professional sports" means sports played for money. Do pro golfers, who are playing for prize money, throw tournaments, purposely shanking balls out of bounds or yanking putts off-line? Playing an individual skill sport where betting (at least on the British Open) is legal and pervasive, golfers more than any other athlete could easily, undetectably, corruptly throw a tournament. If we trust golfers, why not others? Why is Pete Rose banished from the game for playing for money when we allow other athletes to wave their winnings around on cam-

era? For goodness sakes, he's baseball's all-time leading hitter. All
he did was bet. Let the poor man into the Hall of Fame.

The Biggest Game of All

Congress has passed and the President has signed a new federal
law that prevents banks and credit card companies from transfer-
ring depositors' funds into online gambling sites like Party Poker.
Going a step further, the state of Washington has criminalized trans-
mitting gambling information over the internet. In addition, federal authorities have recently arrested major on-line poker magnates
when these American expatriates returned to U.S. soil. So it looks
like momentum is building to attack online poker. I love playing poker
(as the TV ads say, for instructional purposes only; I like to give
lessons). I also love not living in prison. I suspect there are a few
out there who share my preferences.

Maybe I underestimate the power of the pen (referring both to
a writing instrument and to jail), but I cannot believe any act of
legislation, even when coupled with the threat of imprisonment,
will be able to put this genie back in the bottle. Poker websites are
all over the internet, and ads for these websites permeate the sites
of respected news, sales, and informational organizations. This is
a huge, multi-billion dollar industry. Moreover, the customer base
appears enormous, in the U.S. and even more so in Asia. Will these
many millions of people just go back to passively watching television (itself populated by a number of poker shows)? Should online poker be stamped out? I suspect these bans are pro forma and
will never be enforced against individual players, who will find
means other than a credit card to fund their poker accounts.

The obvious question is why the state and federal legislatures
would single out online poker sites but leave intact other gambling
opportunities, including lotteries, horse tracks, video poker and
fantasy sports. Some have charged hypocrisy. But that's never a fair
charge against a legislature, which cannot act with a single, unal-

loyed purpose. It's all compromise and vote-trading. In other words, don't look for logical consistency from a legislature.

With that said, it is difficult to discern a plausible rationale for the statute. Two have been mentioned: the need to protect citizens against scams or fraud perpetrated by the gambling sites, and the need to preclude behavior that leads to addiction. As to the first, it bears repeating that this is big business. Why would Party Poker or these other huge businesses want to cheat their customers out of at most a few hundred dollars when, if discovered, that cheating could collapse their entire business? Their "reputational bond" is plenty large enough to give these outfits every incentive to treat their customers favorably. This justification, if you buy it, seems more plausibly to support regulating the industry, rather than criminalizing it. As to the addiction rationale, there are better solutions than a nationwide ban. Many forms of permitted conduct can harm both the doer and others. (Just like driving.) Couldn't poker players be licensed upon minimal qualifications and instruction and forfeit their license for egregious behavior?

The other rationale, less frequently mentioned, is that gambling constitutes a moral wrong. This is problematic. The argument is that gambling is wrong because it wastes time, is an attempt to get money without working, is inherently covetous, and produces bad side effects. However, this position misses the point, maybe not for all betting, but at least as far as poker is concerned: few who play poker recreationally realistically hope to win money. Poker is not about the money, it's that money happens to be the "tokens" the game uses to make moves and to keep score. Money has to be the token, to make the bets meaningful, and the size of the bets must vary according to the player's individual affinity for money. For some of us, winning even a few dollars is cause for celebration, not for the money, but for winning the game.

The Difficulty of Profiting from a Corrupted Referee

The big story this summer concerned an NBA referee with a gambling problem who attempted to fix game outcomes to favor his gambling cronies to whom he was apparently indebted.[12] At this point none of us know the full details, and we probably never will. Nonetheless, the media reaction to this development has been apocalyptic, and that's putting it mildly. I've heard the event described as the biggest American sports scandal since the Black Sox;[13] some commentators have predicted the demise of the NBA itself.[14]

Time to get a grip everyone. A game-fixing scandal is not that big of a deal. But if it becomes one, what I fear is not the scandal, but the measures that the NBA (and potentially other sports leagues) will take in response. If this scandal leads to the demise of the NBA, it won't be because of the rogue actions of a particular referee. It

---

12. Tim Donaghy's wagers occurred throughout the 2005-2006 and 2006-2007 season, and involved thousands of dollars. The Elias Sports Bureau reported that "Donaghy officiated 68 games in the 2005-06 season and 63 games in 2006-07." There are also allegations that Donaghy has connections to members of organized crime. "Donaghy Under Investigation for Betting on NBA Games." 20 July 2007. *ESPN.com.* http://sports.espn.go.com/nba/news/story?id=2943095.

13. In 1919, eight White Sox players were accused of throwing the World Series against the Cincinnati Reds. Supposedly, one of the players, Chick Gandil, offered to throw the game for $100,000. Despite being acquitted of the charges by a jury, the players were banned from baseball for life. "History Files — Chicago Black Sox." 1999. *Chicago Historical Society.* http://www.chicagohs.org/history/blacksox/blk3.html.

14. NBA commissioner David Stern stated that after twenty-three years as commissioner, "I can tell you that this is the most serious situation and worst situation that I have ever experienced either as a fan of the NBA, a lawyer for the NBA or a commissioner of the NBA." 25 July 2007. "Stern: Bet Probe 'Worse Situation that I Have Ever Experienced.'" *ESPN.com.* http://sports.espn.go.com/nba/news/story?id=2947237.

will be because David Stern, perhaps pushed by an irate Congress or an over-reactive public, makes a profound error in judgment.

The Black Sox scandal was such a big deal because, well, who knows. It's part of the lore and legend of baseball, and, like many such memories (see the "Curse of the Bambino," for instance), the scandal is probably oversold in its significance. Well within the memory of players and fans at the time of the Black Sox was the practice of "hippodroming," which in the early years (before the formation of the first professional baseball league) involved two club owners staging private baseball games for the benefit of local gamblers. So baseball was no stranger to gambling, and only in the wake of the 1919 World Series and the trial acquittal of the White Sox players did the major league employ a commissioner to eradicate betting. So the famous scandal became notorious not because it was shocking or novel, but because it marked what came to be regarded as a turning point in baseball's history. (Somewhat like Paul Revere's ride in that its contemporary significance paled in comparison to the importance the ride is given in the common historical narrative.)

Other sports have had their scandals, even involving game fixing, and have survived intact. College basketball, probably the most corrupted sport given the number of instances of fixing that have surfaced over the years, appears to remain unblemished in the public eye. Why do these commentators, so upset about the possibility of an NBA game being fixed, happily watch college basketball? One solution already proposed to the NBA scandal is to give the referees a pay raise so they wouldn't feel the need to supplement their income through illicit means. How perplexing that move would be for the refs. Here they are, cowering in their off-season homes with a worried eye on the developing story, and then the hammer comes down: pay raises for everybody! That will teach them. More money would give the refs a greater investment (performance bond) in doing a good, honest job, but on that theory we should give a raise to college athletes (who are paid some, in effect) and to everybody else in a position to fix a game. Besides being expensive, how much is enough? At what point does a referee or player make enough money to forgo the bribe? At what point would a person risk shutting down his career to make some immediate cash? I don't know, I suppose the amount would vary quite a bit. Raising everyone's pay seems problematic at best.

Lots of games are fixed, in a sense. Just consider wrestling or horse racing. Given the willingness of some players and teams to use performance enhancements, isn't it just as true that games involving those teams are fixed too? The probability of a particular outcome (victory by the druggies) is enhanced. Reading recently about the drug scandals surrounding bicycle racing teams in the Tour de France makes clear to me that certain teams were pre-ordained to be competitive or to have no chance, depending entirely on their decisions to use illicit drugs or not. Aren't baseball games involving Barry Bonds fixed, in that Bonds' alleged steroid use gives the Giants a (big) leg up on the opposition? Does not the Giants' management, well aware of Bonds' drug use, essentially pay Bonds a large salary precisely because his cheating enhances the Giants' chances? A referee can't guarantee bettors a particular outcome; he can improve the chances, perhaps significantly, and so in the betting world, where even slight edges are worth lots of money, bribing a referee pays off. But does it pay off more than other inside knowledge, such as knowing a particular pitcher is doping, or knowing a wide receiver is having marital troubles, or realizing that a particular guard, in a contract year, will shoot the ball even to his team's detriment? The point is that lots of games are fixed in this broad sense, yet we still love to watch the games and seem to enjoy them just as thoroughly.

If baseball can survive an entire generation's worth of sluggers and fast-ballers shooting up with steroids, basketball can survive a rogue referee's slip to the dark side. Steroids affect every aspect of a sport, from the batter's performance to the pitcher's arm speed. Every game, every day. Even a referee hell-bent on fixing a game will have to overcome the compensating calls made by his two fellow referees, plus overcome the fact that, no matter how many fouls one calls, on some nights one team just beats another, sometimes badly, and there's not much a ref can do about it. Plus some referees are corrupted, not by a bribe, but by the screams of the home crowd, the reputation of the players, the speed of the game, and so on. No, these refs are not corrupted in their intention (as is a referee who is bribed), but the result is the same. Part of the NBA's appeal is the fan's chance to comment directly on the performance of the referees. Unlike football, where many actions that lead to penalties are hidden from public view beneath the mass of linemen's bodies, in the NBA most actions subject to foul calls are nearly as evident to spectators (especially those watching at home) as they are to the referees. Now, along with incompetence and mistake, fans can cite intentional corruption in their catty remarks.

How often would a corrupted referee fix games? Imagine you're a gambler controlling an NBA ref. It is likely you made a large investment in getting the referee to the point where he'll try to fix a game at your request. You wouldn't want him making it too obvious. Once the ref were exposed, your investment would be lost, along with all the future games from which you could profit. Instead, you'd probably look for games likely to be close (so the ref's corruption might better affect the game outcome), and that involved enough betting action to allow you (the fixer) to get down a large amount of money without that bet being traced to a single source. (Bookies know what suspicious games look like too, just from the bets that are made.) Probably you'd pick out three or four games, hoping the modest edge your "fixed" ref gives you allows for the game outcome in the majority of them to be tipped in your favor. My point is, we don't need to search through meaningless Hawks versus Bobcats contests to look for objectionable calls by the corrupted referee; look at games where a lot of money was down. Even then, good luck finding corrupted calls; basketball fouls are intractably subjective, and people see what they want to see. (Some people even claim to see losing NBA teams "tanking" for draft position, even where all logic and anecdotal evidence is to the contrary. More on that later.)[15]

---

15. See Chapter Twelve.

Here's what will happen: after as much detail as possible is learned, the NBA (and other leagues, I predict, will follow suit) will "get tougher" on referees who gamble. Given that the current rule prohibits all gambling and calls for the single sanction of immediate termination, I'm not sure what more the league can do. Perhaps refs will be given periodic lie-detector tests; perhaps also referees will be required to make detailed disclosures of their financial statements to alert the league to unusual gains or losses. Similar restrictions on players, who are equally able to fix games, might follow. At this time, all the leagues prohibit players betting on their sport; some also prohibit sports betting entirely. None, outside of the NCAA, prohibit all gambling activities, and if the story is right, it is non-sports betting that got this particular NBA referee into trouble. Could many contemporary professional players, flush with cash and with a proclivity for wagering action, plausibly be prohibited from engaging in any gambling activity at all? Would the NBA or any pro league really suspend a notable player just for playing cards on the team plane or at the local casino? My point is that taking the anti-gambling rules much further brings the leagues into a position with which few of us would be comfortable.

Here's what should happen. The NBA should investigate, find and fire the miscreants, and move on. The FBI and the U.S. Attorney's office can take care of any violations of federal law. Gambling in general is not that bad. There are lots of ways referees and players can get into deep financial trouble, and some of them involve perfectly legal bets like stocks, bonds, real estate, and business start-ups. A player or referee, by having some (marginal) control over game outcomes, always has the potential to sell that control to a bettor or to others who may be interested. For instance, couldn't wealthy boosters of a college football club be just as likely to fix a game by bribing the opposing quarterback as would a gambler? Even people in no particular financial difficulty might be inclined to sell their control over game outcomes, just to make some money. So there's really nothing the NBA can do to legislate away financial troubles, and little the league can do about the opportunity referees and players have to sell their valuable ability to marginally affect game outcomes. At the end of the day the league has to trust people, and we fans implicitly know that every once in a while that trust will be broken. It's not a shocker; the league won't fail. That a trust given will occasionally be broken is an expected aspect of the human condition, a fact of which everyone except certain notable commentators seems well aware.

One oddsmaker argues that an NBA referee, although unlikely to be able to dictate game outcomes in terms of victory, would be more able to influence the total points of the game.[16] Betting "totals," or the "over/under," is another common bet proposition, along with bets on the winner. Two problems with betting totals present themselves.

First, totals bets are not as widely available as are bets to win. Some bookmakers don't like to offer totals, much like they don't like to offer any wagers on more obscure games featuring unknown teams, simply because information (which gives professional oddsmakers their edge) is harder to come by. Second, a major bettor (and I would assume any bettor who invested in corrupting and controlling an NBA referee would be a major bettor) would want to get down some very heavy action on the particular game his corrupted referee were under instruction to try to influence. Big bets on totals are hard to get down. Most sports books limit the size of these bets much more than they do the size of the bets to win (for that same unpredictability and information reasons). Now, to most of us, a betting limit of $2,000 or $5,000 or whatever sounds like

16. ESPN held a question and answer session with Brandon Lang, whose life story was captured in the film "Two for the Money," and considers himself "the best big-game handicapper in the country." Lang has never lost a Super Bowl in his career, with a record of 15-0-2. Lang also provides wagering advice on his website www.BrandonLang.com. The Q&A session addressed the topic of how referees could have been able to fix bets. Drehs, Wayne. "Expert Explains the Many Ways a Crooked Referee Could Fix Bets." 23 July 2007. *ESPN.com.* http://sports.espn.go.com/nba/news/story?page=expertexplainsNBAbets.

no limit at all. To a professional gambler looking to get down a quarter million dollars on a total bet, this limit can pose a real problem. Plus, even to get down a bet at or near the book's maximum, most gamblers need to have a prior, established relationship with the bookie. Bookies only maintain losing relationships, if you get my drift. A successful bettor with inside information would have a seriously difficult time getting his bet down, even through cut-outs (other people placing bets for the big bettor). Bookies are very watchful of their customers. Worse, once the bookies figure out the bettor is winning, the spreads or totals will move with his bets instantaneously, thus making it progressively more difficult for this bettor to get the action he needs to make this venture profitable.

I'm not saying money can't be made from a corrupted NBA referee; of course some can. I'm again suggesting that this scandal might not be as substantial as some are assuming it to be. Having inside information (a biased referee) and making money off of it are two different things, much like having the ability to access illegal drugs and making (and laundering) proceeds from it involve two different levels of complication. The money part is a lot trickier.

The Dubious Crime of Referee Tim Donaghy

Although details remain sketchy, we are now learning how NBA referee Tim Donaghy went afoul of the league's prohibition on gambling. One of Donaghy's sins was to alert his cronies as to the composition of the refereeing crew for each game. Each referee tends to call fouls a little differently, with some more whistle-happy than others. So knowing in advance the identity of game referees could assist gamblers, who would bet the "over" side in a game officiated by referees who call tight games, or could wager a "side" (pick the victor) on the team with better free-throw shooters. Donaghy apparently also passed on player injury information and details about how certain players interacted. Not sure who would care much about the latter, but clearly injury information can matter a lot in basketball, where only a few players see the substantial bulk of the playing time and even fewer take most of the team's shots. Finally, although I'm not sure about this, I've read that Donaghy may have made some bets on his own account. Donaghy got paid by his co-conspirators for successful bets, at about $5,000 per game.

So as this scandal begins its slow passage into history, the NBA will undoubtedly "learn" from its mistakes. Undoubtedly the league will tighten up its oversight of referees, players and other league employees. Hiring and retention criteria will be reviewed and augmented; policies will be rewritten; financial disclosure and review obligations will be enhanced, all in an effort to prevent this tragedy from ever happening again.

But has the NBA learned the correct lesson? Does the NBA need to impose more regulation to eliminate game fixing? How about deregulation instead?

In effect, Donaghy was betting on his own account. Regardless of whether or not he put his own money on the line, the fact that he was paid only for successful bets gave him an interest in the outcome of a game equivalent to a wager. I don't think there's a lot a referee can do, in the average game, to influence the ultimate outcome in terms of victory. But he may systematically put the game into the "over" category. What Donaghy could do was call games tight (which it seemed he did), hide the fact that he was to referee a game (the NBA took care of this for him, not publicly revealing the identity of game referees until the last minute), bet the over, and then profit from the tendency of games he worked to go over the total. Given the preference that the NBA league officers seem to have for tightly called games, Donaghy's habit of calling games tightly, instead of raising suspicion, actually put him in good stead. Ironically, Donaghy's gambling interests helped him earn a high league rating.

Donaghy's betting was made possible by the NBA's decision to hide certain information. Hiding information makes it valuable and allowed Donaghy to profit from it. What if that decision were reversed? What if the identity of the referees and player injury information had been publicly disclosed? Donaghy would have had nothing to trade. With available information, gamblers and other people interested in game outcomes would study referee tendencies and player injuries. Point spreads and total scoring lines would be adjusted accordingly, much as they are for (known) player injuries, player talent, scoring averages, home-court advantage, and so forth. Making information public renders it comparatively worthless.

Why did the NBA feel it necessary to shield the identity of game referees? Maybe there are competitive reasons (perhaps discouraging teams from preparing game plans to play to the particularities of certain referees), but they seem slight. On the other hand, clearly this practice infuses the seemingly innocuous "game referee" information with value, making this inside information a target for those who stand to profit from even slight betting edges. Think of all the people who had to know referee assignments well in advance of games: besides the referees themselves, there are referee and league supervisors, travel agents, family members, close friends, traveling companions, and perhaps others. A determined gambler would have a multiplicity of targets. But these people are targets only because the NBA made referee assignments a secret in the first place. Let the public know ahead of time and that information would be factored into the over/under total line and would have value to nobody.

Much the same can be said with respect to player injury information. The NFL (a betting league if ever there was one) is diligent in requiring teams to disclose player injuries, even going so far as to mandate that teams classify the severity of the injury. Remarkably, this classification of an injury must be made not according to the actual severity of the injury. Instead, teams are obliged to describe player injuries along the dimension of the player's likelihood of appearing in the forthcoming game. This practice can only be designed to assist bookmakers in setting the gambling line precisely right. (Fans with game tickets are not going to skip the game because the tight end is "doubtful.") Why should the NFL care about the integrity and accuracy of the betting line? Why should it be so concerned about teams disclosing even minor injury information? Because the NFL is well aware that gambling permeates its game and wants to make sure that no valuable "inside" information exists: if all is disclosed, all temptations for insiders to profit from information is gone. Disclosing this information publicly takes away the opportunity and incentive for players, trainers or others to conspire with gamblers.

Imagine a world in which information about referees and player injuries were disclosed. Without any inside information to sell to gamblers, Donaghy's only option, were he determined to make money from wagering, would be to officiate a game in a manner at odds with his normal performance (since his "normal" level of foul calling would have been factored into the total), hoping by excessive foul calls to push the game into the "over." (It is unlikely that Donaghy would risk much on a side bet on the victor: it would seem too hard for a lone referee to dictate the winner; players making or missing shots would be beyond his control.) Even if this strategy were successful, the referee had better place a large bet, for his officiating in this abnormal manner would draw attention to him and signal his interest in the point total. No way a referee would risk forfeiting a $200,000 per year job for a $5,000 payoff. The risk of salary loss would provide for a substantial and automatic check on any incentives to profit from game fixing.

Instead of relying on disclosure and risk of salary forfeiture to prevent game fixing, the NBA imbued their referees with valuable gambling information and then told them not to use it. The league was playing with fire. It will be lucky if the scandal stops here.

By the way, Donaghy did violate some laws, but for the federal prosecutor to charge him with fraud (to which he pleaded guilty) is just stretching the law in a bad way. Donaghy didn't trick anybody out of anything (unless we're to worry about his counterparties on the illegal bets). The government's theory was that Donaghy tricked the NBA out of the loyal and honest services he owed. In other words, the government's fraud allegation implies that any time an employee acts disloyally or dishonestly toward his employer, or breaks some company rule, that employee is not just in trouble with his employer, but he's also committed a federal crime. Nice way to criminalize the fiduciary obligations of employees. (Better listen to that boss next time.) This theory has admittedly been enshrined in federal law for a while but still makes no sense to me.

Chapter Seven

Sports as Property

Property law has an undeservedly poor reputation. Most of private civil (non-criminal) law concerns consensual transfers of goods. Everything from small consumer items to real estate is transferred by contracts of some form; estates are passed on or not by virtue of writing on a will; labor and other business relations are regulated by the terms of agreements; even torts, the world of non-consensual interaction, proceeds largely according to a fictitious "social contract" model. But property law is different. It doesn't concern itself much with how property (even real estate) is transferred. Rather, property law starts with the question of what it means to own something.

Property law creates property rights. Unlike property rights, most rights that we have are good only against the person whose promise created that right: a contractual promisee has a legally enforceable claim against the promisor, but no one else. Property law, by contrast, creates a legally enforceable claim against the entire world. Except for rare governmental needs, no one can take our property without our consent. Property law thus seems anti-social and is not favored by people who view the social entity as paramount. But property has its virtues. Giving a person unblemished ownership of an item gives that person an incentive to hold that item until another person offers him a price exceeding his personal valuation. Property law is the bedrock of the capitalist system.

Now in the contemporary sports world of collective bargaining agreements, league constitutions, commissioners and free agent players, one might wonder how much the basic market model of property-law capitalism can help explain and perhaps resolve seemingly intractable issues in sports. What would sports be like if it were more open to the unblemished property ownership and unbridled property exchanges of American capitalism? What are the limits of the capitalist model in the world of sports? Let's go for a ride on the free market side.

Treating Players like Property

Back in 1976, baseball's "reserve clause," which effectively bound a player to his club for his career, was coming to its end. Faced with the prospect of losing some of his star players for nothing, Oakland Athletics' owner Charles O. Finley sold outfielder Joe Rudi and pitcher Rollie Fingers to the Boston Red Sox for $1 million each and pitcher Vida Blue for $1.5 million to the New York Yankees. Commissioner Bowie Kuhn, however, voided the transactions as not in the "best interests" of baseball, specifically citing the danger to the league's competitive balance from the prospect of wealthier clubs purchasing players from comparatively poorer clubs.

Now, 30 years later, Kuhn's decision seems almost quaint. Today, free agency enables any club willing to dedicate the funds to stock its roster with players at all levels of quality. Clubs willing to pay even have advantages in trades; veterans in the final years of large contracts are often exchanged, cheaply in terms of talent, for inexpensive rookies or minor league players. Although rare, clubs can even compete financially for the Japanese star "posted" to the American major leagues.[1]

---

1. The posting system is a player transfer system that currently exists between the Nippon Professional Baseball of Japan and Major League Baseball. "When a player under contract with a Japanese team wishes to play in Major League Baseball, he requests that the team make him available for posting. If the team consents, the team informs the MLB Commissioner's office that one of its players is posted. The MLB Office of the Commissioner then holds a four-day-long silent auction among its teams.

So money is clearly the bottom line in modern player movement. Yet dating back to the Fingers-Rudi-Blue sale, baseball still retains its limitation on the direct sale of major league baseball players. Kuhn set the maximum at $400,000 for all cash deals; Bud Selig has raised the number to $1,000,000. Now, in the wake of the Matsuzaka deal,[2] surely some struggling MLB clubs eyed with envy the neat $51 million check the Red Sox mailed the Seibu Lions for the right to negotiate a contract with the young pitcher. Just as surely these struggling MLB clubs hold much of their capital in player contracts. These clubs (and their player contracts) would be worth more if the clubs were able to sell contracts for cash to clubs willing to pay.[3]

Why does MLB limit the sale of player contracts? I like the posting system for Japanese players so much, I think it's time to import something new.

It is axiomatic that an item of property is more valuable if the owner enjoys the right to sell it. Among other reasons, the ability

---

The highest resulting bid on the player is sent to the Japanese team, which may or may not choose to accept it. If the bid is accepted, the bid amount is publicly revealed and the winning Major League team is granted the exclusive rights to negotiate with the player. If the player and the Major League team come to terms on a contract within 30 days, the Japanese team receives the bid amount as the transfer fee." "Posting System." *Wikipedia.* 29 June 2007. http://en.wikipedia.org/wiki/Posting_system. The Japanese posting rules are examined at length below.

2. The Boston Red Sox won the bidding war to obtain the rights to negotiate with Japanese pitcher Daisuke Matsuzaka for an astonishing $51.1 million. The Seattle Mariners paid the Orix BlueWave a $13.1 million bid for the right to sign Ichiro Suzuki. Bloom, Barry. "Red Sox Win Matsuzaka Bid." 15 November 2006. *MLB.com.* http://mlb.mlb.com/news/article.jsp?ymd=20061113&content_id=1739983&vkey=hotstove2006&fext=.jsp.

3. The two largest player contracts in all of team sports include Alex Rodriguez who signed with the Texas Rangers in 2000 for an unprecedented $252 million over ten years. At number two on the list is Derek Jeter who signed a ten-year contract for $189 million in 2000. "List of Largest Sports Contracts." *Answers.com.* http://www.answers.com/topic/list-of-largest-sports-contracts.

to sell an item ensures a measure of liquidity and helps owners get out of acquisitions that, in retrospect, didn't pay off. Liquidity is good. Let's say a baseball team is in contention late in the season; adding an additional bullpen pitcher could put the team over the top. But pitchers are expensive. To raise the funds needed to pay a pitcher, this team decides to sell some of its prospects. It then takes the sale proceeds and purchases the pitcher. Is this scenario problematic? Does it threaten the integrity of the game? Clearly this exchange could happen today (within the trade period) but only if the prospects were exchanged directly for the pitcher. The cash limitation would not apply; no matter what amount the pitcher's compensation, the prospects could be accepted in trade.

But if the team with the pitcher wanted cash instead of prospects, the team could receive no more than $1 million. Or, if the team wanted prospects or players other than those available from the trading partner, then a third team with desirable and surplus prospects would have to be located. Why prohibit a team from doing directly (exchanging prospects for cash to acquire the pitcher) what it may do indirectly (by trading the prospects for the pitcher) or more indirectly (by involving a third team and cash and extra players)? The fear, cited by Commissioner Kuhn, that relatively wealthy clubs would translate their financial advantage to competitive advantage seems trivial. Wealthy clubs have plenty of avenues to use wealth to their advantage. Wealthy clubs can and do buy players through free agency and through their willingness to absorb expensive player contracts in trade.

If MLB allowed the direct sale of player contracts, without commissioner-imposed cash limitations, the marginal competitive advantage would accrue to poorer teams, not richer ones. The Yankees and their like already have ample liquidity and can use that liquidity in free-agent player acquisitions. Poorer teams hold most of their wealth in player contracts. Yet MLB's cash trade restrictions inhibit the liquidity of player contracts. To move a player to the Yankees for a pennant run, a team like the Royals must take their payment in players and prospects (and the limited permissible cash). Their trade acquisitions will be limited (practically speaking, given the difficulty of three way trades) to players and prospects who are owned by the Yankees and who are in some sense surplus players for the Yankees.

In addition, trading an established major league player for some surplus prospects or players is dicey business, given the failure rate of minor league baseball players. Wouldn't the Royals prefer to get a check from the Yankees for some number like the $20-50 million paid this fall to the Japanese clubs in exchange for what appear to be quality major leaguers, and then be able to use that cash to acquire established major league players from any club where they are in surplus? Liquidity is good; cash is king. The rich clubs have plenty of both. Allowing the poorer clubs to sell players would help, not hurt them.

It costs a ton of money to develop young players, especially starting pitchers. Most prospects don't make it to the major leagues, never mind major league stardom. So investments in developing young players are risky propositions. Which clubs are better able to absorb the risk inherent in investing in prospects? The wealthy teams. Yet the current system basically makes the poorer teams carry this risk, as they trade their newly established players for uncertain prospects instead of for cash to acquire more proven players. A risk is a cost. So, in effect, the limitations on cash deals make the poorer teams carry risks they may not want; the restrictions on cash make the poorer teams poorer.

The result of poorer teams carrying the risk of prospects is that the poorer teams inevitably function like farm clubs. Look at it this way; today, the Red Sox draft players and send them to the farm club in Pawtucket. In a few years, once some of the prospects appear ready to help the parent club, the Sox call them up, sending new draftees to take their place. That's the farm system. Now, change the name Pawtucket to Kansas City and what's the difference between a farm club and the Royals? Both take prospects and develop them and, once the successful prospects are identified, exchange them for more prospects. The Royals, unable to trade the best of these prospects for cash, will always draw poorly (who wants to see a

AAA team lose so often to superior major league teams?) and so will always be poor and will always have little choice but to take back inexpensive prospects in trades.

Except for very sure things (Jonathan Papelbon), wealthy clubs like the Red Sox will never want to bear the risk of prospects. The large profitable market the team has created for itself in New England means that the club's and the league's revenues will be maximized by putting proven players on the field to produce perennially competitive teams. Even the Royals profit from this arrangement, given revenue sharing. So it may well be that the Royals willingly play the role of the farm club; just food for thought. In other words, one could argue that MLB restricts the sale of players in order to make the Kansas City's of the league into de facto farm clubs. But this would be odd given the vast farm system MLB already has and given that the continued profitability of the revenue-sharing clubs depends in part on rival teams like the Royals fielding competitive teams.

Even as a perpetual farm club, a team like the Royals would still be better off if it could sell players for cash, if only to pour that money into a greater number of prospects, furthering the odds of some of them paying off with major league success while they were still comparatively underpaid. MLB also prohibits the alienation of draft rights, which also impoverishes those clubs that hold the highest draft positions. (In baseball, the highest draft positions go to the biggest losers, usually poorer clubs.) The right to alienate property is a valuable attribute of property ownership. Why does MLB continue to impoverish itself?

The Price of Ballplayer

Sure, the price of ballplayers is going up, way up, judging from the Red Sox bid for Daisuke Matsuzaka.[4] It's going so far up, some

---

4. As noted above, the Boston Red Sox won the bidding war to obtain the rights to negotiate with Japanese pitcher Daisuke Matsuzaka for $51.1

say, that the so-called "small-market" teams cannot compete for
free agents, despite generous revenue sharing.⁵ Do you ever get

million. Bloom, Barry. "Red Sox Win Matsuzaka Bid." 15 November 2006.
MLB.com. http://mlb.mlb.com/news/article.jsp?ymd=20061113&con-
tent_id=1739983&vkey=hotstove2006&fext=.jsp. Despite all that money,
I honestly don't view ballplayers as overpaid, not if they are compared to
other performers like movie actors and singers. They're getting paid a portion of the revenue they help to generate. Winning teams make the most
money; the best players are those who most help teams win. It troubles people that athletes are paid more than the people who run the country. It's
rarer to find a coordinated 6'10" athlete than to find someone who can
get himself elected and sit through Congressional committee meetings.
Scarcity commands higher prices.

5. Fewer star players than ever find their way to free agency nowadays
due to revenue sharing: "small market" teams, funded basically by the
Yankees and the Red Sox, can now afford to retain their home-grown
stars. The comparatively wealthy clubs, with the usual cash to spend,
have few players available on whom to spend it. Thus revenue sharing
diminishes the financial advantage of the wealthy teams. Assume that finances translate to wins (debatable). The big-market teams will therefore win less. (It's a zero-sum game of course.) Does MLB really want to
hinder the success of teams residing in its biggest markets? Baseball was
not pretty during the "down years" of the Yankees, when about all they
had was Don Mattingly. Of course I hate the Yankees as much as the next
guy. But baseball's probably best off keeping a strong team in the Bronx.
Perhaps the Yankees, simply because they can profit so mightily from a
strong team, will always enjoy a solid collection of the best players, no matter if they can acquire them nearly costlessly (through free agency) or ex-
pensively (through trades of prized prospects). Free agency greased those
skids, starting baseball on decades of Coasean exchanges that resulted in
a virtual all-star team in pinstripes. But revenue sharing will damage free
agency and thus thwart exchanges. Even the Yankees might be limited in
trading assets; I've always wondered, however, why the Yankees or other
wealthy teams don't more often simply purchase top prospects from needy
clubs. Couldn't the Yankees take ten million and purchase the half-dozen
or so top prospects from any number of organizations and then have
plenty of tradeable assets?

In any event, I suspect that revenue sharing may well be a league rule
that MLB lives to regret. And so may the players. Currently the view of
the union is that revenue sharing is beneficial because it creates more po-

tired of this constant whining and worrying over small-market teams? Let's stop whining and consider this problem like grownups.

What exactly is a "small-market" team? In terms of population, Boston is smaller than Philadelphia, San Diego, Detroit, Baltimore, and Milwaukee. Boston is about the same size as Kansas City, and nearly every other major-league city. Yet Kansas City, Milwaukee, and Detroit are typically depicted as poor small-market teams that need our sympathy and maybe need revenue sharing from the Red Sox. Folks, these small-market teams are small because the teams have failed to create a larger market. Sure, Boston proper is part of a larger metro area (as is Detroit, for instance), and the Red Sox today are a regional attraction in New England. But it wasn't always the case. The largest difference today is that the Red Sox are compelling, have captured the attention and loyalty of generations of fans, and so Boston fans care: they attend games, pay premium prices, watch telecasts, listen to radiocasts, and follow their beloved team for a lifetime, no matter where that life takes them. Why subsidize teams in commensurately large metropolises because they've accomplished less?

Competitive sports are a joint good, which means attracting fans to Red Sox games requires that there be good competition. A long Red Sox season of uninterrupted blow-out victories would get old (although we should try it, as an experiment). But there is no reason to think that the competition today in MLB is insufficient. Baseball attendance and revenues remain high and are increasing.

---

tential bidders for a player's services. True, but by marginally impoverishing the wealthiest teams the player loses out on the potentially highest bid. It's an auction, highest bidder wins (or loses, if you consider regret).

Revenue sharing makes more sense in the NFL. Pro football is fundamentally a different product than MLB. MLB games are local productions, except for big rivalry games or the playoffs. NFL games are national events, even if the teams are not the best. So in the NFL it makes more sense to ensure that good players are distributed to all the teams. Less so MLB, where the best players "should" be placed on the biggest stages, to maximize revenue.

Plenty of teams other than the Red Sox or Yankees have recently had winning seasons and even won championships. The Red Sox's high and continuing revenue stream virtually guarantees that the club will field a competitive, contending team nearly every season. The less-wealthy teams need to play it smart, pooling assets in order to make a run at a title periodically. That's about the entire difference. The Sox and Yanks will always face stiff competition from the poorer clubs, just not from the same precinct every season. What's wrong with that? Why can't the Royals put together a competitive team every third season or so? The Marlins, Tigers, Twins, A's, and other teams seem able to do it.

What's wrong with being a fan of a team that pools young assets to compete on occasion? The accident of birthplace made me a life-long Red Sox fan. But I would have no problem rooting for a team like the Marlins that features a host of young, cheap, talented players and that will likely be a very competitive team in just a few seasons. Not everyone can win. Fans can wait years, even generations, for ultimate victory; it's part of the fun of being a fan. I waited years for the Patriots; I'm waiting now for the Celtics. I waited my whole lifetime for the Red Sox.

Of course the Red Sox have to pay a ton of money for Matsuzaka. Because all the "small-market" teams have been handed revenue sharing cash, the only way for the Red Sox or other financially successful teams to extract profits from their loyal fans is to leverage their profits even more than ever. The Sox had to raise the stakes for free agents in order for their competitive advantage, namely money, to be useful. Without revenue sharing, the price of free agents, especially those at the middle-level of major league ability, would have remained lower, and the wealthier teams could have easily outbid the poorer teams had they chose to do so. Now, with revenue sharing, the top teams have to bid very high for the top free agents (especially with fewer top players even reaching free agency, again due to revenue sharing). More mid-level players will be affordable by the less financially successful clubs. These "poor" teams should be happy that the Sox will have to spend a lot on one player.

Poorer teams can afford big-time free agents. Houston (a small-market team that, of course, plays in a city about three times the size of Boston) just paid around $70 million to keep Roy Oswalt. The Red Sox's total payment (posting plus salary) for Matsuzaka won't exceed that price by much. Let's stop using Bud Selig's language. "Small-market team" is a misnomer.

It's not a permanent condition. Let's call them "less successful" teams, perhaps to encourage improvement. And let's stop setting baseball policy to cater to the need of the least successful clubs in the game.

Posting, Japanese-Style

Japanese baseball star Daisuke Matsuzaka is making his way to the United States, much like Ichiro Suzuki and Hideo Nomo did before him. The process these Japanese player transfers take is, well, quite foreign to American baseball. Here are the relevant rules. When Japan's professional clubs have a year remaining on a particular player's contract, the club can "post" the player, which means they can offer the player to auction by MLB clubs. The auction is conducted by sealed bids with each bidder kept in ignorance of the other bids. The selling club is not made aware of the identity of each bidder. The highest bid is accepted and the winner announced to the MLB commissioner, who then authorizes the MLB club to negotiate a contract with the player within the next 30 days. If a contract agreement is reached, the winning team may keep the player or trade the player to another team (as the Padres did with Hideki Irabu, who went to the Yankees). Only if a contract is agreed to does the American club have to pay the posting fee. If no contract is reached, the player returns to his Japanese club for his final year. The following year the player is a free agent, able to sign with any club, anywhere.

This is a curious system, to say the least. The commissioner's office polices the clubs for evidence of collusion, as provided in the agreement between the Japanese and American professional leagues.

Nonetheless, collusion is a real possibility with this type of auction. After all, the U.S. Treasury used to sell debt this way, before it wised up after the bidding scandals in the early 1990's.

Offering a high bid raises the probability of winning but lowers the value of the player to his new team. So in a sense, teams are bidding against themselves. An American club appears to have a large incentive to offer an exorbitant bid; it's a free swing. If the bid is accepted, the American club has a cost-free option to sign the Japanese player for the coming year. The winning club also controls the right to trade the player for that year, and presumably recover its posting fee, along with some players, from the trade partner. The winning club at worst keeps the player from his rivals for the coming season, without losing the right to bid on the player in the following year's free agency period. Plus, because of the anonymous bidding system, clubs can offer over-large, non-serious bids each auction with apparent impunity.

Compelling incentives appear to exist for the Japanese club and its star player to collude, too. A club whose player cannot reach an agreement with the winning American team forfeits that very large posting fee. Surely the club will consider slipping some of that fee back to the player to induce him to accept the American bid. If no contract is reached, the Japanese club essentially "pays" (in the sense of foregone payment) the player a huge fee for one year's service. In Matsuzaka's case, his Japanese team would essentially pay $51 million for one year of his service. An astute bargainer could easily play the Japanese club off against the Japanese player.

In essence, when a team bids for a player like Matsuzaka, it is trying to hit the top of the market. The team understands that the high bid is costless and entitles the bidder to either negotiate the price downward with the Japanese player or the Japanese club, or trade the player. The system seems designed to elicit very high bids without very high seriousness.

Is the Posting System Legal?

Reports say that the Red Sox and Scott Boras, agent for Japanese baseball star Daisuke Matsuzaka, are oceans apart on coming to terms. Boras has made known the possibility that if no deal is reached, he will challenge the Japanese-American posting system in court, in an effort to have Matsuzaka declared a free agent or get some other relief (perhaps re-posting) that allows his client an opportunity at a more lucrative deal. So here's the $51.1 million question: could Boras win? Is it legal to sell players like a piece of property?

Let's assume Boras decides to file a claim in American court under the federal antitrust law, arguing that the posting system amounts to an unfair restraint of trade. (I suppose a suit in Japan under Japanese law is another option, but since I know nothing about Japanese antitrust law, I'll just ignore the possibility.[6]) The first obstacle is baseball's historic antitrust exception. The exception comes from a rather quaint (and factually wrong) judicial decision that held that baseball did not constitute interstate commerce (even though every other professional sport does). Over the years Congress has been unable to decide whether or not to overturn this wacky decision, so the courts reaffirmed the initial decision on the basis of Congress' implicit indecision. Whatever. In 1998, Congress did revoke the exemption to allow MLB players to sue over agreements "directly relating to or affecting employment of major league baseball players," but nothing else. So, Boras' first issue will be to

---

6. I do know that the Japanese law is a post-WWII creation of American governorship and so does have something in common with U.S. law. Japanese antitrust law applies a similar "unreasonable restraint of trade" standard as U.S. law. That much I know. Now, on the question of whether or not Japan would reach the same outcome as a U.S. court in deciding what is "reasonable" I have no idea. I do recall the Japanese players did strike a few years ago and that the fans generally supported the job action, perhaps suggesting a more "pro-employee" public perspective than might have been the case in years past.

argue Matsuzaka qualifies as a "MLB player" and that his suit involves an employment issue.

The first issue is a tricky one and provides a real hurdle for Boras. Boras' argument is that, although Matsuzaka is not currently an MLB player, Matsuzaka is seeking to enter the MLB, and so, like rookies, free agents and other players who are not yet in the league but seek to be in the league, he should be considered a MLB player under the act. I'm thinking of the Wood vs. NBA decision, which held that even a player not currently in the bargaining unit is nonetheless represented in the bargaining unit.[7] However, there's a meaningful distinction between concluding that a non-member is in effect a member of a bargaining unit and saying that a non-member fits under a federal statute that carefully limits standing to "MLB players." Boras' contention will be that, if Matsuzaka is denied standing to challenge the Japanese-American posting agreement, then effectively no one could challenge it (since American players cannot be posted to Japan). Maybe Boras can prevail here, maybe not.

Easier to satisfy is the second requirement that Matsuzaka's suit involves an employment issue. The Japanese-American posting system appears to qualify, since it could have been the subject of bargaining when the current collective bargaining agreement (CBA)

---

7. 809 F.2d 954 (2d Cir. 1987). The trial court in the Maurice Clarett case, Clarett v. NFL, 306 F. Supp. 2d 379 (SDNY 2004), held that Clarett had "standing," despite not being a member of the NFL, to sue under antitrust law. In granting standing, the judge reasoned that the NFL eligibility rule denied all players in Clarett's situation from selling their labor to the NFL. The other issue in the case had to do with the so-called "nonstatutory labor exemption," which basically is a court-devised rule that precludes certain labor issues (those subject to collective bargaining) from being challenged under antitrust law (hence the "exemption" for "labor"). On this ground the appellate court reversed the trial judge's finding that the exemption did not preclude Clarett's suit. Clarett v. NFL, 369 F.3d 124 (2d Cir. 2004). I don't think this exemption would be a problem given the 1998 "Curt Flood" statute that specifically withdrew MLB's antitrust exemption for employment issues. But I could be wrong; it's never good business to try to predict court decisions.

ends at the end of this season (although of course the issue is moot with the new CBA extension). Clearly, it's hard to classify Matsuzaka's issue as anything else that is listed in the 1998 act. Stipulation city.

So now let's assume that Boras can overcome these first two "standing"[8] issues and get his case heard in a federal court. If antitrust law were to be applied to the posting system, the application would be somewhat relaxed; courts have long recognized that strict application of antitrust laws to sports leagues makes no sense. Teams, although separate entities, must cooperate in order to run a joint enterprise (the league), and this cooperation will entail a degree of anti-competitive behavior (such as revenue sharing, restrictions on player movement, etc.) that would be condemned if practiced in other industries. Courts instead apply the rule of reason to assess whether or not this cooperative act of the MLB clubs has the "ancillary effect" of unduly or unreasonably restraining trade. In this case "trade" would refer to the tendency of the posting system to reduce output (reduce the number of Japanese players able to enter the US) and thus frustrate consumer (fan) demand for the best players. In short, the test will be whether the posting system enhances or inhibits consumer welfare. Testifying experts, begin your billing.

There are at least two ways of looking at this issue. One view starts

---

8. "In the common law, and under many statutes, standing or locus standi is the ability of a party to demonstrate to the court sufficient connection to and harm from the law or action challenged to support that party's participation in the case. In the United States, for example, a person cannot bring a suit challenging the constitutionality of a law unless the plaintiff can demonstrate that the plaintiff is (or will be) harmed by the law. Otherwise, the court will rule that the plaintiff "lacks standing" to bring the suit, and will dismiss the case without considering the merits of the claim of unconstitutionality. In order to sue to have a court declare a law unconstitutional, there must be a valid reason for whoever is suing to be there. The party suing must have something to lose in order to sue unless they have automatic standing by action of law." "Standing." 11 July 2007. *Wikipedia.* http://en.wikipedia.org/wiki/Legal_standing.

with the fact that Matsuzaka was at the time under contract with the Seibu Japanese baseball club. Seibu owned his contract, much the way the Red Sox own David Ortiz' contract. In theory, the team that owns the contract can customarily trade that contract for whatever price it can get (although MLB clubs are somewhat limited in how much cash they can receive in trade). So, the fact that the Red Sox are willing to pay a large amount to Seibu (without any of that money going to the player) doesn't matter, although that fact nettles Boras. Acquiring any player (short of a free agent) involves both an acquisition fee (in the form of traded contracts), plus the assumption or renegotiation of the acquired player's contract. In this view, the posting system is no more a restraint of trade than is the practice that player contracts can be moved among teams via trades consented to by the respective teams. Daisuke, it's our country; love it or leave it.

The opposing view focuses on one peculiar (and perhaps unforeseen) aspect to this posting system: the system can be "rigged" to effectively curtail or even eliminate the possibility of player movement. Here's a wild hypothetical: assume MLB had two highly wealthy and unusually competitive teams. Assume a very valuable Japanese player became eligible for posting. The posting rules allow for one of these rivals to bid wildly high for the player (just throw a number out there, say 51.1 million), then knowingly offer a submarket bid, knowing the player will likely reject the offer. The result? The player goes back to his Japanese club and is kept away from the rival for an additional baseball season. Hmm, it just might work, no? And if it did, well, now the Japanese-American agreement appears to diminish consumer welfare and thus restrain trade by keeping quality players out of MLB. Scott Boras, call your office.

Sure, Matsuzaka could just try again next year. But what are the limits to the Red Sox' bid? Since the Commissioner is involved and seems to have some supervisory role over the bidding, I would assume the bid must be plausible in light of the financial assets of the bidding club. But given the Sox's vast financial capabilities and large payroll, a very large number is very plausible. Who's to say that the Red Sox couldn't write $75 million on next year's anonymous bid sheet, just to keep the player away from the Yankees? And maybe, if Daisuke really does want to spend some time in the major leagues, he'll have little choice but to accept the sub-market contract offered by the Red Sox.

This posting system bears some comparison to baseball's annual waiver-wire claims. Under MLB rules, after the trade deadline has passed, only players on waivers may be traded (see, another restraint of trade). So, the custom has developed where teams will place much of their roster on waivers so that either they can shed bad contracts (if a claim is made) or make a player eligible for trading. Alongside this custom has emerged another: teams will make waiver claims on the best players, not because they hope to acquire the player, but to keep the player from being traded to a rival. Only middling players make it through the waiver process. I think the Sox and Yanks do this to each other pretty much every season. So there's a history of these clubs exploiting baseball's rules to thwart the aims of their chief rival. With the Matsuzaka episode, the greatest rivalry in sports has been taken to the international stage. One day, soon I think, each team will drop the charade of "friendly competition" and will align its interests with distant warring factions, using its finances and worldwide connections to funnel arms and mercenaries to allies. Then we'll really see the Sox and Yanks do battle. Let's settle this score once and for all.

Hunting and the Law of Property

Central Oregon constitutes one of the best patches of earth in the country, without doubt. And the very best spot in the area is the gorgeous little town of Sisters.[9] But it turns out that in this seeming western utopia, all is not always well. Even endless outdoor

---

9. Sisters, Oregon, obtained its name from its location close to The Three Sisters Mountains, nicknamed "Faith," "Hope," and "Charity." The town has a population of approximately 1,745 as of July 2006. "Fast Facts

recreational opportunities can lead to trouble. This is a story of "elk stealing," where two hunters join in downing an elk and then disagree over the ownership of the animal.

In a nutshell, here's what happened: Hunter One wounded an elk to a mortal degree (his view); after the wounding, the elk ran off, and was eventually downed by Hunter Two (apparently a rascal from Sisters), who quickly tagged the animal and commenced field dressing. Hunter One showed up, claimed the animal as his own; tempers flared, and Hunter One grabbed his ... pen and wrote the account described above. The lesson of his story, imparted to his son (who had accompanied him on the hunt) and indirectly to the reader, is that Hunter Two's conduct had violated the ethics of hunting and thus brought shame upon the otherwise fine inhabitants of this little cowboy nirvana in the mountains.

Just a minute, there, partner.

Although it's hard to tell from the newspaper account, it seems that the elk ran off quite a ways after the first shot. I'm not an elk hunter, but that fact seems inconsistent with the claim that the elk was mortally wounded. Hunter One's account concedes that mortally wounded elk don't run much. If the elk was in fact not mortally wounded, and Hunter Two in fact imparted the mortal blow, then Hunter Two has a proper claim to the animal. Clearly Hunter Two had an obligation to finish the wounded animal off; it's inhumane to prolong suffering.

In the eyes of the law, the hunter who deals the mortal blow to the animal has legal claim to the animal. This rule of law (called the law of capture) comes from the law of natural resources and makes sense in that context. We want to encourage actual harvesting of resources, so the property right is accorded to the person who can actually manage to bring the resource to market (here, reduce the elk to meat), not the person who (unsuccessfully) tramped over

---

about Sisters." 2007. *Sisters Oregon Guide Online.* http://www.sistersoregonguide.com/sisters-facts.htm.

hill and dale trying to harvest the resource. To the victor goes the spoils.

Yet the rule of capture is inapposite to hunting. Hunting is a sport, not an effort to harvest resources. Here's where non-hunters, including the lawyers and judges who devise legal rules, get utterly confused about hunting. They see hunting as killing (as resource harvesting). Yes, hunting involves killing. However, the goal of hunting is not killing, at least not in this day and age, where we don't need to kill to eat. The goal of hunting is killing in a certain way, according to certain practices and ethical rules.

If the goal of hunting were killing, then many of the ethical rules that hunters voluntarily adopt and inculcate into novices make no sense. Just to give a couple of examples of hunting practices, the rule of "fair chase" (a fundamental hunting norm) dictates that hunters only attempt shots when the prey has a reasonable chance to escape. Thus, one doesn't point a shotgun at a bird on the ground or in the nest; one waits for the bird to "flush" (take flight) and then tries to shoot the bird out of the air. Similarly, hunters have ethical obligations to avoid wounding animals; thus hunters must practice their shooting, take only reasonable shots, pursue wounded game, and so forth, all to make sure that unnecessary suffering is avoided. I could go on, at length. The point is there are a lot of constraints on hunting, constraints that hunters voluntarily place on themselves, and constraints that inhibit the killing of animals. This is because hunting is a sport, not an effort to kill. (Hunters make a mistake when they refer to hunting as "harvesting" because that term suggests that hunting is another form of resource exploitation.)

But the law regards hunting as killing, not as a sport. That's why the legal rule of "capture" does not comport to the reality of hunting, even as it regulates it. That's also why Hunter Two was "right" to claim the elk (assuming that he delivered the mortal blow) in the eyes of the law, but wrong to claim the elk in the eyes of fellow hunters. Hunting is a sport.

Yes, I hunt. Why? Try it once and you'll see. I take my boys (who have their own shotguns, have been trained, certified, and are very good shots) out to very rugged terrain far from any towns or cities. We hike all day through canyons, fields and streams in wild, gorgeous country, attuned to the workings of the tireless dogs. Our hearts race when the dogs come to a point; my boys and I, alone in this vast wilderness of creation, take positions consistent with safe zones of fire. The pheasant or chukar flushes, and who gets the shot is dictated by the bird's direction and movement. I've seen my ten-year-old take down a flighty chukar with a crossing shot from a 410 shotgun at 20 yards. I've seen my older boy patiently wait on a bird to dive toward a canyon, taking the shot at the last possible instant, bringing the bird down at the edge. We hunt, we clean, we spend the time outdoors, away from the video and information revolution, at least for a few days, just us, alone. We create memories, instill confidence, and bond in a way that no other sporting activity can match. Sports are part of our lives, like they are for many parents and their kids. But for most dads, participation is limited to cheering for your child from the sideline. Hunting is just as hard for me as it is them (harder, actually, as I can't hit anything; bad eyes). We share this sport and this experience. That's the true purpose of hunting, whether the law (or Hunter Two) recognizes it or not.

Wisconsin and Its Motion W

The University of Wisconsin has asked Waukee High School, just outside Des Moines, Iowa, to stop using the "motion W" on the side of its football helmets. UW claims this letter belongs to the university and no other.[10] What? Can we start claiming trademark in letters? (I tried to register the letters "TSLP" for football helmets,

---

10. University of Wisconsin director of licensing, Cindy Van Matre, said in an interview: "You can't put a dollar figure on the value of the motion W ... but we have to protect it so it doesn't become a generic type of logo. If it's not associated with UW, anyone can say you haven't controlled the use of it." Walker, Don. "UW Targets Schools Using Its Helmet Logo."

but found out that the teams from Tulane, Stanford, Louisville and Paraguay beat me to it.) Okay, I understand, it's the "motion W" that Wisconsin owns, not the letter W, and that's a whole different thing. Right? Well, maybe not.

For a sign or symbol to qualify as a trademark it has to be distinctive. Is the "motion W"? Go find it on the web; you be the judge. It looks like just a "W" to me, maybe a little fancy, but hardly something that people are going to identify as distinctive from any other "W." I'm sure the University spent a ton of money getting someone to come up with this trademark (hey, let's try a "W!"), but investment doesn't matter; the question is whether or not the mark is distinct from the ordinary appearance of the letter. But it's difficult to make a single letter into a trademark simply because, if one monkeys around too much with the letter, it ceases to be recognizable as a letter and has no usefulness. (See the contrivances to which Major League Baseball clubs put their team letters to ensure distinctiveness; I never knew what the shape on the Montreal Expos hat was supposed to be.)

Plus, it's just a W. How many schools have "W" on the side of their helmets? The W is descriptive of the University of Wisconsin. A "W" is also descriptive of a lot of other schools. And a "W" can be quite generic, as all of these schools beginning with a "W" probably use the letter in their school acronym. Terms that are merely descriptive and generic cannot properly be registered as trademarks. Now to be clear, I'm not saying Wisconsin's "W" is not a valid trademark; however, I will say it looks to me like a close call.

Even granting the proposition that this "motion W" is indeed special and distinctive and non-generic and thus qualifies as a trademark, in my view trademarks and university sports are inimical. The purpose of trademark protection is commercial; to preclude unwary customers from being misled as to the origin or quality of

---

2 December 2006. *Milwaukee Journal Sentinel Online*. http://www.jsonline.com/story/index.aspx?id=537657.

a product. I can understand UW protecting its commercial interest in selling merchandise. If the Waukee booster club were selling sweatshirts with the funny "W" then I guess UW had to put a stop to that. But is the same thing true with symbols on football helmets? Is anyone watching the Waukee Warriors high school football team going to say, "Gee, I wonder why the Wisconsin Badgers are playing football on a Friday night here in rural Iowa?" There's no consumer confusion possible, so there's no consumer protection needed.

MLB allows Little League baseball to use team logos, hats, and jerseys. That's why your little kid gets to play on the Mets. The real New York Mets understand that the purpose of trademark law would not be served by refusing to license kids to wear the big league hats; only a loving parent watches his nine-year-old play baseball and thinks he's seeing a major league player. Why can't UW see things the same way?

Who Won "The Big Game"?

Apparently the NFL's not making enough money. Now comes news that the NFL wants to trademark the phrase "The Big Game," which I guess refers to the Super Bowl. The NFL is reacting to the advent of what is called "ambush marketing." Some product sellers, unwilling to pay the very high price for being licensed to use the phrase "official product of the Super Bowl," are nonetheless taking advantage of the attention the event draws by using the phrase "the Big Game" to draw notice to their products (for example, "get your new television in time for the Big Game").

It seems the NFL has a problem with its proposed trademark; the annual Cal-Stanford football game has been termed "the Big Game" for about a century. So what happens? Does the NFL get its desired mark? Can it prevent ambush marketers from selling their goods while capitalizing on the Super Bowl? Will the NFL have to pay Cal-Berkeley and Stanford Super-Bowl levels of money? Nothing gets TSLP angrier than rich people trying to stop other rich people from getting even richer. I'm a selfless crusader for the big man. So which big game is the real big game?

Modern trademark law makes no sense to me (hence I'm perfectly willing to give an opinion on it). The point of trademark protection is not to protect the owner of the trademark. It's to protect the consumer. So, when I buy the little TSLP's some "official junk food of the Super Bowl," I know I'm getting the genuine junk food, not some flimsy substitute. However, is there any real chance of consumer confusion when an advertisement urges me to buy a new television before "the big game?" Will a consumer likely think that the new set comes with the official endorsement of the NFL? Probably not (as in, no way).

But here's the problem: modern judicial decisions have twisted the primary purpose of trademark protection. Yes, I'm talking judicial activism, but not the kind that gets people all upset in the constitutional law field. I'm talking real judicial activism, without which our contemporary sports franchises would be worth a lot less money. These cases, starting with a 1975 decision (yes, that's "modern" to me) protecting the beloved and famous "B" of the Boston Bruins, decided that sports teams and other owners of trademarks had in effect a property right in their mark. This is a big deal, as any NFL owner could tell you (it will have to be you they tell, because NFL owners won't talk to me after this). Property means the owner owns the mark, and the rest of us can only use the mark for a commercial, non-journalistic purpose when we have the owner's permission. So if I want to describe my television as "the best one for viewing the Super Bowl," I can't, because the NFL owns the phrase "the Super Bowl;" I can't do it, even though there's not a chance in the world anyone's going to think that my television, although good for watching football, is somehow endorsed by the NFL.

So under this (crazy) property theory of trademark, trademarks become not a means of precluding customer confusion but a means of making money. Sports are full of trademarks of words and images that denote games or leagues or teams. You may have noticed one on the front of the last team jersey you popped $120 to purchase. The property aspect to trademarks is the key to the sports merchandise business. In other words, this is very big business. When the NFL says it wants to trademark "the big game," the NFL is going after big game.

Forget about Cal and Stanford. Even though their game was the Big Game long before the Super Bowl got its first Roman numeral, if the NFL's game came to be called "The Big Game" through the words of people or entities other than the NFL, then the NFL is not responsible for ascribing to its game the label "the Big Game." If the NFL is not responsible, then Cal and Stanford cannot assert that the NFL can't trademark "The Big Game" as referring to its Super Bowl. Who is responsible? The "ambush marketers." By ambushing the Super Bowl with the phrase "The Big Game," the ambushers gave the Super Bowl a second name, so to speak. A few years ago this same issue got litigated with respect to "March Madness," which of course refers both to the annual Illinois high school basketball tournament and to some other big basketball tournament that escapes my memory for the moment. The Illinois tournament had used the phrase forever, but in the end couldn't stop the NCAA from trade-marking it because CBS and others had come to call the NCAA tournament "March Madness," and not the NCAA.

Probably the best Cal and Stanford can hope for is joint ownership, which probably is all the NFL wants. The NFL doesn't really expect to open a whole new marketing venture based on licensing use of "the Big Game" to refer to the Super Bowl. It just wants to stop others from making money, even where these others are not making money at the NFL's expense. Got to love the NFL. Why in the world should United States law help sports leagues prevent ambush marketing? It's just marketing, just fancy talk. There's nothing illegal about it. At least not yet. But the NFL's legal tactic, if it succeeds, promises a future where the sports leagues will attempt to trademark whatever phrases ambush marketers use to associate their products with sports events.

This development will effectively render ambush marketing illegal. A body of law that was designed to protect the consumer against the predations of producers will be turned on its head, diminishing the advertising information that reaches consumers in order to protect the producer. The constant river of sports merchandising profits that accrue to leagues and franchises all flows from this dubious extension of trademark law.

I Want My Direct TV

Troublesome news at the TSLP home space. Come to find out that Major League Baseball's "Extra Innings" package, the league's season-long, every-game television coverage, will henceforth be available to subscribers to Direct TV and to no one else. Like most people, we have cable, and I refuse to screw a radar installation onto the roof of my house. So it looks like the Red Sox will have to play the coming season without me. This is disappointing to me and to the little junior miscreants, who have been so far socialized into Red Sox Nation that it wasn't until they turned seven that they figured out we don't actually live in Boston.

Needless to say, a lot of people are beefing about this. These special sports packages are just the thing for transplants. What can be done to rectify this injustice?

It's not an injustice. Why shouldn't the leagues be able to structure their television packages to elicit the most lucrative rights fees someone will pay? From what I've read, the satellite company basically offered a better deal (in terms of cash, broadcast channel for MLB's own channel, and so forth) than did the company that offered the package through both cable and satellite networks. This result reflects what freedom of contract can produce. We have to live with it (or without it, if you don't want to drill holes in your roof).

On the other hand, although it looks like freedom of contract, the law does put some limits on contracts. Specific to this situation is the antitrust law.[11] The relevant part of that law prohibits "contracts in restraint of trade." Sounds perfect. The problem is that all contracts that are worth writing will involve some future performance ("I pay you today to deliver your goods to me tomorrow"), and all contracts involving future performance are, in essence, a restraint on trade. That's the point of a contract, to restrain trade. A contract in which the seller promises to deliver his goods to the buyer restrains trade, in that the seller may no longer (with impunity) deliver his goods to someone other than the buyer, and, by the same token, another person who wants those particular goods may not have them. This contract restrains trade, if only by limiting trade to the contracting parties. But Congress couldn't have intended to outlaw all contracts when it wrote the antitrust law, only some of them. So Congress left it to judges to determine which contracts are in fact restraints on trade and which are not. (By the way, it was the judges who figured out that Congress gave over this authority to the judges. Judges aren't troubled by obvious conflicts of interest that would embarrass the rest of us.)

Is the Direct TV deal an illegal restraint on trade? Courts will uphold contracts that restrain trade as long as the restraint is "reasonable," which basically means that the contract promotes consumer welfare. Does the TV deal? Does denying the consumer what he wants promote the consumer's welfare? Yes. Here would be MLB's argument: the league needs a competitive balance among its teams. No one wants to see some wealthy team, like the Boston Red Sox, blow everyone else away all season on their way to another World Series title (although we should try this for a season, just to con-

---

11. The Sherman Antitrust Act was enacted on July 2, 1890, and was the first action by the United States government to limit monopolies. The Act provides: "Every contract, combination in the form of trust or otherwise, or conspiracy, in restraint of trade or commerce among the several States, or with foreign nations, is declared to be illegal." "Sherman Antitrust Act." 27 July 2007. *Wikipedia.com.* http://en.wikipedia.org/wiki/Sherman_Antitrust_Act.

firm this theory). Players are pricey. So the league needs to maximize its revenue streams and spread the wealth out among the teams so they can afford players, thus making games and seasons competitive, thus eliciting maximum fan interest, thus allowing MLB to compete with the other outlets for our time and money such as golf, movies, golf movies, internet surfing, and so forth. Consumers get a better sports television product by not being able to see it. Sounds a little crazy, but the leagues have done pretty well with arguments just like that in litigating over player rights for the past century. In short, if the antitrust issue got litigated, don't think it a foregone conclusion that MLB would lose.

But maybe this argument loses. Most likely, MLB will never have to make it. That's because MLB enjoys its historic "antitrust exemption."[12] The U.S. Supreme Court gave baseball that exemption and has never taken it back, basically daring Congress to do it. Congress did, as far as labor issues go, with the Curt Flood Act of 1998.[13] But arguably (and this is a close argument), baseball's antitrust exemption extends to MLB's other business dealings (apart from dealings with its players), such as television contracts. So it's likely MLB will never have to defend its Direct TV contract in a court of law. Baseball is exempt from the law. (Must be nice.)

What about football? How does the NFL get away with sticking its game package on Direct TV? Simple. Congress, when no bloggers were looking (it was 1961), gave the NFL an antitrust exemp-

---

12. The exemption arises from a 1922 Supreme Court decision based upon the rationale that baseball games "were local affairs, not interstate commerce." "Ending Baseball's Antitrust Exemption." 26 November 2001. *Baseball Prospectus Online.* http://www.baseballprospectus.com/article.php?articleid=1286.

13. The Curt Flood Act passed in 1998 "partially repealed the antitrust exemption to give the Players Association the same rights as the unions in the other major sports." "Ending Baseball's Antitrust Exemption." 26 November 2001. *Baseball Prospectus Online.* http://www.baseballprospectus.com/article.php?articleid=1286.

tion too! The NFL's is more limited than baseball's historic exemption; basically the NFL is exempt from the antitrust laws with respect to it's (drum roll please) television contracts! Perfect. No one can be sued.

Maybe the members of Congress, angered because they can no longer get free game tickets, will at least want to watch the games too and will act to revoke these antitrust exemptions (in time for Opening Day, please). Alternatively, we'll see highly trained legislative assistants climbing on the roof of the Russell Senate Office Building following the installation steps for the satellite dish. Someone's got to back down; either MLB or the U.S. Congress. This is going to be a rough summer otherwise.

The Solution to the NFL Network Problem

Like many sports fans, I was a little upset at the prospect of missing the big Patriots-Giants game that closed out the NFL's 2007 regular season. The reason for this prospect was the NFL's decision to allocate these games to its fledgling NFL Network in an effort to boost channel subscribers. More to the point, apparently the NFL and the cable television giants could not agree on a proper fee for featuring the NFL Network as part of the schedule of channels for "standard" cable service, much like is ESPN. Had these particular games been available to the "free" television networks, undoubtedly both would be nationally televised.[14]

Commentators have described this problem as a stalemate between two business giants (the NFL and Cable TV) over the last dollar, with each side waiting for the other to yield. This characterization is true, but falls so far short of the whole picture as to be mislead-

---

14. In the end, of course, the NFL wavered in its commitment and decided to allow the NFL Network broadcast to be shown simultaneously over both NBC and CBS, thus making the game viewable by everybody.

ing. What's missing from the picture is the law's role in creating this mess. As usual, the law is guilty as charged.

Start from the premise that clubs own the right to broadcast their games. By this I mean individual clubs, and not the collection of clubs gathered together to form a league, own their games. So the legal right to televise a particular game between the Cowboys and Packers is owned by the Cowboys and the Packers, the teams that will engage in the contest. This legal right is an intellectual property right, an intangible asset, and is based on a very questionable reading of the law. Federal copyright law precludes the "re-broadcast" of the particular versions of games broadcast over the air. But as to the initial broadcast of the games themselves, under federal law when Brett Favre completes a pass to a receiver for a touchdown, it's just news. Anyone who's aware of the news can broadcast the news, even simultaneously with another "permitted" broadcast, without violating copyright law.

What prohibits alternative, competing, bootleg broadcasts of live NFL games? Just the following historic judicial decision. In 1938 a local radio station decided to broadcast Pirates' games from vantage points outside the fences at Forbes Field. The Pirates had sold radio broadcast rights to NBC. When the Pirates sued to enjoin the local competitor, a lone federal judge stated that "it is perfectly clear" that broadcast rights belong to the Pirates. No citation to legal authority was provided to support this wild claim. The judge just said it was perfectly clear and that's that: the Pirates, and every team in history thereafter, has enjoyed a "property right" to broadcast its games. The court grounded this property right in a theory of unfair competition: that if other broadcasters could compete with NBC, then the Pirates would not be able to profit from their investments in the team and the event. Now it may be true (although very contestable) that the Pirates "need" to have this property right in order to field a competitive team, but generally speaking the legal protections for intellectual property are devised by statute and are pretty carefully circumscribed. Why? There is a large public interest in having ideas and information disseminated. Yet here, in the absence of a statute, a judge in Pennsylvania created a property interest out of whole cloth. Go Pirates!

In any event, teams have this property right, but have chosen, under league agreements with the NFL, to allow these rights to be sold as a group by the league: hence the mega-monstrous national television packages the NFL enjoys. But, here's the rub: there is a strong case to be made that this arrangement wherein the teams pool their rights for collective sale to the networks (and thereby to the public) is a violation of federal law, not copyright law, but antitrust law. So while enjoying the law's (judge-invented) property right, the teams are using those rights in arguable violation of the (Congressionally mandated) antitrust law. Gave them an inch, they took the mile. Is there any reason to believe it's an antitrust violation? In 1953 the United States itself sued the NFL on this very point, and won. The judge in that case issued a series of injunctions against the NFL that basically told the NFL to stop violating federal law. Yes, the NFL broke the law. (If Roger Goodell had been commissioner, he would have suspended himself for one year or until he could convince himself that he had learned his lesson.)

In the wake of the judge's historic 1953 ruling that the NFL was in violation of the antitrust law, did the NFL mend its ways? No, it did what any rich kid does when in trouble: it pulled strings, running off to the Congress to get a special exemption from antitrust law in the form of the Sports Broadcasting Act of 1961 (commonly called the "SBA"). This act allows the NFL to sell the teams' individual broadcast property rights as a group. But there's a limit: NFL teams may join together to sell their broadcast rights as a group, but only for what the act calls "sponsored telecasts" of games. This is obviously pre-Information Age language, but basically what the Congress had in mind, as NFL Commissioners have conceded, is free, over-the-air, received-with-rabbit-ears-held-by-duct-tape, old-fashioned network broadcasts. (Somehow not even the federal Congress foresaw the rise of cable, ESPN, and the internet, even though young Al Gore was around and could have been asked.) In short, it's pretty clear the SBA doesn't protect the NFL from antitrust scrutiny when it ventures beyond network broadcasts, as the NFL has done with the NFL Network.

So the solution to the Battle of Big Business is for someone to sue the NFL for violating the antitrust law in creating and broadcasting its games jointly over the NFL Network. Maybe those fans who sued and made millions over the Direct TV NFL package could make some more money on this one. Or maybe the United States government could stop worrying about the election and turns its attention to a problem that bothering millions of Americans. Or maybe even Jerry Jones, no stranger to suing the NFL, could find his way back into court to reclaim his ownership of the broadcast rights to this game and sell them to the highest bidder. The solution to the problem lies with holding the NFL's corporate feet to the fire. Now the NFL might well prevail in an antitrust suit: a contemporary court may not agree with the federal court's 1953 decision. But in any view, the league's collective marketing of these game rights poses a close question; it might be nice to get it answered. And quickly. I'd like to see next year's big games.

Chapter Eight

Private Life and
Public Responsibilities

The financial and public-relations success of the modern athlete, particularly at the professional level, has brought the athlete to a position of prominence that rivals that of leading politicians, movie stars, television actors and other celebrities. Although Hollywood's leading figures have long been accustomed to the intense scrutiny of the "paparazzi" press, for sports stars the media's transition from its traditional deference to today's aggressive investigative reporting has come as something of a shock. Long gone are the days of the beat reporter for the local paper writing glowing tributes to his subject's athletic prowess before joining the boys for a game of cards in the back of the bus. Today's pro teams, particularly those located in large media markets, are covered by sizable press contingents, sometimes including foreign reporters, who are in active competition for new stories and new angles to attract readers.

Athletes displeased by the overbearing attention devoted to their off-field conduct blame reporters, and surely the reporters' zeal is the direct antagonist. But fans are complicit. Reporters are feeding a demand that appears insatiable. For those who are indifferent to the personal lives of celebrities, this demand appears inexplicable. But there's no accounting for taste. Still, assigning some responsibility to the inquisitive interests of fans, along with the press in choosing to cater to it, brings into question the proper role and appropriate interests of spectators, who, unlike the media, usually escape blameless. Redirecting our consideration to the rightful place of the fan in contemporary sports culture allows more refinement in defining the obligations of the athlete to the media and the fans. Athletes carry a lot of responsibility, but as we'll see, their responsibilities to the rest of us are not unlimited.

Athletes as Role Models

With an NBA referee having pled guilty to game-fixing charges, pro quarterback Michael Vick convicted of dog fighting and suspended from the NFL, and Barry Bonds' home-run record having brought to the fore baseball's perduring problem with steroids, now seems as bad a time as any to reconsider the bromide about superstar athletes serving as role models for youngsters. Should parents point to these law-breaking, drug-ingesting, bet-placing, fan-despising, spoiled, pampered rich athletes and tell our children to be like them? Are athletes role models? Are they good ones?

Yes, on all counts.

First let's define "role model." It's not just "model," it's a model of a specific "role." This is an important limitation. None of us are models for children in an unlimited sense; even we parents should be humble enough to hope that our children do not mirror our behaviors completely. We all want our kids to share in our good qualities, not the bad.

Athletes are role models for children, but only for the role of "athlete." Athletes display the athletic virtues: diligence, perseverance, the value of training, fair play and sportsmanship, grace under pressure, and the pursuit of excellence. The best of our athletes exhibit these virtues abundantly, in full public display. How familiar is the story of the gifted athlete whose rise to stardom is fueled by endless practice, peak performance on notable college teams, and diligent perfection of his professional game? How common is the athlete who has overcome a deeply difficult upbringing in single- or no-parent homes amidst neighborhood poverty and crime? This time of year I daily help my young children organize themselves to arrive on time, fed and properly dressed for baseball practice. What chance would my kids have were a parent not available to make sports participation easy? It amazes me that many of our accomplished professional athletes were able to put it all together and excel. One can watch any professional game in any sport and see role models at every position.

Yet some fans and commentators apparently want more. They want athletes to be more than a model of a role; they want athletes to be a model of all personal and public virtues. Why should we expect athletes to exhibit non-athletic virtues to any greater degree than we or others model such qualities? Virtues such as honesty, integrity, self-control, humility, kindness, generosity and the like are immensely important, but they are no more important to the athlete than they are to the rest of us. Why should I expect to point to an athlete or other celebrity to show my children an example of humility or generosity, more than I should live a life where I can point to myself? But when the lesson is about the pursuit of excellence and the need to practice or the possibility of overcoming obstacles or the determination needed to succeed, well, professional sports players are exemplars. What more can we ask of them? That a person pursuing his own life's goals can unintentionally be a paragon of excellence for others is the best role model possible.

Of course some athletes fail to model the role that they have assumed and that we can rightfully expect from them. We can't fairly ask our sports stars to be especially kind or honest, but we can ask them to exhibit good sportsmanship and a commitment to fair play. I am personally dubious about the logic behind the ban on performance enhancements, for example, but rules are rules, and players who flout the rules cheat the game, much as talented players who squander their innate gifts cheat the duty they owe to their employers and, by extension, their fans. Athletes are models for their roles, and like any role model they can succeed or fail at that role. But it is on that singular and limited dimension, as an example or model of the specific role of the athlete, that we should judge our professional athletes, and no more.

Children understand my point implicitly. I can point to Kobe Bryant's wonderful form on a jump shot as worthy of emulation without my children taking my comment as an implicit endorsement of Bryant's alleged broken adherence to his marital vow. I can (one day perhaps) mention Michael Vick's success as an NFL quarterback to evidence the possibility for a person to overcome certain physical limitations (in his case, inferior height for the position) and perform athletic tasks competently, and do so without endorsing mistreatment of helpless animals. And so on. I suspect strongly that the claimed worry about kids ("What can we tell our children?") that one hears when the foibles and errors of star athletes are once again brought to public light is nothing more than an invention, something we say because we can't bring ourselves to speak the truth.

The truth is this: we're not really worried about our children. We fans are worried about ourselves. We spy, pry, and obsess about the private lives of people who "choose" certain occupations, such as athlete or movie star, and deep down we know this is voyeurism. And then we think that our decision to watch them (and spy and pry) justifies our holding them to a standard that we ourselves do not always meet. And that if they, the stars, don't like our spying and prying, then they (we say) should not have chosen to be in the public arena. Wrong. We watchers made the choice to watch, and it's a new decision each time we buy a ticket to the game or turn on the television. The basketball player will play (if that's his best occupation) whether it's in front of a small crowd or an international television audience. The player chooses to expose that much of his life (his playing of the game) to our scrutiny. The rest of the prying and spying is clearly not the athlete's choice; it's ours. Should we be surprised when that part of the athlete's life that the athlete did not choose to be held open to public scrutiny fails to measure up to the virtuous excellence we want to see (and very often do see) on the playing field or court?

We should be ashamed of ourselves for our constant, envious nosiness into what is often not our business. All of us "go public" with certain aspects of our lives, if only to advertise our businesses, apply for a job, or write a book. Should that limited act of consent mean that all aspects of our life are now fair game for the prying eye? If not, then why should this be the case for the athlete?

Of course it's news and newsworthy when a high-profile athlete is accused of a serious crime or of cheating the game, much as would be the case for any other citizen. But our legitimate interest in the private lives of our celebrity athletes does not go much further. We need to allow these young men and women to try and fail at the "non-athletic" human virtues as much as we permit everybody else. We ask enough of these athletes to achieve perfection in the athletic virtues. That they accomplish these athletic virtues so often and under such pressure is testament not to the demise of professional sports in this country, but to their success. Long gone are the days of baseball players drinking beer during games or basketball players using cocaine before the tipoff. Few today are the gifted athletes who negligently or lazily squander away their talent. Our professional athletes are more virtuous and yes, better role models than they have ever been. That we fans and observers fail to recognize this, and instead demand even more of them, creates a vision of a "role model" that is unrealistic and unreasonable.

Offensive Team Nicknames

This is a tricky topic. On the one hand, the NCAA, in announcing its categorical prohibition on indigenous American nicknames, has come off as officious, doctrinaire and blindly adherent to the silly dictates of political correctness. On the other hand, the NCAA has a point. Some of these nicknames seem little more than slurs. I detest the political correctness movement in the same instinctive way I abhor any totalitarian claims. But still, basic charity and politeness suggests some of these teams should find a new identity.

One issue with the Native American nicknames is that they're caricatures (much like "Cavalier," "Pirate," "Yankee," etc.). For instance, the nickname "Braves" would seem an accurate, descriptive and dignified word. Yet the term captures an image of a tomahawk-bearing, war paint-wearing, horse-riding male member of a plains tribe with which the American immigrants and settlers came in contact as they moved west. I've met a number of Native Americans in my work (mostly from the river tribes of the Northwest) and have yet to see one adorned in anything close to such garb, and unless I attend a ceremonial event, most likely never will. The "Braves" conjured up in our minds aren't contemporary Indians; they're historical artifacts, or maybe a caricature of historical artifacts.

So one question is whether or not non-Native Americans should have access to or appropriate those artifacts for their own (largely commercial) purposes. Or instead do the tribes "own" these artifacts? One attribute of ownership is the right of alienation.[1] Could an Indian tribe sell the right to these artifacts to a sports team? If the answer is that a team need not purchase an "Indian" nickname from an Indian tribe, then that fact is strongly suggestive that the tribe does not own these historical caricatures. A new sports team tomorrow could call itself the Braves or even the Sioux or Seminoles, apparently without further obligation. (Ironically, the sports teams that appropriate the Indian names have asserted intellectual property rights in the name; you can't just start marketing "Florida Seminoles" football jerseys without a license from the University.)

If it's true that the contemporary Indian tribes do not own their ancestral caricatures (no more than I, as a native New Englander from Protestant stock, own "Yankee"), should they be offended when sports teams employ those caricatures as nicknames? Can

---

1. "Alienation, in property law, is the capacity for a piece of property or a property right to be sold or otherwise transferred from one party to another." "Alienation (Property Law)." 4 June 2007. *Wikipedia.com*. http://en.wikipedia.org/wiki/Alienation_%28property_law%29.

one be offended by another's legal conduct? Yes, of course. However, requests for amelioration of the slight are not grounded in legality but in good manners or polite social relations. That is why the NCAA's clumsy employment of a strict rule seemed so heavy-handed, given the nature of the perceived slight.

With that said, judgment is needed. Some nicknames are unnecessarily offensive and should be done away with. It is difficult to understand "redskin" as anything but derogatory. Historically, Indians would refer to their own race as "red," in contrast to the "whites." But in contemporary social intercourse, describing a person along the dimension of race or color is rude, both because it draws attention to an immutable characteristic and because it threatens to set the person apart from others. No one who was raised right would refer to a group of Native Americans as "those red skins." Even if one wanted to identify the group as a group, one could refer to their tribe membership in terms that didn't draw attention to perceived skin color.

In the same vein, some of the historical caricatures sports teams employ also seem unduly unkind. Images of Indian braves in full headdress, howling, mouth agape, do not present a pleasant picture; of course contemporary Indians will not like it. Again, legally speaking no one has to make that change; we can make fun of each other as much as we want, pretty much with impunity. But let's be reasonable. The historical treatment of the natives by the white immigrants was, in many cases, utterly shameful. I now live in the Northwest, and the deal the Nez Perce got was about as raw as could be. This is a tribe that was nothing but helpful to early American settlers, and without whose help these settlers and the preceding Lewis and Clark expedition would never have survived the difficult immigration over the Rockies and the harsh Bitterroots. Yet, to put it bluntly, this large tribe was forcibly kicked off its designated reservation (where it had been located forever) once the settlers realized they had allocated to the tribe some very nice real estate. Let's be honest, white people: there's something owed to Native Americans. We can go a little out of our way to be considerate, especially on something as inconsequential as the nickname for a sports team.

I have read that some tribes have consented to the use of their name (the "Seminoles"), and in that case, the continued use is legitimate because the team is using the specific name of a specific tribe. More generic nicknames (Braves, Indians) cannot be subject to consent because the group is too diffuse. So I only buy the consent defense in limited cases. Plus, some of the more objectionable images are coarsening and affect more people than just Native Americans, so the consent of one tribe may not suffice for the rest of us.

White Men Can Jump

ESPN commentator and former star receiver Michael Irvin goes on one of ESPN's national radio programs and suggests, albeit in jest, that Tony Romo, the Cowboys (white) new quarterback is so athletic that he must have "some brother" in his ancestry, perhaps when his "great-, great-grandmother" had a romp in the hay with a black man.[2] Irvin's comments were crude, to be sure, but a fireable offense? Not if I'm the boss.

Irvin's comments call to mind similar statements on "racial athleticism" a few years ago by NFL commentator Jimmy the Greek[3]

2. Michael Irvin specifically stated: "I don't know if some brother down in that line somewhere, I don't know who saw what or where, his great-great-great-great-grandma ran over in the 'hood or something went down." He continued: "If great-great-great-great-great-great-great-great grandma pulled one of them studs up out of the barn, 'Come on in here for a second,' you know, and they go out and work in the yard. You know, back in the day." "Michael Irvin Says Tony Romo's Athleticism is Due to Black Ancestry." 22 November 2006. *FanHouse.com.* http://sports.aol.com/fanhouse/category/cowboys/2006/11/22/michael-irvin-says-tony-romos-athleticism-is-due-to-black-ances/.
3. Jimmy the Greek was quoted as saying "if blacks ever take over coaching like everybody wants them to, there is not going to be anything left

(which, by the way, caused an immediate and non-stop media firestorm and resulted in Jimmy's rapid job termination). For some, it also brings to mind Rush Limbaugh's comments on Donovan McNabb.[4] So should Michael Irvin get the Jimmy the Greek/Rush Limbaugh termination letter?

No. Irvin gave voice to a stereotype, and stereotypes are by definition inexact and (at times) counterfactual generalizations. However, it's a stereotype that (warning: stereotype coming, so if you're easily offended, stop reading now) white people are repeating/generating/stating all the time; the stereotype of the non-athletic white man. What was the movie "White Men Can't Jump," but the embodiment of exactly that sentiment? A two-hour joke about white people's lack of athleticism and how that assumption allowed the

---

for the white people." White, Jack. "Of Mandingo and Jimmy 'the Greek.'" 1 February 1988. *Time.com.* http://www.time.com/time/magazine/article/0,9171,966590,00.html.

4. Limbaugh chastised the media (claiming that the liberal media wanted a black quarterback to succeed, and thus overrated McNabb), accusing the media of slanted coverage on a racial issue, and made no comment on race as a predictor of athleticism. Thus Limbaugh attacked the media for racism. Why Limbaugh's comments were considered a transgression, and what standard or piety they transgressed, escapes me. Given the repeated calls, some time ago, for the NFL to give black quarterbacks a chance (including articles in the media disparaging the NFL's habit of switching black college QB's to other positions), wouldn't it make sense that these same commentators would be rooting for those black players who were given a chance at QB to succeed? Don't you think some of us (including me) who have called on the NFL to give minority coaches a chance also root for the success of those minority coaches once they are given a chance? It's only natural and indeed logical. If your team drafts a rookie and you become a big fan of that rookie, don't you make excuses or stand up for that player when other fans say he's not playing too well? This motivation amounts to nothing more than being a fan, that's all. Now, it may be that Limbaugh underestimated McNabb on race grounds. That may be, I don't know. I do think people can say so-and-so is no good, even when that claim is demonstrably wrong, and have that claim have nothing to do with race.

white basketball player to trick money out of blacks who (operating on the same stereotypical assumption) bet they could beat him. Do you think a movie titled, "Black Men Can't Think" would have been green-lighted? No, we'd be up in arms, appropriately. So where was the anger over the "White Men" movie? Why do numerous sports commentators, bloggers and others casually repeat the pejorative "white stiff" in referring to tall, white basketball players? My point is, white people (by and large) have made the "unathletic white man" stereotype part of our contemporary lexicon. Irvin implicitly invoked it in his comments. If Jay Bilas (ESPN's NBA draft analyst) said of a white center, "he's not a white stiff," no one would give that comment a second thought. Why should Irvin be precluded from making such a comment because he's black?

Message for white people: stop invoking this stereotype. Not only is it demeaning, it's factually incorrect. You can't just scan the racial composition of the NBA and assume that whites are unathletic. Look at some other sports. Ever try surfing? Don't laugh until you've attempted to stand up on a board in a turbulent ocean. How about sitting on a dirt bike and flipping over backward through the air? (Yes, TSLP does that all the time.) How about hitting a good curveball? I could go on. I look at these sports and I see lots of whites doing these very difficult athletic activities very well. (Some) whites are very athletic; the same is true for (some) blacks.

Some black comedians, presumably for shock value or to get a cheap laugh, have more or less made the "N" slur part of their act. To me, it's like a comedian using the "F" swear; it's a crutch to cover up material that is not always funny. People can say what they want, but what angers me is that the audience will laugh at non-funny jokes simply because the comedian filled his delivery with slurs and curses. Why not make the comedian come up with something that's actually funny? Yet we laugh, just as we're happy to repeat racial stereotypes instead of actually going to the trouble of saying something interesting and insightful about Tony Romo or a college basketball center. Michael's message about Tony Romo was not a product of racial thinking; it's a product of the stereotypes that

Michael reads and hears about every day. Let's stop pretending we're offended.

Why is job termination always and reflexively the remedy of choice for every transgression of the political correctness law? Is this some kind of mandatory minimum? Don't we understand how serious this sanction is? Jimmy the Greek never worked in television again. Termination is the workplace equivalent of capital punishment. If we "throw the book" at Michael Irvin for this single episode, what are we going to throw at more serious offenders? Wouldn't a reprimand and some supervisory instruction suffice?[5]

Love Children

TSLP's personal favorite, Patriots' quarterback Tom Brady, recently became the proud father of a child with his former girlfriend, actress Bridget Moynahan. Another TSLP favorite, young Lebron James, will soon be parent to his second child, who will also be born outside of wedlock. Babies are everywhere in our sports world, but not so many marriages.[6] What's going on with our contemporary athletes? (I guess the answer is obvious.)

---

5. Ultimately, ESPN decided to let Irvin go after the controversial statements, announcing on February 17, 2007, that he would no longer be working at the network. "Michael Irvin." 22 August 2007. *Wikipedia.com.* http://en.wikipedia.org/wiki/Michael_Irvin.

6. In 1998, *Sports Illustrated* did an issue on the "epidemic" of "out-of-wedlock births." The article stated that "one of the NBA's top agents says he spends more time dealing with paternity claims than he does negotiating contracts." This same agent said, "there may be more kids out of wedlock than there are players in the NBA." Specifically, the article highlighted Larry Johnson, who has five children by four women, Shawn Kemp, with seven children but remains unmarried, and many other players who have been a part of paternity suits. Crane, Paul. "This Week's SI: An Inside Look." 29 April 1998. *CNNSI.com.* http://sportsillustrated.cnn.com/features/1998/weekly/980504/insidelook.html.

Why is everyone so afraid of this subject? We'll stick a micro-
phone in any athlete's face and hound him around the clock if
there's even the slightest whiff of a drug issue. Gambling scandals
have always been good press. Nowadays, our rough-talking athletes are even being held to the standard of contemporary political
dogmatism, not the standard of the locker room, in their speech.
No behavior or comment of a prominent athlete goes overlooked
by the aggressive media or omniscient commissioners, except for
one thing: the athlete's mating habits. Why can a pro athlete run
around and father children by multiple women all over the country with barely a mention, but let him pause in his love-making to
utter some politically insensitive comment, and certain public interests and commentators (and maybe me) will take turns telling us
how upset we are with his behavior? Why is the fearless press so
reticent?

There are a lot of athletes I'm criticizing here; at least it seems so
to me. The "news" that an athlete has fathered children casually, or
by his girlfriend, appears so commonplace that it hardly rises to the
surface. TV announcers or magazine article writers will so easily,
even glowingly, mention that an athlete is proudly expecting a child
by his unmarried paramour that, in my mind, it becomes as much
a comment or reflection on the commentator as it is on the athlete.
Doesn't anyone realize or care to bring to mind that a child born
into an unstable marital situation or incomplete home life starts out
with a significant hurdle to overcome? That irresponsible sex is, well,
an act of substantial irresponsibility? That kids, at least whenever
possible, deserve to have the benefit of a well-grounded family situation? The ideal is not always possible, of course, and children can
and do overcome this deficit regularly. But no one's going to say
that having estranged, unmarried parents is better for children. Even
a dad who is rich and famous and on television every week but lives
one thousand miles away is not likely to be the equivalent of a regular dad getting paid by the hour and coming home every night.

A lot of debate crops up from time to time on whether or not it
is appropriate for people to regard athletes as "role models," or in-

deed even for athletes to think of themselves in this way. As dubious as I am of this expectation, it is clear that the professional leagues are of a single mind on this question, expecting their players to represent the league in both their on- and off-field conduct. Morals clauses in the standard player contracts, coupled with the suspension power of league commissioners, reflect the leagues' concern. So why are players and others corrected for verbal insensitivity or recreational drug use, while this other aspect of a player's conduct goes unaddressed? Which is more harmful, saying bad words in public (or smoking some marijuana) or fathering children around the country toward which one has no plausible expectation of being a decent parent? At least the victims of insensitive words can defend themselves.

I'm not saying athletes who father illegitimate children should be suspended. But when such conduct, especially if it's adulterous, comes to the attention of the commissioner, it needs to be addressed as a serious, irresponsible matter. I realize that male pro athletes, unlike law professors, are particularly subject to the attention of beautiful young women, and that the long hours on the road leave plenty of time and energy for romantic pursuits. But we commonly claim that people in the public arena must be held to a higher standard that comes with the decision to assume such celebrity. Why not here? Maybe if athletes were less promiscuous, the frequency with which young women made themselves available to them would diminish. Perhaps a certain amount of protection of the player from fans needs to be considered. Sound unduly paternalistic? Our professional leagues take many steps to keep athletes away from drug dealers, bookmakers and gamblers; they police what the players wear to games and what they say to fans. Requiring NBA or MLB hotels to keep adoring bar patrons away from visiting athletes would not be much of a step. Maybe the unions are active on this front, but this is also a financial issue. I doubt too many male athletes are thrilled to find out they are financially responsible for a child of a woman with whom they had only a fleeting relationship.

I realize that many pro athletes are themselves products of unions outside of wedlock. But so what? I don't buy the argument that this fact of birth makes them unable to live life differently. These are men; young men, but not infants. They can make decisions and are smart enough to see that sex (even "protected") can have serious consequences. Self-control is always an option.

Lawyers, Liars, and Football Coaches

Alabama football coach Nick Saban will earn $32 million over the next eight years, not counting additional bonuses for bowl games. Along with his salary, Saban has earned extreme vitriol from fans and others angry with his departure from the Miami Dolphins. His crime? He said he was staying, and then he left. Even old sage Don Shula blasted him.[7]

Is it wrong to tell a lie? No, not always; not here. If Saban was guilty of anything, it was practicing law without a license.

It is wrong to take a sharp instrument and stab somebody in the chest. (That solves that dilemma.) Yet surgeons do it every day. They hurt us in the hope of making us better. Lawyers also, in a broader sense, injure the body politic by lying. To use the simplest example, criminal defense lawyers lie when they argue that a person they know to be guilty is innocent. A lawyer lies when the lawyer suggests that a witness the lawyer knows to be a truth-teller is in fact lying or mistaken. If the lawyer's argument is successful, a guilty person goes free, which makes things worse for the rest of us. Yet we collectively risk this injury in the hope that we'll be better off (by

---

7. Don Shula stated that Saban has "run away from the challenge. It's unbelievable. There were four or five direct statements that were blatant lies. That tells you a little bit about the guy." Shula added that "[t]he guy likes to talk and then doesn't follow up on what he says." "Shula Blasts Saban for Quitting Dolphins." 4 January 2007. *MSNBC.com.* http://www.msnbc.msn.com/id/16469936/.

helping to ensure that the non-guilty are not convicted). It's utilitarianism. We injure ourselves (surgeons cut; lawyers argue for counterfactual innocence) in the hope of gaining a net benefit.

The fact that lawyers tell lies is ethically permissible because our justice system asks them to do so, at least in the criminal defense function. It is the lawyer's "role" as a lawyer that permits conduct that would be unethical in most other walks of life. Lawyers may lie at work, so to speak, but not at home.

Football coaches have to lie too. (They don't have ethical theorists justifying their lies, as lawyers do, so this modest contribution will have to do.) Essentially, their role requires them to lie, and since football coaching is a role society obviously condones and even venerates, then implicitly, society condones their lies. Nick Saban's lies were ethical.

Assume football coaches have contractual freedom to change jobs.[8] As a practical matter, the only way a football coach can change jobs is by lying to the press and everybody else when asked about his intentions. If a coach admits, truthfully, that he is looking to leave, bad things happen. For a college coach, recruits sign elsewhere, assistant coaches update their resumes, and presidents go down their private list of replacements. For a pro coach, assistant coaches and free agents might go elsewhere, general managers may look to replacements, the commitment of

---

8. Usually people can change jobs even in the middle of a contract. Courts will not enforce employment contracts by "specific performance," which is an equitable remedy forcing a person to honor his employment contract against his will. The reason courts historically have refused to enjoin workers to work against their will is our long-standing prohibition against peonage (forced labor to pay off debt) and involuntary servitude. Courts may remedy broken employment contracts with damages, and sometimes courts will impose an injunction directed at the new employer should there be specific limits in the employment contract against re-employment in the vicinity, such as a non-competition clause.

remaining players may wane, and fan ticket renewals may suffer. Even a non-answer or "no comment," given in response to a direct question about the coach's interest in another job, basically admits the truth, and thus substantially undermines that coach's present position with his team, and perhaps will cost him his job anyway. Additionally, a truthful answer, by more or less eliminating the coach's chances to stay with his present team, torpedoes his negotiation leverage with his new team. The new team will know the coach now has little choice but to accept their terms.

By steadfastly, "sincerely" (and untruthfully) denying his interest in another job, the coach preserves his position with his present team and helps maintain that team's momentum in keeping coaches and acquiring players. Indeed, the coach's present employer would actually prefer that the coach lie, even to the employer, about his intentions, if only to preserve the team's coaching and player recruits and sales momentum. Even the players, supposedly the "victims" of the coach's prevarications, would prefer him to lie, to help the team attract additional players to improve the team's performance.

That's not to say that no one is hurt by the lie. Ostensibly the coaching and player recruits, some of whom came to the team to work with the coach, might feel misled, as may some ticket buyers. But these folks made their decisions knowing (at least they should know by now) that even coaches on multi-year contracts sometimes will break that contract and leave for another team. We all make employment decisions this way, betting on the future of the company. Fans are hurt too. But all of us commonly make purchasing decisions in the face of uncertainty, paying money now in exchange for performance in the future. We know that when we buy an item to be delivered months into the future that we bear the risk that the seller may go bankrupt in the meantime. We probably even get a discount to compensate us for that risk (much like ticket renewals are often discounted if purchased by an early date). So fans aren't really victims if they're paid for the risk they bear.

There is pain from the lie, but there's also benefit. If the latter exceeds the former (as we think it does with defense lawyers and surgeons), usually the lie is considered ethical, even though we look the other way when it happens. Even with surgery, we don't know for sure beforehand that the benefits will exceed the costs; sometimes they don't, and the surgery itself ends up killing an otherwise non-terminal patient. So we have to do our best to guess. Since there's no law against lying to the press, at least not about one's job intentions, the better guess is that the damage caused by the coach's lie, although not trivial, is outweighed by the harm the coach's lie avoids. Coaches may lie, ethically.

Don Shula is no stranger to the flexibility of coaching contracts. He was the very successful head coach of the Baltimore Colts back in 1969, the team having played in the Super Bowl the previous season. As the 1969 season neared a close, the Miami Dolphins surreptitiously contacted Shula about the possibility of his coaching their team. In a complaint to the league, Baltimore accused Miami of tampering, successfully, and the league forced the Dolphins to give the Colts their first-round pick as compensation. His position with the Colts undermined by his flirtation with Miami, Shula was allowed to resign from Baltimore and take the Dolphins' offer.

Eating Cornbread

Boston Celtics' radio announcer Cedric "Cornbread" Maxwell is a thoughtful and funny guy, usually. But trouble loomed when, laughing about a presumed erroneous foul called by an NBA referee, Maxwell cracked that the referee "should go back to the kitchen" and "fix me bacon and eggs." The referee in question, of course, was the NBA's only female referee, Violet Palmer. Max was the one in the kitchen afterwards, namely in boiling hot water. He issued an on-air apology, but this being Boston, that wasn't enough. Commentators called for him to lose his job.

I watched parts of the Academy Awards last year and saw comedian Ellen DeGeneres describe actress Penelope Cruz as "Mexican," state that Dame Judi Dench was off getting a "boob job," that without "blacks, Jews and gays" there would be "no men named Oscar." I also witnessed some comedians make reference to "having sex all alone." Some award winner for visual effects made some flat joke to the effect that critics said that "four blind kids" could do what they did. My point? More than a few off-color, inappropriate and insensitive remarks (and a lot fewer than in usual years), none of which I suspect got as much as a ripple in the next day's news. Why not?

Why did Cedric Maxwell receive such a different reaction? The man was making a joke, offering what he thought to be a clever, witty comment on the alleged incompetence of the female referee. A lame joke, one that referred and drew attention to her sex, on par with some of the equally lame jokes at the Oscars that also drew attention to certain aspects of people, but still a jest. Can we separate out Maxwell's joke from, for instance, Ellen's joke about men named Oscar? If anything, Max's comment appeared spur-of-the-moment; Ellen's was presumably scripted and therefore more blameworthy. Yet, let's imagine a black or Jewish referee named Oscar; what if Maxwell, in commenting on the referee's call, had uttered Ellen's joke, that if it weren't for blacks (or Jews), there would be no people named Oscar? I suspect he'd have been fired by halftime. What's the distinction? If there is a distinction, does it make the situations different? Is it such a compelling difference that Maxwell should receive a substantial job penalty while Ellen gets invited back to host again next year?

Should sports announcers make jokes? A few years ago ABC hired a comedian, Dennis Miller, for its Monday Night Football franchise, and he bombed because he had trouble fitting his cerebral, wry brand of humor into the vortex of an NFL football game. ESPN once hired Rush Limbaugh to offer "political" football commentary; that experiment ended as soon as Limbaugh said something political. Tony Kornheiser announces games, playing the role of the bombastic opinionista full of himself (and I like Kornheiser a lot, but only on "Pardon The Interruption," and only in conjunction with the more circumspect Michael Wilbon). The point is that sports announcers today are part expert explainers of events and part entertainers. As entertainers, they should be accorded the same latitude we implicitly allow Ellen at the Oscars.

I watch a good deal of NBA games. I think many of the referees have their "blind spots" or certain calls that they do not make well. Violet Palmer sticks out as the league's only female referee, and so I will admit that I probably notice her calls more than I do other referees. (I am sure this is the case with other observers too; I am sure her job is a very difficult one, given the focus she draws.) Palmer, in my view, has a great deal of trouble making the offensive charge/defensive foul call, probably the most difficult call in basketball. She's not alone in that weakness, but still, that's her weakness. That's exactly the call that spurred Maxwell to make his joke. He's a commentator. The pressure's on him to say something clever about Palmer's mistake other than the commonplace "bad call."

People, even sports announcers, need room to step around and occasionally across the lines of sensitivity that people have staked out for others to abide. Comedians (or all of us when we attempt comedy) need even more room. Comedy's social role, at its best, is to use humor and irony to pick at our hubris and make us question our presumptions and commitments. Often, one might respond to a witty joke with a laugh and the comment, "good point." See, comedy makes a point.

Maxwell's point? Lots of possibilities. Maybe his point is that women should not be refereeing NBA games. Or maybe that Violet Palmer, in particular, should not be refereeing NBA games. Or maybe that women should not work outside the home. But I suspect it was none of the above. In my view, Maxwell was just invoking a historical stereotype (women in the kitchen) as a rhetorical device to say that Palmer made a bad call. He wasn't endorsing the stereotype or recommending it; he was using it rhetorically to make a statement about current events. Here's another example of invoking an historical stereotype as a rhetorical device to make a statement about contemporary events: "without Jews, there would be no men named Oscar." Ellen didn't mean that literally (that we need Jews, blacks and gays to promulgate the name "Oscar"); instead, she meant to refer to the importance (in her expert opinion) of Jewish people in the production of Academy-Award caliber films. The name thing was a play on words and a play on a stereotype. Maxwell also didn't mean literally that Violet Palmer should quit her job and go make Maxwell breakfast; instead, he meant to refer to her incompetence for the workplace position she currently holds. He referred to her sex in doing so, using her sex and the historical stereotype of that sex as the fulcrum of the joke, much like Ellen used the ethnicity of the winners as the fulcrum of her joke. That's a strong comment by Maxwell, to be sure, but one in his place to make, as an expert analyst.

Now certain historical stereotypes do not serve well as rhetorical devices, simply because the conjured image ("greedy Jews") is so off-putting and jarring that any hope of rhetorical mileage will be lost. But it's a close question when such historical artifacts pass from the usable to the unusable category. And it's the comedian's exact role to make us question the lines we've drawn. Personally, I would never use Maxwell's device in making a point (at least not without a lot of explanation), but then I'm not a comedian whose job is to prick people's conscience. But in law school, often the subject matter does call on the discussion leader (that would be me) to broach and discuss difficult and sensitive perspectives. I have the luxury of the class hour to make my qualifications clear. Maxwell had a punch line. I once heard a comedian give a long and hilarious riff on "greedy Jews," using the stereotype as rhetoric, as joke, as wordplay, as metaphor, and everything in between. (Since you'll want to know, yes, he identified himself as Jewish.) I've heard of black comedians spending a lot of time on racial stereotypes. So even distasteful, troublesome stereotypes can be put to use rhetorically. I suspect that's what Maxwell had in mind.

Chapter Nine

What If the Rule Were Otherwise?

The most fun for a law professor (admittedly we lead a sheltered life) is to ask a student this simple yet always challenging question: what if the rule were otherwise? It's the ultimate test for why we have or don't have certain rules of law: if rule "A" is a necessary rule, but were changed to "not A," then all hell would break loose. So rules have a purpose, and it's the job of the lawyer to probe that purpose constantly. If rules could be changed to their opposite without much ill-effect, then perhaps the rule is unnecessary in the first place. Rules are costly: they inhibit personal freedom that might produce personal satisfaction and socially valuable goods, they have to be crafted carefully to avoid over-inclusion, and they have to be enforced. So no one favors adopting rules unnecessarily. If a lawyer can show that the same or similar beneficent ends can be generated without the imposition of a rule of law, then the rule of law is unnecessary, and legal analysis would dictate its abrogation.

The world of sports features rules and practices that are as old as the concept of organized sport itself. Yet sometimes organized sports are "over-organized," and contain a few strictures or prohibitions that, upon examination, do not appear to serve an important purpose any longer, if they ever did. My position on one of these rules, the prohibition on gambling, received its own chapter. In this chapter we come across a number of other prohibitions, the existence of some of which may surprise you, and ask (at times semi-seriously) if these quaint limitations perhaps need to be reconceptualized. As we shall see, the arcane and endless rules of the great game of golf have earned particular attention.

For some of these thought experiments, I bring back to life notable sports events from yesteryear. As we shall also see, once a rule is changed, imagination runs wild.

Why Can't Michael Play?

As every sports fan knows, the highlight of the 2010 NBA season was those precious seconds that *Time* magazine has called "The Greatest Moment of the New Millennium." The Washington Wizards had called a timeout with 7.5 seconds left, trailing the Los Angeles Lakers by one point in the deciding championship game. The sellout crowd stood in solemn silence while the seconds ticked away on the Wizards' garish new "timeout clock." And then, with less than a minute to go before play resumed, the crowd erupted in a shout that shook the building.

As he had done on several occasions during the regular season, the Wizards' owner, his Airness himself, Michael Jordan, sprang from his private box, stripping away his business suit as he ran to the floor in the glare of a large spotlight. As was Jordan's custom for big games, he was wearing his team uniform under his outer clothing. When Jordan's unerring jumper from the left wing sailed through the hoop as time expired, not only had the Wizards won their first championship in decades, not only had the NBA enjoyed its biggest year at the box office in memory, but we had just witnessed a moment that will be remembered as long as humankind walk the face of the earth ...

Oh, wait a minute, sorry. That moment will never happen. Michael Jordan can't play for the Wizards[1] because the National

---

1. Jordan used to own a share of the Wizards before he divested himself of the stock to take a management role in the Charlotte Bobcats. In the thought experiment, however, I pretend that Jordan is still connected with the Wizards, simply because the Bobcats, as a recent expansion team, have no history and no former players. It's okay to pretend counterfactual things in a thought experiment.

Basketball Association has a rule against team owners playing in its games. Why? Why not let Michael play? I guess the league is afraid of this story:

Disgusted by what he called his team's lack of hustle during a dreadful second period against the Phoenix Suns, Celtics owner Wyc Grousbeck spurned his halftime highball and sped down to the locker room. The audible dismay of the Boston faithful, Grousbeck wore Bob Cousy's retired No. 14 when he came out in uniform for the second half. (At least the fan reaction was more subdued than the infamous night against Miami when Wyc donned Bill Russell's sacred No. 6 and touched off a small riot.) After the Celtics began the third period by missing several ill-advised three-point attempts, Grousbeck signaled Coach Doc Rivers that he was ready to go in. Point guard Rajon Rondo was clearly miffed to be taken out once again — for a player whom Rondo has termed "my personal white shadow" — but at a mere 5'8", Grousbeck has made it clear that playing the point is his best and safest position. Although he failed to score, Grousbeck did seem stronger last night than he was earlier in the season against the Detroit Pistons. Then defensive-minded Chauncey Billups hounded him all over the court, and team doctors feared he might suffer a heart attack. Stripping off his headband, wrist bands, knee pads, and socks after last night's game, Grousbeck vowed that his team would "get into shape" or he'd find a coach "who can get it done" — fueling speculation that Grousbeck plans to fire Rivers and take the coach's reins himself.

Okay, so there are a few problems with letting owners play. But why can't players own? Players can coach, as two championship rings among the eleven that adorn Bill Russell's fingers will prove. And coaches can own: Rick Pitino owned a bit of the Celtics when he coached the team. So players can coach and coaches can own, but players can't own, so owners can't play. Since the owners themselves devised these rules, what motivates them to limit themselves this way?

Perhaps the reason for this prohibition goes no deeper than a concern that owners of professional sports teams, consisting mostly of fabulously rich men with a salient preference for athletic entertainment, might try to relieve their childhood frustrations by inserting themselves into games. Why shouldn't Ted Turner, when he owned the team, take over center field for the Atlanta Braves near the end of a blowout, late-season loss? Turner once took over managing the team for a few games until the league made him get back to business, so he certainly might have the interest. Things could get out of hand. What better way to impress a prospective son-in-law than by letting the lad start for the Montreal Canadians or call for the ball in the post at Madison Square Garden? Why not let all your pals play? After all, it's not as if they'll have to guard Tim Duncan and Manu Ginobili; those guys will be riding the pine in favor of their owner's sons too.

Clearly, owners who play themselves or their surrogates diminish the value of their teams, but maybe some won't care. Why would Bill Gates play basketball at the local YMCA if he could buy the Seattle Supersonics and hoop it up with Kevin Durant? Would he care about losing a few million in franchise revenue? More likely, the prohibition on owners playing is aimed to maximize joint returns: teams need their competitors to field quality players in order to produce the rivalries and excitement that stimulate fan interest.

But surely the need to ensure player competence could be met short of an outright ban. The rule against owners playing may be explained by something that the leagues fear even more than the owner-player: the player-owner. For if owners could play, then players could own.

Why not let the players own part of the team? In other words, why shouldn't owners pay their highly valued employees with stock options, like everybody else does? A few years ago, an NBA draft choice demanded a rookie contract pretty close to $100 million. The only problem was that the whole franchise was worth $77 million. In a small bit of humor that rookie didn't quite appreciate, the owner offered to give the player the franchise if the player would give the owner the salary. But why kid about it?

For many reasons, paying athletes with ownership makes sense.

Often we read of players who strive only for individual statistics, to the detriment of team goals. Sprinkle some Class A stock on those selfish players and watch them pass the ball now! If you think the point would be lost on modern athletes, remember that Michael Jordan himself purposely took much of his Nike pay in stock options.

Of course, there might be some downside. Since all but the best players tend to be short-term employees, years of doling out stock options could substantially dilute the majority owner's control. Player movement might be hindered too, when getting a quality left tackle requires two draft choices and a squeeze-out merger with appraisal rights; however, such things can be handled. The ubiquity of employee stock ownership plans shows that issues like transfer and dilution need not unduly impede business decisions.

So c'mon, NBA, think of the possibilities of a world in which players own and owners play:

Skip (play-by-play): What a battle this one's been, folks! The Celtics had that big lead, but the Wizards have clawed their way back into it. Jordan came in to start the fourth quarter, and he's been lighting it up! And now the Wizards are bringing in Elvin Hayes!

Red (color commentator): The Wizards need to take the ball inside. And even at age 52, Hayes still can make his patented bank shot from the left block.

Skip: But is he rusty? When's the last time Hayes saw action?

Red: Elvin played the final few minutes two months ago against Minnesota. He's been on vacation in Europe since, but I'm glad to see him back. I see Wes Unseld on the bench tonight—a little heavy, but I bet he could still get 15 rebounds. And is that Gus Williams over there, the Wizard himself? Maybe he'll want to play!

Skip: Wait a minute, the Celtics are countering. Who's this? It's Larry Bird!

Red: No way, he's general manager of the Pacers!

Skip: Yeah, but he cleared his conflict of interest by divesting himself of Pacer's stock. If the Celtics can knock off the Wizards tonight, the Pacers will secure the final playoff spot. By the way, I heard

*a rumor today that Kareem might buy a piece of the Knicks.
That would certainly help their championship run.*

*Thurston (legal affairs commentator): Well, the Knicks better make
sure that Kareem pays fair market value. Otherwise, they'll end
up like the Nets when they sold shares to Magic Johnson at a
huge discount just to get him on the team. The tax bite alone
almost bankrupted the franchise, never mind the pending share-
holders' derivative litigation.*

*Skip: Oh no, is that Bill Russell walking around over there? If he puts
on his jersey, the Celtics will control the boards for sure. Quick,
someone call Manute Bol and see if he's still awake. We might
need the height!*

I would love this game. Why should storied franchises like the
Celtics and the Wizards have to go through lean years with anonymous journeymen players? Why not motivate the legendary greats
to continue playing, even just once in a while, to keep up stock
price? Then franchises could really battle it out on the greatest scoreboard of them all, the New York Stock Exchange.

Can You Hear Them Now?

ESPN took a bold step a few seasons ago by introducing political commentary to football. But soon after Rush Limbaugh uttered
his first political critique, he was out of a job, and ESPN was knee-
deep in controversy. In my view, the network should have been
commended for its innovation. It's about time the world of sport
got a taste of political debate. Here's how my "Sunday NFL Countdown" show would run, once political commentary was fully inte-
grated into football:

Rush: "The media go easy on Donovan McNabb because he's black
and the media want a black quarterback to succeed."

Howard Dean: "I condemn your offensive introduction of race into a discussion of sports! And why aren't there more black head coaches?"

Al Sharpton: "Whitey can't run. That's why the African-American man dominates sports."

Arnold Schwarzenegger (reading):
"Skinny black man no match for me.
I terminate all competitors!"

See, that would be a lively program. Honestly, televised sports could use a little more pizzazz. Bare-knuckled political analysis might be just the thing. Why merely criticize the coach for bad play calling when his entire worldview could be torn apart?

Bud (play-by-play): "Three minutes left, and the Lakers lead by 10. They just need to run down the clock, and they'll pick up the win."

Red (color): "True. But Coach Phil Jackson refuses to play the ball-control game."

Bud: "Is Jackson worried about turnovers?"

Red: "No. He's a committed libertarian who refuses to give directions to his players. He's the Zen Master. This is anarchy!"

Bud: "Frankly, it's a shame we lost Pat Riley. His Irish Catholic Democrat roots made him comfortable with taking total control of his team."

Red: "That's why again I call for more of a political centrist as coach. Let's hope Joe Lieberman turns down the ambassadorship to France and becomes available."

Now that's insightful commentary, linking a coaching controversy, political philosophy, and international relations. But why stop there? Law professors have free time, lots of complicated ideas, and a powerful urge to pontificate.

Chip (play-by-play): "Wow, listen to the crowd! If the Cubs rally again, Wrigley will explode!"

Judge Richard Posner (color): "I wonder why they care."

Chip: "Your Honor, what? Why do they *care?* These Chicagoans are some of the best consumers of baseball in the whole league! They love their Cubs!"

Richard: "But what makes you think the fans of the game are the consumers of the game? They're not. The consumers are the people who buy the items advertised during the telecast. The game and its cheering fans are the products! They're the lure that brings the shoppers to the advertising. Because the fans are products, we're justified in imposing any quality controls on them that we want, to ensure that the product comes out right. That's why the exploding scoreboard messages that constantly instruct the fans to make noise and stomp their feet are so useful. Why leave the quality of the product to chance? We should make sure these fans "explode" whether the Cubs rally or not! In fact, we could more efficiently produce viewers for the advertisers if the games themselves were carefully scripted to maximize dramatic twists and turns. Professional wrestling appears the best analogy here."

Chip: "Anyway, the first pitch is high for ball one."

OK, bad idea. The subtle, overheated mind of the law professor won't mix well with the blunt athletic world. After all, sports are about competition, which professors abhor. (Once tenured, a law professor's only real competition is death, and even then a busy dean might not realize there's an opening for a semester or two.) But the sports fan loves competition. And who better to bring him the complicated message of the law than those practiced denizens of the courtroom, the plaintiff's lawyers?

Trip (play-by-play): "It's gone! Home run, Derek Jeter. The Yankees now lead Tampa by eight runs."

Gerry Spence (color): "This isn't a contest! The Bronx Bombers' financial advantage and personnel superiority make this game a mockery of the sport! Yet with the typical indifference of the rich, the Yankees have now added insult to injury. Why is Jeter still in the game? I submit to you, Mr. and Mrs. America, that your good judgment will lead you to root against this greedy plundering of the poor by the wealthy! The arrogant Yankees must be stopped, and only you can send that message!"

Trip: "Here comes the Devil Rays' manager out to the mound. I think he's going to make a change."

Gerry: "To whom, I ask you? To which reliever can the Rays turn now? The cupboard's bare! The wolf's at the door! Yet why must Tampa be left to its own meager resources? The Yanks are loaded. Look at all these relievers in their bullpen. Let Tampa Bay take from the Yankees! Bring Mariano Rivera to the mound right now!"

Integrating legal argument into the sporting scene would open up entire new subjects for athletic commentary. But, my apologies, I've fallen into the characteristic arrogance of the bar: If lawyers can comment on sports, why can't sports commentators opine on legal practice?

Greta Van Susteren: "This is a surprise. The prosecutor has offered the defendant's secret diary into evidence! If it's admitted, the jury will learn about the defendant's sinister plans."

John Madden: "It was like, Pow! The prosecutor brought out the diary and offered it right up, just like that. Bam! That's how it should be, you know. Just get the evidence and put it in. No dancing around, just straight ahead."

Greta: "Here's the replay. There was the diary on the prosecutor's desk."

Joe Theismann: "Watch this. The prosecutor grabs the book off the desk! See? Now he brings it over to the defense team, and they inspect it. Now he brings it over to the judge. See that? Right to the bench, hands it to the bailiff. That's what I like to see, just do it."

Greta: "Wait. Defense counsel Barry Sheck is on his feet! He's objecting! We're going to have an argument!"

John: "You gotta love the shape Barry's in right now. He took some time off to rest up, and he's come back stronger than ever."

Joe: "Have you seen Barry with his shirt off? Wow."

Will sports and politics begin to merge? People used to complain about the politicization of the law. But look at what it has brought us: unapologetically biased juries, self-important law-making judges, and wild, rancorous confirmation hearings. In other words, trials of the century, Court TV, "Law & Order," John Grisham, and tons of money to spread around. Politics pays.

Now professional athletes appear to have an unusually strong preference for money. As soon as the jocks realize the profit potential of politics, Rush will fill the anchor chair permanently on "Sunday NFL Countdown" and political sports commentary will be routine. Let's end the unnecessary discontinuity between Sunday morning political talk shows and Sunday afternoon football talk shows. To wit:

Rush: "Welcome back. We'll start our halftime report with Paris Hilton on the sideline."
(Camera shows Paris Hilton for a few moments. Then back to the studio.)
Rush: "Ok, thank you, Paris. Now let's watch this highlight from the first half. It's second and long. Daunte Culpepper looks away from his tight end and throws it to the wide receiver. Did you see that? He refused to throw it to a white man, and instead favored a fellow black with the reception. I'm not saying Culpepper is racist. I'm just saying he's racially motivated to discriminate against white people."
Ralph Nader: "It's not about race, big guy. It's about conflict of interest. The wide receiver has a bonus clause for receptions; the tight end doesn't. Is Culpepper taking a payoff? Follow the money, Rusheroo!"
William F. Buckley: "If your only tool is a hammer, then every problem is the nail, eh, Ralphie? You are correct that this excrescence is about corruption, but not the corruption of a bribe. It's about the corrosive effect of the immiscible egalitarian jape that plagues this country. The tight end already received several passes. Culpepper's misguided sense of justice militated in favor of letting the leporine wideout find the

hemocoel of the defense and catch one, too. Culpepper's bankrupt Weltschmerz not only diminishes the Vikings, but also imperils the crucible of Western democracy itself."

Dan Dierdorf: "Um, before we go back to Paris, I'd just like to say I thought Culpepper made a pretty darn good throw right there."

Don't Play Pro Se

With golf's British Open having returned to famed Carnoustie, focus again returns us to poor Jean Van de Velde who, in perhaps the biggest mistake in sports history, lost a major championship that was his for the taking. Why did he lose it? Not because of poor golf swings or even poor judgment, as is commonly understood. No, Jean lost the Open because he failed to exercise his right to counsel in a timely manner. Yes, if only a lawyer instead of a caddie had carried Jean's clubs that day, the Claret Jug would have been his. Let's look at how, if the rules were otherwise and lawyers were permitted to accompany golfers on the world's links, Jean Van de Velde would be a major champion.

The Rules of Golf, which golf professionals are somehow expected to master along with driving, chipping, and putting, are about as understandable as the writ system. Playing a long shot from a deep sand bunker is a cakewalk compared to taking on the intricacies of Golf's Rule 27.[2] Had Jean had a lawyer by his side as he played the fateful 18th hole at Carnoustie, he might have won, despite his poor judgments and poor shot execution.

Recall the troubles. Our doomed Frenchman carried a com-

---

2. Rule 27 governs a ball lost or hit out of bounds, in addition to procedure for hitting a provisional ball. United States Golf Association. "Rule 27. Ball Lost or Out of Bounds; Provisional Ball." *USGA.org.* http://www.usga.org/playing/rules/books/index.html.

manding three-shot lead into the final hole of the Open. A simple par, a routine score for a professional, would mean the famed Claret Jug would be brimming with expensive Bordeaux within the hour. But even a one-over-par bogey or a double bogey, the mode score of hackers everywhere, brings the Jug to France. Now, ending with a double bogey is not winning in the classic style, to be sure, but who cares about convention? An offhand wave of the Gauloise accompanied by an insouciant smile, *c'est la vie*, and that double bogey is forgotten forever.

But Jean wants it all, he wants to arrive in fashion, so on 18 he uses too much club on the drive, his first shot. Of course, Jean hits his drive errantly (a lesson there for us all), but he's lucky! His ball somehow lands and stops on a small isthmus of land surrounded by a ball-swallowing stream, the Barry Burn, well off the fairway, but safe and dry, the ball lying perfectly on a flat patch of groomed and mowed grass. Of course, now we understand that Sartre was right, *il fait necessaire*, it must be. There is no reason for that patch of land to be groomed and mowed and flat but to catch and coddle Jean Van de Velde's stray shot at this moment in time. Jean would win the Open no matter how much we mere mortals tried to interfere.

Certainly, Jean must have understood all of this. How else to explain his next shot? Jean decides to use a long iron[3]—for most players, the most difficult club in the bag—to carry the ball over the same burn, which circles back over the fairway about 200 yards away, with the idea of rolling his ball onto the green in regulation. A successful negotiation of the burn at this point all but seals the

---

3. Irons numbered 1 through 4 are typically considered the long irons. These clubs have a small degree of loft which makes them useful from longer distances; however, the low loft also makes the clubs more difficult to hit. Most players opt to hit a fairway wood or hybrid due to their higher loft making them easier to hit. "Golf Club (Equipment)." 20 August 2007. *Wikipedia.org.* http://en.wikipedia.org/wiki/Golf_club_%28equipment%29.

victory, as most players, from skilled pros to overweight cart-riders, can two-putt on most greens at most times. But as golf history will forever record, Jean tempted fate once too often. His shot did fly over the burn, but veered to the right at the end, and in an abrupt reversal of luck, struck a grandstand rail and bounced sharply backward, toward the burbling burn, bouncing off a rock and ending up in the long hay grass and gorse that passes for rough on Open courses. Now in a hopelessly impossible situation, Jean stumbled his way to a triple-bogey seven, ending up in a three-way tie playoff that he was unmistakably scheduled to lose.

What Jean should have done is this: moments after his second shot caromed off the grandstand and into the tall grass, Jean should have handed his two-iron back to his caddie. He should then have planted his feet square to the target line and made a full shoulder turn to his left to consult his golf lawyer, who would have by now researched and prepared a legal opinion on how to proceed under the Rules of Golf. The golf lawyer — or GL, as they will one day be called — would have told Jean to try it again.

That's right, Jean, drop another ball and try to hit it straight this time. What the rules of golf call a "provisional," though in the hands of a skillful lawyer really amounts to a free do-over, universally known as a "mulligan." Had Jean's provisional shot been correctly struck and ended up on the green, the GL would have told Jean to hurry to his provisional ball and two-putt to a victory.

Could it be true? Do the Rules of Golf, that long and picky list of do's and don't's issued jointly by the most stuffy of ruling bodies, the U.S. Golf Association and the Order of the Royal and Ancient, really allow for a good old mulligan on the last hole of a major championship, just like you get on the first hole every Saturday morning? You bet. It's a bit complicated, but that's why we pay lawyers.

Our path to a free mulligan begins with Rule 27, pertaining to lost and provisional balls. A ball is "lost," according to the rule, when, well, it's lost. No one can find it within five minutes. Under

the same rule, a ball is also "lost" when the player puts another ball
into play, even if the original ball is not lost in the first sense. So even
if the original ball is sitting in the middle of the fairway, if a player
drops another ball and hits it, without declaring it to be a provisional
ball, then the first ball is lost, and the provisional ball is now the
ball in play—albeit lying there after a one stroke penalty for a lost
ball. None of this would have helped poor Jean, who on the advice of his GL, would clearly have declared his mulligan to be a
provisional ball before dropping it at the spot from which his original shot, the second shot on 18, was struck.

But Rule 27 doesn't stop there. For some reason, a third definition of "lost ball" is provided, and here's the one on which Jean's
golf lawyer would have rested his finger in explaining matters to
perplexed officials as Jean hoisted the Jug. Strangely, under Rule
27 an original ball is deemed lost whenever a player plays his provisional ball from the place where the original ball is likely to be
lost or from a point nearer the hole than that place. So as soon as
Jean smoothly strokes his provisional ball for the second time (after,
presumably, it has come to rest on the green, which is a point nearer
to the hole than the place where his original ball is presumed lost),
then at that moment Jean's original ball, snuggled in an unspeak-
ably long rough, is lost—even if thousands of spectators are looking at it, Bob Rosburg is assessing the merits of its lie for the
television audience, and Curtis Strange is calling Jean stupid for
hitting it there. Jean putts his provisional ball for his fifth shot (after
taking his one-shot penalty), taps in for the double bogey, hugs his
gleeful wife, and prepares his gracious acceptance speech.

Sound implausible? As they say in golf, it will work. A player
may play a provisional ball as long as the ball may be lost outside
a water hazard. The player's belief on this point must be a reasonable one, according to the USGA's "Decisions on the Rules of Golf,"
which provide what purport to be authoritative interpretations of
the rules. These numerous decisions resolve dilemmas involving
balls being stolen by animals, balls hit by thrown clubs, and all
other sorts of wild mayhem and improbable luck that might happen

on our otherwise sedate golf landscapes. With Jean's ball lying in the tall grass, his decision to declare and play a provisional would seem reasonable.

So Jean drops and hits his provisional shot. If the provisional shot was well-struck, Jean could proceed to play it, forgetting about his original ball. If the provisional was as bad as the original, then Jean could simply have abandoned his provisional and played the original, no harm done. Wait, the weekend player might say, this isn't just a mulligan, it's the coveted "Murphy," one better than a mulligan, because Jean can actually hit two balls and pick the better. That's right. Jean had a chance to try the shot again with impunity. Indeed, in interviews after the tournament, Jean said that, for him, a long-iron shot from the perfect lie where his drive ended up was actually an easy shot. Jean's claim was probably correct, given that the young Scot, Paul Lawrie, the eventual winner, attempted successfully a very similar shot about one hour later in the playoff, and he did so holding but a one-stroke lead. So we have good reason to conclude that Jean's second try would have sailed true, and Jean would have had an easy choice to make.

Could Jean really have putted out a provisional ball? Decision 27-2b/1 of the USGA discusses in question-and-answer format a player continuing to play his provisional ball without searching for his original ball. Here's the question, which of course is on the lips of every golfer whenever the provisional stroke turns out far better than the original:

Q: At a par-3 hole, a player hits his tee shot into dense woods. He then hits a provisional ball which comes to rest near the hole. In view of the position of the provisional ball, the player does not wish to find his original ball. He does not search for it and walks directly towards his provisional ball to continue play with it. His opponent (or fellow competitor) believes it would be beneficial to him if the original ball were found. May the opponent (or fellow competitor) search for five minutes for the player's ball?

A: Yes, provided that in the meantime the player does not play a stroke with the provisional ball, it being nearer the hole than the place where the original ball is likely to be. The player is entitled to play such a stroke. If he does, the original ball is lost under Rule 27-2b and further search for it would serve no purpose.

You see, it's a race. Jean hits his provisional shot, the ball rolls onto the green, and then, acting under legal advice, Jean moves quickly to the green. Heck, it's the Open! Run, Jean, run! As long as Jean plays his next shot before his first ball is found by his fellow competitor, forecaddie, or some official, then his provisional becomes his ball in play and his original ball is lost.

Indeed the rules are even more specific. Even if Jean's ball is found, Jean may still stubbornly proceed to his provisional and play it, as long as he has not actually been told that his original ball was found. Look at Decision 27-2c/2, "Original Ball Found: Player Wishes to Ignore It and Continue Play with Provisional Ball":

Q: At a par-3 hole, a player hits his tee shot into a heavy thicket and, since his ball may be lost, he hits a provisional ball, which comes to rest near the hole. In the circumstances, it is advantageous to the player not to find his original ball, in which case the provisional ball would become the ball in play. Accordingly the player does not search for the original ball; he walks directly towards his provisional ball. While the player is on his way to his provisional ball, his original ball is found by a member of the Committee, a forecaddie, his opponent, or a fellow-competitor. The player is advised that his original ball has been found. May the player ignore the original ball and continue play with the provisional ball?

A: No. The player must inspect the ball which has been found and, if it is the player's original ball, he must continue play with it (or proceed under the unplayable ball Rule). The provisional ball must be abandoned.

So putting these two decisions together, as long as the player has not "been advised that his original ball has been found," he may dash forward and hit the provisional ball for his next shot. Once he plays the shot, the original ball is lost no matter who finds it and when. Jean's golf lawyer could have helped here too, engaging meddlesome officials and rerouting troublesome forecaddies who might want to help Jean find his original ball while Jean quickly lined up his approach putt.

And why not? This is the British Open, for goodness sake. Tiger Woods once had a two-foot high boulder carried out of his way, with the assistance of spectators, as a "loose impediment" and that was a comparatively meaningless PGA tour stop. Why shouldn't Jean use the Rules of Golf just as aggressively? The only "violation" of the rules Jean would have committed by quickly hitting his provisional ball again is playing out of turn, which under stroke play competition results in no penalty at all.

Check out this delicious variation. What if Jean's provisional ball had rolled into the cup? As his GL, I'd advise him to sprint to the green. Surely he'd be faster than the rotund Craig Parry, his playing partner for the day. Consider Decision 27-2b/2:

Q: At a short hole, A's tee shot may be out of bounds or lost, so he plays a provisional ball, which he holes. A does not wish to look for his original ball. B, A's opponent or fellow-competitor, goes to look for the original ball. When does the provisional ball become the ball in play?

A: The provisional ball becomes the ball in play as soon as A picks it out of the hole, provided his original ball has not already been found in bounds within five minutes of B starting to search for it.

And they say golf is not a sport! This decision could have restated more realistically as follows: the moment A's provisional ball falls into the cup, A and B take off like mad-men down the fairway. B dons his golf gloves and dives headfirst into the thicket, hoping to find A's original ball at first look. For his part, A, having trained for speed, sprints to the green, coming to a sliding stop right at the hole. He plucks his provisional ball from the hole and holds it aloft moments before B screams out, "I found it!" And A records a routine par 3.

Jean had the championship right there in front of him. Not on the 18th green, but in Rule 27. What could officials have said had Jean played a provisional and then hit it again? The Rules and Decisions of Golf actually permit a Murphy; a chance to hit the shot again and then decide, after seeing how good the second try was, whether to play the original ball or the provisional. Nothing would have prevented Jean from playing the provisional with the one-stroke penalty—a trade Jean would have been delighted to make, given the fate of his original shot.

Poor Van de Velde. One day, in a better world, professional golfers won't have to face the perplexities of the Rules of Golf without adequate legal counsel. Until that day comes, pro golfers, like victims everywhere, will have to suffer the injustices meted out by unseen tyrants. *C'est la guerre, Jean, c'est la guerre.*

How a Lawyer Plays Golf

I'm not a bad golfer, so frequently my fellow lawyers will ask me how to play the game. Most golfing lawyers, when asked for such advice, do little more than hand the eager novice a copy of the United States Golf Association's Rules of Golf (and Decisions on the Rules of Golf). This is like tossing a client who needs tax advice a copy of the Internal Revenue Code. I for one prefer to practice golf law with a little more care. In my experience, a newcomer who has been clued in by some sage hand to the critical Rules of Golf (and Decisions on the Rules of Golf) is already halfway to the putting green. So here goes.

The first thing you need is a set of clubs. Bring your clubs with you to the golf course. Be very careful not to spit on them, or else you will be immediately disqualified. *See* USGA Decision 4-2 (Applying Saliva to Face of Club). Then buy some golf balls. Don't spit on them either. Decision 5-2 (Foreign Material on Ball). Spitting is not allowed in golf. If you prefer to spit, try baseball.

Carrying your (dry) clubs and balls, head out to the first tee. Swing the club and hit the ball. Then look at the club. If the ball is stuck to the face of the club, peel the ball off and drop it at the spot where the ball first stuck to the club. Take a two-stroke penalty. Rule 1-4 (Ball Adhering to Club Face After Stroke). If you're lucky and the ball does not stick to the face of the club, then it must be in the air heading ... somewhere. Watch it carefully. If your ball flies in the direction of another golfer who is in the middle of swinging his club, and that other golfer's swing hits not only his ball, but your ball too, and he knocks your ball out of bounds or into some dense thicket, then you have to take a one-stroke penalty and hit the ball again off the tee. Decision 19-1/2 (Player's Ball Deflected by Stroke of Player in Another Group). So don't hit your ball if some other duffer within range is about to hit his ball. After he's finished, you may hit at him without penalty.

This being the first hole, it is likely that your tee shot was errant, and ended up either in or next to the nearby clubhouse. The clubhouse now interferes with your next shot. Although you've paid good money to play this game, the Rules of Golf would penalize you two strokes if you moved the clubhouse out of the way. Rule 24-2 (Clubhouse an Immovable Obstruction; Two-Stroke Penalty for Moving It). It goes without saying that hitting a golf ball from within or around the clubhouse would needlessly endanger the well-being of innocent people. Lives should never be put at risk for a silly diversion like golf. Instead, the proper procedure is to open the clubhouse window first. Decision 24-2b/14 (Window of Clubhouse Opened and Ball Played Through Window). When playing full shots from inside the clubhouse through open windows, remember to keep your left wrist stiff through the impact zone. Experience has taught me that shots played off clubhouse carpets tend to hook. I also advise you to yell "fore" immediately after you strike the ball, so that someone coming down the hall from the grillroom does not interfere with the line of flight of your shot.

Now that you've escaped the clubhouse, go find your ball. Many times, it will be lying in the fork of a tree. Climb the tree to take your stance. Plant your feet on the weaker branch to take advantage of the "trampoline" effect, which will give your shot extra distance. You'll notice that when you stand on the weaker branch, the branch will sag, having the effect of moving your ball closer to the ground. That is permissible; no penalty incurred because even though your ball has moved closer to the earth, it hasn't moved around in the tree. Movement of the golf ball is measured in trees. Decision 18/3 (Ball in Fork of Tree Moves in Relation to Ground But Not in Relation to Fork; No Penalty). Now go ahead and play your shot, remembering to turn your shoulders fully with a complete follow-through.

But first check for litter. Sadly, sometimes trash will be left on our beautiful golf landscapes. Before hitting the ball, always examine the litter carefully to make sure that there are no plastic bags. It is essential not to hit your ball into a plastic bag. If the wind blows the bag with your ball in it, thus moving your ball, you have a real problem: Did the wind move the bag, thus moving the ball, or did the bag, which was being moved by the wind, move the ball? How did you do in your college philosophy class? If the wind moved the ball, drop the ball where the bag lies now; if the bag moved the ball, drop the ball where the bag lay initially. Decision 18-1/7 (Ball in Plastic Bag Moves When Bag Blown to New Position by Wind). If you get this problem wrong, take a one-stroke penalty. My stern advice is to never hit your ball into a plastic bag. Most of the top teaching pros emphasize the same point.

Newbies, who can be unduly pessimistic, often ask me what happens when they swing at the ball and miss. Nothing happens. You missed. Oh, and as far as your score goes, the swing doesn't count. Many accomplished players, even professionals, misunderstand this basic rule. If you intended to hit the ball and missed, then, sure, you must add one to your score. (I believe some USGA rule says that somewhere). But who can say what intent lies hidden in the secret recesses of the human heart? Lawyers know that the best evidence of a person's intent is his actual conduct. The fact that your swing actually missed the ball provides compelling evidence that you intended to miss. Even if you started your swing with the intention to hit your ball, you can change your intent at any time. Decision 14/1.5 (Intent to Strike Ball Ceases During Downswing; Club Not Stopped But Path of Clubhead Altered to Avoid Striking Ball). This is the best rule in all of golf. Personally, despite declaring my intention before I swing to strike the ball (my playing partners frequently ask me for such a declaration, for some reason), I often change my mind at the very last moment as the head of my club speeds down toward the ball. Golf is not a game that puts a premium on decisiveness, nor should it be. Instead, thoughtful, relaxed deliberation over one's next shot is a traditional and enjoyable part of the sport. For many golfing lawyers, that agonizing contemplation continues right up to the moment just before the clubhead strikes the ball. "Should I strike this ball or not?," we ask ourselves repeatedly. Don't decide too hastily.

By about now your ball should be on the putting green.[4] It's been a rough first hole. Nonetheless you must control your temper. Do not, when you pick up your ball and throw it into a lake, claim that the ball sucks. That's a two-stroke penalty. Decision 5-3/3.5 (Player Lifts Ball on Putting Green, Throws Ball Into Lake and Then Announces That Ball Is Unfit for Play; Two-Stroke Penalty).[5] So hit

---

4. Unless, of course, some practical joker has moved the flagstick to the wrong green. When this happens, you get no relief and are left on your own to redirect your ball back to the correct green. Decision 1-4/3 (Flagstick Stuck Into Green Some Distance From Hole by Practical Joker). You can't even use a compass. Decision 14-3/4 (Use of Compass to Find Hole Prohibited). Although I know many will differ, in my opinion this particular "practical joke" should not be tolerated, and is ruining our wonderful game. Please, for the good of us all, never include a practical joker in your foursome.

5. I have also recently received many questions from beginning golfers about vegetable gardens being planted on putting greens. These are hard times, I answer, and groundskeepers must do what they can to provide. If you are hungry, you may, of course, pick the vegetables—unless they

your putt toward the hole, using a steady stroke with minimal wrist action. Typically the ball will come close to going in, and then stop—tantalizingly—at the very edge of the hole. What is the correct procedure now? The usual response of most golfers is to throw their putters at the ball. There is no penalty for doing this, naturally, as this is just human instinct. Decision 1-2/4.5 (Player Leaves Putt Short and Instinctively Throws Putter at Ball; No Penalty). But here's a twist: It will surprise many readers to learn that if the thrown putter actually hits the ball, then the golfer must record a penalty stroke. I will admit that many times I have hit the ball with my thrown putter (I have good aim), but have failed to add the requisite stroke. I'm sure others will have similar confessions to share.

But lawyers will ask me: With the ball teetering on the hole's edge, may the golfer jump up and down, thereby causing the tectonic plates beneath the earth's surface to shift, thus inducing the golf ball to fall into the hole? Of course not. Decision 1-2/4 (Player Jumps Close to Hole to Jar the Earth and Cause Ball to Drop). Not only would this be cheating, but millions could die from the tidal wave you would release on China. The proper procedure with the ball at the edge of the cup is to cast your shadow over the ball. By blocking the sun, the planetary wonder that sustains all forms of life, eventually you will cause the grass to wilt beneath the ball, which will then tumble towards the hole. The USGA has given its approval to this procedure. Decision 16-2/3 (Casting Shadow on Ball Overhanging Hole to Cause Ball to Fall Into Hole Permitted).

I realize that some purists have been complaining about slow play caused by golfer-lawyers casting their deadly shadows on the grass. I say, let them wait. You'll save par.

---

are mushrooms. Mushrooms have a sacred status to golfers and may not be touched without penalty. Decision 16-1a/15 (Mushroom Growing on Line of Putt Cannot Be Picked).

Chapter Ten

Vice Law

Left to their own devices, athletes will use drugs that enhance their performance. If tomorrow Major League Baseball or some other professional league eliminated its prohibition, most serious athletes would rush to their doctors for prescriptions to improve their physical ability to play their sport. Why not? The risks of most of the drugs in question, such as steroids, hormone therapies, and the like, although potentially serious, appear manageable, especially if administered under the care of a physician. Plenty of people willingly use illegal drugs that carry greater health risks and lack socially redeeming benefits. With respect to steroids and the like, the socially redeeming benefits are obvious: players who perform better draw more fan interest. They also earn substantial salary increases. Athletes get compensated for performance enhancement, thus providing an unmistakable incentive for them to use any permissible means to achieve it.

It is not necessary to argue that athletes are particularly "risk-preferring" or indifferent as to their future health to conclude that they would likely take advantage of all permissible substances. Wouldn't many of us take some health risks in exchange for fantastic financial and career success? People take health risks for all kinds of comparatively trivial benefits, if only driving too fast to make it home in time for the big game. If assured by a competent doctor that the drug could be administered with minimal and controllable side effects, a needle or a pill seems an easy way to get ahead. Unlike in most occupations, compensation for athletes is allocated exclusively to very few people, the few who survive the lifetime

competition. Fewer than 400 basketball players are on NBA rosters, for instance. In a winner-take-all tournament, the incentive to
use every means available to win is pronounced.

The same "winner-takes-all" incentives lead sports figures to
adopt other means to get ahead. Thus, the bans on steroids and
other performance enhancers is not the only prohibition the leagues
or associations impose on athletes. Also prohibited are various activities that might give rise to an improper advantage in the contest. The line between improper advantage-taking and the
permissible utilization of superior playing or coaching acumen can
be difficult to find, as we shall see.

For better or worse, the desire of sports leagues to regulate the
"vice" of their players and employees extends to conduct that has
little, if anything, to do with the actual competitive activity of the
game itself. Sports sells ideas, in part, and the idea that the owners wish to bring to market does not include athletes who conduct
themselves in criminal or immoral ways. As a result, criminal conduct that violates the various "morals" clauses commonly found in
standard player contracts[1] or in league constitutions[2] is prohibited.
Nonetheless, players will on occasion violate these prohibitions,
often enough to attract the attention of the public. League commissioners have to step in to enforce their rules. When they do,
they act with large discretion. How should they exercise it?

---

1. In the Major League Baseball Uniform Player's Contract, the club has
a termination right if the player "neglects to conform his personal conduct to the standards of good citizenship and good sportsmanship." The
player also pledges to "conform to high standards of personal conduct."
2. The NFL's recently revised "Personal Conduct Policy" prohibits players from undermining or putting at risk "the integrity and reputation of
the NFL."

Performance Enhancement Needed

I once saw Roger Clemens pitch in Fenway Park. He was a rookie for the Red Sox and got hit pretty hard, but it was obvious that he had tremendous natural talent and was not afraid. And he was big: not weight-room "built" big, but a rawboned, strapping body that seemed to this New England boy just the kind of pitcher a rugged Texas upbringing would produce. The years passed and Clemens moved through the league in search of his payday. Unlike many Boston fans, I never begrudge an athlete his contracts. There are millions at stake and the professional career, a product of years of great effort and training, is so short. But for Clemens it hasn't been short, and he remains among the top echelon of major league pitchers despite being well into his forties. The big body has remained too, although long ago the rawboned, supple strength of youth has been replaced with what is simply bulk; bulk in the legs and hips and across the chest. Bulk that speaks of a career spent building muscle for strength and adding size for endurance. Bulk that also suggests illegal supplements.

It is a mistake to point to the body change as convincing evidence of the use of illegal performance enhancements. Most of us in our forties have traded the natural limber and musculature of youth for quite a bit of added breadth. Something more is needed, and apparently more has been provided, if the report that Senator Mitchell read to an enthralled America is true.

Mitchell's committee report has been widely attacked for lacking better evidence in support of its claims. But the committee lacked any formal authority to compel answers to questions. It also lacked subpoena power, which means it could not even order anyone to show up at one of its meetings. Players were "interviewed" by the committee only if they agreed to the interview, and even then could choose which questions to answer and how. Of course few players bothered to show up.

The commissioner's office could have given this committee some real punch: Bud Selig could have ordered all players to comply with the committee's orders and to answer all questions. He could have invoked the powers of his office, which are broad and include discretionary authority to protect the "integrity of the game," and imposed suspensions on all players, coaches, staff or front office executives whom he deemed less than fully forthcoming. Selig could have tested the limits of his authority, fought the union, and found out who exactly used what and when, or lost his office trying. Instead, Selig gave Mitchell complete independence, and bragged about it, as if complete independence were strong medicine. Complete independence is needed when the overseer, here Selig, is himself potentially complicit. To think the Commissioner was actively involved in this drug distribution scheme is absurd. This committee didn't need independence; it needed Bud Selig. The problem shouldn't have been foisted off onto a committee in the first place.

But it was, and the report bears comment. First, Senator Mitchell repeatedly admonished the Commissioner and baseball's fans to "look forward," and not back to baseball's immediate past. This statement was both naive and wrong. It's naive because this search for truth is meaningful to everybody: it involves recent events, salient players, and a subject that matters to many sports fans. The Mitchell report, which relies a lot on non-testing evidence, only begins this search; the report's broad claims about a past "steroid era" hardly satisfies legitimate curiosity. The report's admonition is also wrong: you don't tell someone shocked by bad news your prescription for preventing recurrences. The aim of the report was to expose the past, not make it irrelevant. The better advice is to ignore the report's prescriptions, most of which are described in general terms and are subject to collective bargaining. The focus of our attention should be on baseball's immediate past.

The report also names a lot of players; presumably many more are involved. At some point the law of diminishing returns kicks in and we no longer care. (Is Barry Bonds all that bad of a guy now that we know how widespread was the abuse?) What comes to mind is Jose Canseco's book.[3] Clearly Canseco's public image has moved from pariah to prophet. Canseco, who by his own claim more or less introduced supplements to major league baseball, casually suggested eighty percent of players used. Mitchell insisted in his press conference that the abusers were "a minority" of players; what if Canseco (again) is proved correct? What if entire teams had rosters nearly full of players using enhancements? We can be pretty sure as we sit here today that entire competitions in some sports, such as track and field, were heavily populated with dopers. Were the events less enjoyable? Are we fans of competition, or fans of "drug-free" competition? Baseball's huge popularity in the midst of widespread knowledge of baseball's steroid culture does call into question the basis for legal (and private) prohibitions of performance enhancers. There is some evidence that, in mature adults, human growth hormone is a medically safe treatment that promotes healthy living. If that proves true, look for baseball's rules to change.

Finally, many commentators have expressed concern with the report's reliance on "non-analytical positives," instead of drug-testing results. Such non-testing evidence includes matters that the law would describe as "hearsay" and "circumstantial," and that in total sum amounts to a quantum of proof that would be less than compelling in a court of law. But so what? This is not a court of law; the Mitchell report is essentially an act of journalism, a public statement in the form of a grand press release. Hearsay is considered and relied on in virtually all walks of life. (What is the media, except a large dose of hearsay?) The Mitchell report's evidence is some proof: not enough to satisfy the "beyond a reasonable doubt" standard of a criminal case, but still proof. It's worth something. It would not be enough for a criminal conviction. But the Commissioner's office, in meting out discipline, is not required to adhere to that most stringent standard. Selig may impose sanctions at his discretion.

---

3. Jose Canseco, Juiced (2005).

One correction to the common wisdom: all this talk about "hearsay" in the Mitchell report is incorrect. Most of the evidence in the report is not hearsay. When a player asks a trainer to order him some steroids, the player's statement is not hearsay. (It is a party admission specifically exempted from the definition of hearsay.) When a player writes a check for steroid purchases, the cleared check is not hearsay (it's a business record, assuming a foundation could be laid, which would be easy). When a trainer states to Senator Mitchell that, some years ago, he supplied or injected a player with drugs, it's not hearsay (the statement is made to the investigator, not "out-of-court," so to speak; in any event, it's also that of a co-conspirator, and thus is exempted from the definition of hearsay). Little of this report is hearsay; for the most part, the report consists of valid evidence. The only question about the report is whether or not the (valid) evidence it gathers is sufficient to conclude the named player actually used illicit enhancements. It's a question of the weight of the evidence, not its validity.

Drug Testing Addiction

Is it inappropriate for athletes, even at the professional stage, to use drugs, even legal ones, to improve their body conditioning and athletic performance? That's a great question, and one that the professional leagues and players' unions have answered in the affirmative. Parties to a collective bargaining agreement can agree to pretty much anything they want. But let's be realistic; there's a lot of pressure on players right now to agree to drug prohibitions.

A big part, maybe the essential part, of the anti-doping regime is drug testing. The extent and mechanics of drug testing vary by sport. Drug testing can include in-season and out-of-season testing. It sometimes includes the need for athletes to register their whereabouts at all times. It includes surprise tests at random moments during a player's day, even away from the sports arena. And by the way, drug testing constitutes a pretty severe intrusion into one's privacy, at least if you consider having another person staring at you while you relieve yourself to be a bit uncomfortable. Again, at least with the professional leagues, all this is a matter for collective bargaining.

But here's the rub: call it freedom of contract if you like, but the unmistakable trend in drug testing agreements is that the leagues will test for so-called "street" drugs such as cocaine or marijuana at the same time they test for steroids and the like. Why does the decision to rid the games of performance enhancers necessarily include testing for marijuana? Should it? What is going on with all this drug testing?

First, be careful with the glib response that refers to the labor agreements and freedom of contract. I know the players make a ton of money and get compensated handsomely for any concessions they make. I'm not infantalizing these people. Yet they are under enormous public and governmental pressure to accede to these particular demands. Despite collective bargaining, some of these testing standards have been more or less imposed by league commissioners, with players importuned to acquiesce. Even when the unions agree to drug testing, not all individual players consent. Remember that unions are the embodiment of an antitrust violation. The only reason unions get to impose such conditions on its members, even those who are in fact unwilling to agree, is that labor enjoys the non-statutory exemption from the antitrust law. I'm not saying that labor issues shouldn't be exempted from antitrust scrutiny; my point is that the claim that the tested player "agreed" to be tested depends on a rather forced understanding of the term "consent."

Note also that some of the pressure on leagues to adopt drug testing is implicit; lawmakers and opinion-makers have looked at the comparatively stringent drug testing rules of the World Anti-Doping Agency (WADA), founded in 2004, whose rules govern Olympic sports, and wondered why those rules shouldn't serve as the template for professional-league rules. Should we use the WADA rules? Remember, Olympic athletes aren't unionized, so they have no negotiating opportunity to limit or even refuse the WADA rules. If Olympic athletes don't like the WADA rules, their sole option is simply to walk away from their sport. Yet the WADA rules, not a product of collective bargaining, have become the gold standard for sports where drug testing, like other conditions of employment, is subject to the collective bargaining process.

These drug tests are conducted for the sake of ensuring a level playing field, by which metaphor is meant that athletes are limited, as far as their bodies go, to natural endowments and non-pharmacological improvements. How did coke and pot get into the mix, so to speak? Neither one improves athletic performance, nor do the leagues claim as much. They probably inhibit performance. Professional athletes have huge financial incentives not to inhibit their performance. It seems doubtful that we need to test for these street drugs to make sure athletes are not doing something they have every incentive not to do already. The leagues appear to test for drugs that do not threaten to tilt the playing field.

On the other hand, it could be thought that the leagues' testing for street drugs helps to ensure the integrity of game competition by making sure all players are at their best. We can't have the running back, high on crack, taking off in the wrong direction. But has this ever happened? Did Doc Gooden or Darryl Strawberry or Steve Howe, all baseball players with notorious drug addictions, ever take the field high? Even assuming it has happened, should there be some requirement that the leagues (or the federal government, which after all lies right behind all of this) demonstrate that we have a problem of some magnitude and scope before we foist mandatory testing on all of the players? Again, the players have obvious financial and team incentives not to impair themselves.

All of this, of course, comes with penalties attached. In the WADA setup, the penalties are mandatory and severe. Again, for substances that give athletes an unfair advantage in the contest, arguably stiff penalties are necessary to deter cheating. But smoking marijuana days before a big event isn't cheating. I'd rather compete against a bunch of pot smokers. (Indeed, I think I did, when competing for grades in college.) Why have swift and severe penalties for a detection of marijuana use when no one gains an advantage? Aren't we living in a day where lots of countries and states are further reducing penalties for personal marijuana use, where it's even punished at all? WADA is supposed to be in the business of chasing down steroid cheats, so why should it be giving attention (and money and focus) to these street drugs?

The sports organizations defend their decision to test for street drugs primarily on a rationale other than cheating. Sports sells both products and ideas, and the leagues want to make sure nothing happens in the second category that impairs the first. Players who use illegal recreational drugs (or at least are caught) give the team and league a bad image, and bad images give the kids bad ideas and slow down the money-making for the league.

This argument, although valid, proves too much. Many professional athletes engage in bad behavior, much worse than recreational drug use, that gets disclosed publicly, yet the public seems unfazed. Kobe Bryant jerseys are the league's best-sellers, and he suffered an (unproven, but never recanted) allegation of forcible rape. (By the way, Bryant was allowed to play without interruption during the entire episode.) So the leagues' need to protect their image often goes overlooked. In addition, a lot of us are role models for younger people, probably all of us at times. Should that be a sufficient legal basis to test people? Usually courts want to see that there is some need, in terms of safety or risk to job integrity, before they'll uphold mandatory drug testing, in cases of public employees. Yes, these are not public employees. But if the government is lurking in the shadows with threats of legally imposed testing standards and drug penalties, shouldn't these private rules be subject to legal requirements?

We have to be careful with WADA-style standards. Under WADA's rules, liability is "strict" and immediate suspension is mandatory, which means if it's in you (and it's not Gatorade) you're in trouble. No excuses, no explanations, no mitigation (although the arbitration panel can reduce but not eliminate the suspension if the drug use was unintentional). What if the athlete drinks from the wrong water bottle? What if a player's food is sprinkled, by an enemy, with a banned substance? Never happen? At the Sydney Olympics, a young gymnast was stripped of her gold medal for taking two teaspoons of an over-the-counter drug for her cold. For pro athletes, strict liability coupled with mandatory suspensions could mean huge financial penalties. Do we really need this response to an athlete caught smoking pot in the off-season?

It's also been said that the leagues need to keep athletes off of street drugs so that they don't get beholden to drug dealers and end up purposely losing games to pay them off. Again, has this actually happened? Is there a genuine problem we're addressing here? Drug dealers are in competition, if only with each other. A (rational) drug user could purchase elsewhere if his dealer tried to extract higher prices from him in the form of game fixing. Plus, why would an athlete trade his career (should he be caught game-fixing) for drug fixes? One thing professionals have is cash. They can use it to buy their drugs.

In case you missed this point, the WADA rules are strict: mandatory drug testing, swift sanctions, little process. One of these years, a U.S. city will again be selected to host the Olympic Games. Will a United States court find that WADA's approach is consistent with federal constitutional requirements? Could WADA treat a U.S. citizen this way? This will be an interesting question, to say the least.

The Investigative Power of the Federal Government

Lurking in the shadows behind the Mitchell Report and the BALCO investigation lies an issue that may one day prove to be of more lasting, if less notorious, impact. It may also teach all of us a memorable civics lesson in the power of the federal government.

The federal grand jury investigating the BALCO steroid distribution scheme and the ten or so professional baseball players who apparently received steroids from BALCO has become interested in the results of Major League Baseball's initial drug tests of its players. The tests were conducted to determine the degree to which steroid use in baseball had spread, in order to trigger further drug testing and sanctions. The players were promised confidentiality in the test results. Apparently about 100 players tested positive. The players' identities and test data were held in secret by several drug testing labs.

A federal grand jury is practically speaking the investigative arm of the federal prosecutor. The prosecutor can ask the grand jury to issue subpoenas that command private citizens to produce documents or other evidence, including testimony. Alternatively, the prosecutor may investigate crime by seeking a search warrant from a federal magistrate to permit police officers to conduct a forcible search to locate the desired evidence. Although non-binding prosecutorial guidelines may inform the prosecutor's decision on whether to proceed by subpoena or search, as a legal matter the prosecutor's decision lies within the prosecutor's discretion.

The federal prosecutor in the BALCO investigation ultimately chose to use the forcible approach. Federal agents, acting pursuant to a search warrant, seized from the testing labs computer files that revealed, once juxtaposed with a master code list, the identities of the 100 or so MLB players who tested positive for steroids. A decision of the Ninth Circuit U.S. Court of Appeals upheld the government's seizure of this computer file, generating brief national news. The court's decision was attacked by the Players' Association and by numerous commentators.

But the United States of America did not do wrong, at least not in the eyes of the law. People can promise each other all kinds of secrecy and confidentiality, but very, very few of those promises can withstand a federal subpoena or search warrant. That's the law today and has been the law for a long time. So the authors of the

Game of Shadows[4] can promise confidentiality to the person who leaked the grand jury testimony, or MLB can promise confidentiality to the players about drug test results, or you or I can commit our innermost thoughts to the privacy of a personal diary, but if a prosecutor wants to find out the reporter's sources or the results of a drug test or the entries in my diary, the prosecutor can. Private promises don't matter, not in the face of a federal criminal investigation. The MLB players seem to have a few lawyers hanging around. Surely the players knew, or should have known, when they agreed to the 2003 tests that a federal subpoena could easily shatter their expectations of privacy. In the wake of Jose Canseco's book and the disturbing Congressional hearing where MLB stars talked their way around admissions of guilt, the players undoubtedly felt compelled to compromise. This was the deal they made.

The Ninth Circuit decision also upheld the Players' Association claim of "standing," which refers to the association's legal right to contest the legality of the seizure. This aspect of the decision seems wrong. The court's premise was that the association had standing because the individual players had standing to contest the use and discovery of the drug testing information that came from their urine. Not free from doubt, but the better answer is that people don't enjoy any privacy interest in their urine once the urine is passed. It's no longer part of our body, and whether the urine is deposited in a cup or in the mystery place deep within the earth to which toilet drains lead, it's gone. The fact that the urine is tested, consensually by the way, probably means that the former owner (the urinator) has given up any plausible claim that he might have to the test results. Admittedly this is a highly debatable point and maybe goes too far, but the answer is that, nearly without exception, the federal courts have been willing to go "this far" for quite some time. Basically if we voluntarily give up something we own,

---

4. Mark Fainaru-Wada and Lance Williams, Game of Shadows: Barry Bonds, BALCO, and the Steroids Scandal that Rocked Professional Sports (2006).

we coincidentally give up our right to claim ownership in it. (As your lawyer, I advise you to hold it as long as you can.)

The key point to the case is that the government officers, when searching for evidence respecting the ten baseball players named in the warrant, came across a computer file with a whole list of test results, including many players other than the ten, and just seized the whole file, with the expectation that it will pore through the file back at the office. It's not a big deal, because the government could have looked through every data entry on this file at the office of the searched party to determine which fit the warrant. The government temporarily seized the file (actually a copy of it) to allow it to search more deliberately back at the station. The appellate court ordered this "offsite" search to be conducted under the oversight of a federal magistrate, who by the way are very capable judges. All non-conforming data was to be returned to its owner (the lab, not the players).

The officers were allowed to review all the test results to determine which matched the materials requested in the search warrant. As they did so, they were entitled to seize any evidence in "plain view." Plain view does not permit a search, but it does permit a seizure of any document or thing that constitutes the fruits, instrumentalities or evidence of a crime, as long as that criminality is immediately apparent on viewing the document. Well, any document that says, in effect, "Player X tested positive for illegal steroids" constitutes pretty good evidence of a crime. The crime could be anyone's crime, not just the crime of one of the original ten players. Even if the police didn't want to rely on plain view to seize all the test results, the officers could simply use what they see when they review the file documents to go get another warrant, this one directed at the records of the new names the file review turns up. Indeed, the appellate court discussed the trial court's quashing of a subpoena designed to elicit precisely that information. On appeal, the subpoena was upheld.

The Players' Association's claims of wild government overreaching and callous disregard of constitutional rights are implausible. The

aim of the fourth amendment is for the government to act reasonably, which in the best case means that the government seek
the approval of a magistrate that probable cause justifies the intrusion. Here the prosecutor got warrants, repeatedly. The judgment of the magistrate to issue the warrants need not be perfect,
only itself reasonable. Thus the heretofore happy and insulated
world of sports is becoming fast acquainted with the unfriendly
people who popular the world of criminal law.

Vick's Sentence Too Long

Twenty-three months in a federal prison without the possibility
of parole.

That's a harsh sentence for quarterback Michael Vick, who pled
guilty in federal court to dog fighting.[5] The federal sentencing guidelines provide for lesser presumptive sentences for conduct that
seems at least equally serious, if not more serious. For example, a
lower base punishment is prescribed for an aggravated assault against
another human being, which means a felonious assault with a dangerous weapon leading to serious bodily injury. Similarly, a lower
presumptive sentence is provided for the crime of abusive sexual
contact, defined as "causing sexual contact with another person by
threatening or placing the victim in fear." Now, to be clear, these penalties are presumptive baselines only, and the guidelines allow plenty
of room for upward enhancements to reflect serious behavior or
consequences. My only point is to make clear that, even under the
generally stiff federal guidelines, Vick's sentence is very substantial. Indeed, the penalty is too much. Vick's sentence should have
been lesser, not greater, than that of his co-conspirators. Twenty-
three months' imprisonment is too long.

---

5. Vick was convicted of one count of conspiracy to violate the Travel
Act, 18 U.S.C. section 1952. The criminal activity underlying the Travel
Act count was dog fighting in violation of state law.

It is the dirty secret of criminal sentencing that an offender's criminal sentence is not derived solely from the offender's criminal conduct. Offenders are also sentenced for their non-criminal, legal conduct. Sound crazy? In my view, it is. Vick's sentence can be (and apparently was) increased because Vick failed to "accept responsibility" adequately for his conduct. Even assuming that's true in this case (Vick did, after all, plead guilty and thus formally accept the prosecution's charges: how much more "acceptance" do we need?), what that means is that Vick was given additional imprisonment for not being cooperative and for having a bad attitude in his dealings with the police and prosecution. I thought we citizens have a constitutional right to fight charges and not cooperate? What if Vick had committed the ultimate act of uncooperation: pleading innocent and putting the government to its proof at trial? Could Vick be sentenced for invoking his constitutional right to a trial by jury? You bet: the guidelines provide for about a six-month term of imprisonment for exercising one's constitutional rights.

The answer to my concern is to cite to the accepted practice of plea bargaining: it is routine, the argument runs, that offenders plead guilty to lesser charges or enter into sentence agreements, and do so in expectation of reduced sentences. In other words, the argument would run, it is common that offenders trade off their constitutional right to be "uncooperative" (and stand trial) in exchange for a reduced sentence. Just because one can plausibly characterize this trade the other way (as offenders getting enhanced sentences for exercising constitutional rights), although semantically correct, is disingenuous, as it overlooks the essentially voluntary nature of the transaction. Thus my position is ultimately demagogic, as the offender is not "sentenced" for exercising constitutional rights; he's merely not given a sentencing reduction for relinquishing his rights.

The problem with this standard position is twofold. One, it makes the criminal sentence into currency. The offender must risk an enhanced period of incarceration should he wish to exercise his rights; no other means of "payment" for standing trial is possible. In Vick's case, if Vick preferred to fight his charges, to be uncooperative, then he must pay in increased time. Why couldn't Vick have been allowed to use another currency, like say legal tender? What if Vick, a wealthy man, offered to pay the prosecution's expenses should he be found guilty after a trial? Could the prosecution still complain about Vick's refusal to plead and about the cost of putting the government to its proof? The prosecution should not always be able to condition sentencing breaks on a defendant's willingness to forgo his constitutional rights.

Second, conditioning sentencing on "acceptance of responsibility" is ineluctably subjective. Here, remember, Vick pled guilty. The government did not have to prove its case; Vick saved the government that expense. Nevertheless, the prosecutor and judge decided that Vick was guilty, not of animal cruelty, but of being uncooperative. No proof beyond a reasonable doubt was necessarily adduced to establish this latter contention, and no jury ever weighed the prosecution's perceptions against Vick's reasons or explanations for his apparent lack of cooperation. The prosecutor refused to recommend a sentence reduction for cooperation, the judge agreed (presumably according to the lessened "preponderance of the evidence" standard of proof), and that's it: Vick gets added terms of imprisonment for his post-crime, post-indictment conduct. (The alleged failed drug test and alleged lies fall in the same category.)

Why should the prosecutor, Vick's nominal opponent in this adversarial system, have it within his discretion to add to Vick's sentence? How reluctant would any criminal defendant be to fight charges knowing that, by the simple act of fighting the charges, one's adversary can unilaterally decide to increase the punishment? In the civil system, which handles less serious, non-criminal disputes, no adversary has any such power over his opponent. In the civil law, each side pays for his own counsel fees, regardless of the trial outcome. Why should our most serious branch of the law, the criminal law, feature a system where the loser pays, as long as the loser is the citizen charged with a crime? (The government does not pay if the defendant is acquitted.) And why must that payment be in terms of a period of one's life, and not something else, like money?

Vick's sentence is in effect much greater than twenty-three months. Vick loses his NFL contract and his endorsement deals. One article estimated the loss at about 142 million dollars. Add to that the fact that Vick will lose most of his opportunities to earn a substantial wage in his livelihood. Should we care? Should any upper limit be placed on the extent to which we will punish and bankrupt a man, even a man who has committed a serious crime? Vick's co-conspirators, who stand to lose no money (comparatively speaking) got less time. If Vick is forced to trade a period of incarceration for exercising his constitutional right to stand trial (or to be uncooperative), shouldn't he also be entitled to have his very, very substantial loss of income be at least considered in the imposition of a sentence? Is the guidelines penalty for this crime twenty-three months, or is it twenty-three months plus complete bankruptcy of a man who has earned his money legitimately? Where does the guidelines say the latter? Nowhere. But that's what Vick got.

The sentence should have been twelve months. That's supposedly the figure the prosecution thought Vick would get in the wake of his agreement to plead guilty. Twelve months in prison is a lot of time, especially when that sentence in reality includes for Vick a forfeiture of his bonuses, his NFL contract and his endorsements. The judge could not have been blind to Vick's situation. Twelve months puts Vick out of the NFL for one season (a large income loss), and allows him to resume some semblance of his pro career. Instead, the twenty-three month sentence takes Vick out of two seasons' play, and leaves him without a job even into the third NFL season. It is a devastating sentence, and probably ends Vick's career.

Vick in fact got a twelve-month sentence: twelve months for dog fighting. It's not true that Vick got twenty-three months for dog fighting or that dog fighting deserves twenty-three months. Vick got twelve months for his crime. He also got eleven extra months for failure to cooperate. Is eleven months too harsh for being perceived to be uncooperative, for being less than candid with the prosecutor, and for smoking marijuana? None of these were charged crimes; indeed not all of these are crimes. That people in this coun-

try are put in prison for failing to cooperate with people who aim
to do them harm remains a scandal and a blemish on the criminal
justice system. I used to teach criminal sentencing. What happened
to Michael Vick is precisely the reason I left it.

How bad is dog fighting? It's bad, in my view. But my stomach
would be equally turned by cock-fighting, bull-fighting, and many
of the other blood sports that are not uncommon, still, in the contemporary world. Michael Vick witnessed a dog fight. So has baseball star Pedro Martinez. Has Pau Gasol (from Spain) witnessed a
bull fight, where the large, sentient creature is slowly and cruelly (at
least it looks cruel to me) put to death through a succession of
pricks, stabs and other wounds? Cocks may not be as sentient and
intelligent as dogs, but still I couldn't watch them fight, pecking
each other to a bloody pulp. Yet people, both men and women, do
enjoy such fights, and I assume the rest of us treat these people
with normal respect and politeness. I see glimpses of Ultimate
Fighting on television, and even though no one's fighting to the
death in that ring, I have seen men fall and their opponents jump
on top of them, pounding them in the head unto submission. Again,
I don't have a taste for such blood sports. But some people do.
Should we deny them that taste? I would. But by the same token,
when they act on that taste and attend a dog-, cock-, bull-, or ul-
timate-fight, I think the rest of us have to understand that a taste
for blood sports is a somewhat normal and (in some places) cul-
turally accepted means of enjoyment.

Why were the dogs killed? The indictment contends that dogs
at the Vick house were killed by strangulation, shooting, drowning,
and the like. What could possibly justify such barbarity? Perhaps charity and humaneness? As I've written before, on occasion I take my
boys bird hunting. Now my boys are excellent shots, seldom missing the birds that flush into their zone of fire (those young eyes are
nice). As for me, with my poor vision I often miss. It's not good to
miss (which is why I never attempt difficult shots and always remind my boys to be ready to fire in case I do miss). Missing can
wound the bird instead of kill it. I have wounded birds and like

any ethical hunter it becomes my duty to track that wounded bird down and finish the job as quickly and humanely as possible. Tired and hungry, my boys and I have crossed much rugged terrain in chasing down my wounded prey. When we find the bird, we don't just shoot it on the ground (sluicing). Sluicing is reckless and dangerous, as you never know how a BB from your shotgun might ricochet; plus you never know what else is hiding in that bush. No, what you have to do is grab that poor wounded bird and twist his neck so he dies. I don't like killing birds that way, but it's the only humane thing to do in the circumstances.

Now, I have no idea why people were strangling dogs at the Vick property. Maybe it was just malignant, and if that's the case, it's despicable. But we might learn that these particular dogs were injured from fights to such an extent that the humane thing to do was to put the dog down, and strangulation or shooting was the quickest and most painless way to end the dog's life. I don't know why these killings happened (and neither do you), but my point is that there might be non-malign explanations. Calling the veterinarian was not an option.

The NFL's Punishment of Michael Vick

With his guilty plea and stiff federal sentence now set, the ultimate fate of quarterback Michael Vick rests with the NFL and its commissioner, Roger Goodell. Goodell has decided to stay his decision on the possible NFL sanction for Vick until Vick's sentence is complete and he has applied for league reinstatement. So what should the NFL do about Vick? Should its penalty be as severe as the federal court's? Not necessarily. The NFL should be careful not to over-punish Vick.[6]

---

6. There has been much public confusion about the NFL's new "Personal Conduct Policy." The new policy gives the Commissioner discretion to impose a suspension, including a lifetime ban. But so did the former,

The NFL's sanction needs to be calibrated in response to the severity of the federal court's response. In other words Goodell, like a judge imposing a sentence, needs to be mindful of the total penalty Vick will suffer. I find pitting dogs against each other in a death match deeply disturbing, as I do cock fighting and bull fighting and certain forms of human fighting (were such allowed by law). I bet Goodell shares my aversion to this sort of thing. But Goodell has to consider more than his personal response. Vick will suffer a lengthy federal term of imprisonment, some lengthy sentence of probation, the largest fine allowable by law, the loss of the remainder of his $130 million contract, public enmity and stigma that will follow him for a lifetime, plus the loss of very large ancillary income from endorsements, post-career job opportunities, and so forth. Surely there must be some limit to a sanction, no? Surely Goodell, imposing a suspension in the wake of the criminal penalty, must consider the severity of that sanction, and the other relevant public and private sanctions, in crafting his response. Indeed, the NFL's new Personal Conduct Policy commands as much, requiring the Commissioner to consider the disposition of the criminal case in setting a penalty.

All crimes are bad; if not, we shouldn't call them crimes. Yet prudence, the limitations of resources, the desire to rehabilitate, and

---

now-superseded policy. The new policy does direct the commissioner to consider "the nature of the incident" in setting his penalty, along with similar factors, but these factors are obvious and would be implicit under the old policy. My point is that the new policy hasn't changed much from the old policy, at least not in any way relevant to the Vick case. The major changes in the new policy are two: the Commissioner may punish players for conduct that is not criminal, but that "undermines or puts at risk the integrity and reputation of the NFL"; second, the new policy obliges the league to conduct an investigation before punishment is imposed and gives the player a right to some kind of hearing afterwards. So despite the popular perception, nothing in the new policy directs Commissioner Goodell to impose more severe punishments under the new policy than Commissioner Tagliabue would have under the former policy.

basic humanity require us to make distinctions among crimes. Not every crime should result in maximum life imprisonment or a sentence of death. It's easy and glib to say, as have many commentators, that Vick should be put away for life or subject to physical torture or the like, but really, would we want that as social policy? If we impose huge punishments for animal fighting, what should we give for spouse abuse, which in my mind can be every bit as disturbing and wrongful as dogfighting, and in many cases worse? What about child abuse? What about child abuse that involves drug selling? See, almost all crimes are bad, and all deserve our condemnation. But even the staunchest advocates of law and order recognize that our punishments have to vary for crimes according to their seriousness. If we punished all crimes at the maximum, then an offender might as well commit the most serious crimes, since the outcome will be the same in terms of legal liability.

It amazes me how often, when an athlete or other public figure has violated the criminal law, I hear people say that that person should lose his job. We have sanctions for crimes in this country: imprisonment, home detention, probation, parole, fines, restitution, death. Why do people want to so easily and quickly add a non-criminal sanction, job loss, to this list? It's one thing if the person, say a politician or lawyer, has abused his office in committing the crime, but that's not the case usually. Why add job forfeiture? Why take away a person's livelihood? Why should one animal abuser (say one of Vick's co-conspirators) get to serve a six-month sentence and then go back to his occupation but Vick after serving his sentence have to lose his, plus suffer the additional penalty of a $130 million contract loss plus a substantial forfeiture of his future income? Many of us have engaged in conduct that could have been a crime, if only driving home from work above the speed limit. That's not usually a crime (not everywhere), but if bad luck comes your way and you hit and kill a pedestrian who wandered into the street, now you're a criminal. You would be deeply sorry, you would plead guilty, you would suffer a criminal sanction. Should you get fired from your job too? We've all driven our cars too fast. Should we lose our job just because bad luck intervened?[7]

Job forfeiture as a remedy for a crime makes no sense to me, generally speaking. If an employee commits a crime entirely unrelated to and outside of the employment but nevertheless the employer "must" (pursuant to our job-forfeiture ethos) fire the employee, then by the same logic and according to the same ethic the next employer must not hire that same employee. The ethic is that a criminal does not deserve a job, either his present one or the next. The upshot is that a criminal offender is permanently disbarred from working for a living. If Vick cannot be hired to quarterback an NFL team, should he be hired by another company? If not, what's he to do for the rest of his life? I'm old school. What ever happened to paying one's debt to society and being done with it?

I'm not saying the NFL is not entitled to add to Vick's penalty. Clearly the league has, and has asserted, its interests in presenting its fans with players who represent the league appropriately. But the NFL's response, as its policy suggests, must include consideration of all the penalties the player will suffer. Despite the common wisdom, Commissioner Goodell has not been a hanging judge. Pacman Jones got a one-year suspension, but his conduct, which consisted of a multitude of bad behaviors and brushes with the law, did not (yet) result in any criminal sanction: the NFL's suspension was all he got. Jamal Lewis did time: he helped set up a drug transaction, was convicted of drug trafficking, and received a two-game suspension. Why so light? Why so brief a suspension for a drug

---

7. I realize Vick's crime was not the result of bad luck, and I'm not saying speeding is analogous to dogfighting. That's not my point with this analogy. The analogy is this: that some crimes (indeed many, it turns out) are the result of bad luck. People do negligent or reckless things all the time, and once in a while that carelessness hurts someone. It's bad luck, but in the eyes of the law it doesn't matter that it was bad luck. It's a crime, just like dogfighting is a crime. Do we want job forfeiture for all crimes, even the (many) "bad luck" crimes? Or do you want job forfeiture only for some crimes? Which ones? There are a lot of crimes.

dealer (who to be clear was but minimally involved in the crime)? Because Lewis also received a two-month term of imprisonment; the NFL moderated its penalty to account for the federal sanction. Tank Johnson got an eight-game suspension in the wake of a two-month term of imprisonment for illegal firearms possession, but in his case there were several other incidents involving firearms, including a shooting involving his bodyguard. Albert Haynesworth got five games for kicking an opposing player in the head, but that conduct was not addressed criminally at all. Vick's dogfighting was terrible, but so was Haynesworth kicking an exposed man in the head with metal cleats.

So Goodell, like Tagliabue before him, has shown some judgment in his penalties, and clearly appears to be mindful of the criminal sanction imposed on a player. What should the NFL's penalty be for Michael Vick? In light of the seriousness of his crime, and due to the public uproar, and with consideration of the precedent of other penalties, it strikes me that a suspension that extends the length of his term of imprisonment is plenty. The penalty should run concurrent with the rest of Vick's sanctions. Two years of job loss is enough, regardless of whether Vick is sitting at home or in a federal penitentiary. Playing in the NFL is a short-term employment. Vick, at age 28, has only a handful of seasons left. In fact, although some quarterbacks can hang on as backups for many years, Vick is an erratic thrower who relies on his speed and quickness to make plays. Surely that athleticism will fade with time, and Vick will be reduced to a pocket passer, a task for which he is not well-suited. Vick does not have many years left. When he comes back after two years he'll be a social pariah, relegated to a backup position on one of the NFL's less-notable teams. He'll be relegated to backup money too, and will never again earn a penny in outside endorsements. He'll live with the stigma of his crime for the rest of his life. A lengthier suspension that took away, for all practical purposes, all chances for the only job for which he has ever trained seems unreasonably harsh.

It's never easy to argue for any sentence, high or low. How much time in prison or suspension from a league is appropriate is always indeterminable. There is no mathematical exchange rate between the conduct of an individual and the official response. Added to the mix is the fact that people respond to the same sanction differently: for one person, even a month in a federal prison might be unbearable; for another, less so. The same might be said of social stigma or job loss: some of us might bear it better than others. But Goodell will not have the luxury of calling the question indeterminable: he has to pick a number that adequately responds to Vick's conduct and protects the interests of the NFL. Vick is currently and will continue to suffer a huge extent from his conduct; Commissioner Goodell needs to take this into account when he imposes his suspension.

Collusion

Recently Donald Fehr, head of the Major League Baseball Players Association, worried publicly about some of the grumbling by baseball executives concerning Alex Rodriguez' stupefying salary demands. (Three hundred and fifty million dollars does seem like a lot of money, at first blush.) Fehr has charged owners with colluding to suppress Rodriguez' salary. Major League Baseball, of course, has a history of collusion in attempting to restrict player salaries, giving the union cause to be worried. But Fehr's reputation as a combative and strident union boss seems to have led him to see hidden monsters on this one. As Time magazine has reported, there is no way teams would collude over just one player contract, right?

Wrong. I never quite believed the MLB owners colluded on player salaries back in the 1980's. But I do believe they could do it now, especially with respect to Alex Rodriguez.

Collusion can happen with respect to just one single contract. In other words, if one player is not offered a contract at a fair market price and that failure is the result of an agreement between bidders, even a tacit agreement, then that's collusive behavior. Moreover, colluding to keep Rodriguez from maximizing his salary makes all the sense in the world from the perspective of the clubs. A-Rod is baseball's best player and will undoubtedly again set the upper benchmark for player salaries. The incentive is palpable to limit his deal. As great a player as Rodriguez is, other players are not far behind in ability. At this point, however, these other great players are far behind in salary, even though Rodriguez signed his record-breaking contract about seven years ago. At some point, soon one would expect, these other great players will be in position to catch up to Rodriguez' salary, escalating star salaries to a new level. From the perspective of the clubs and the union, a lot rides on A-Rod's new contract. The clubs have reason to cheat; the union has reason to be vigilant.

Colluding is easy in this case. Only one player contract is involved; only a small handful of clubs appear to have the wherewithal and revenue potential to pay Rodriguez what he wants. Communications in the digital age are simpler, quicker and potentially more secretive than ever before. A quick call from a cell phone or message from a PDA could accomplish in moments what once may have required travel, secretaries, and phone messages. I'm not saying clubs have colluded here, of course, despite some odd public statements. It is curious, however, that with baseball attendance and revenues at historic levels, Rodriguez is having trouble getting a raise from his year 2000 contract despite remarkable performance. Could his 2000 contract have so far outpaced the market that, even seven years later, he's still overpaid?

What's remarkable is that, in a sense, Rodriguez himself effectively induced two MLB clubs to collude with respect to his last contract. A couple of seasons after signing A-Rod as a free agent, the Texas Rangers escaped the lion's share of the obligation by trading him to the Yankees. So for the last few seasons, New York has benefitted from A-Rod's services at something of a discount (not counting the players and money that went back to Texas in the trade). Two clubs, ostensibly competitors, joined together to pay the game's top performer. Now look at this the other way: assume back in off-season 2000 no single MLB club was willing to pay off the entirety of Rodriguez' contract. By signing with Texas and then departing a few seasons later, Rodriguez allowed the Rangers to split the bill.

Could that arrangement ever be brought about at the outset? In other words, could A-Rod today tell the Yankees he'll play third base for $30 million per season, with but 20 coming from the Yanks and the rest from some other team(s)? No, that's absurd. But that absurdity is exactly the arrangement Rodriguez ultimately wrangled back in Texas. So why couldn't a team like New York sign Rodriguez today, giving him the money he wants, all the while planning that a few seasons down the road the team will trade Rodriguez and remain liable for only a fraction of his salary? Players have been traded multiple times and had their contract paid by multiple teams. Even if no single team could (or was willing to) pay Rodriguez over the course of a 350 million dollar contract, the reality is that several teams (together) could, and that baseball has an explicit mechanism in place (trades) to make that collusive conclusion a reality. My point is: there is or should be a market for Rodriguez and that market should be a a level that is a substantial raise above his last contract because teams know they can for all practical purposes collude with other teams (via trades) to share the burden of a player's contract. So why is the market for Rodriguez not there? There are reasons consistent with non-collusion: team needs, financial limitations, concerns about the player's age and compatibility. But collusion provides a sufficient explanation too.

I've never bought the conventional line on the mid-1980's. Here's the story: that the entirety of the teams of the major leagues acted in concert for the better part of a decade, and with regard to not just a few but all free agent salaries; that these teams concocted, enforced and achieved a league-wide conspiracy to limit player compensation, and that this improbably successful conspiracy would have continued unabated but for the unprecedented penalties imposed by labor arbitrators at the behest of the union. It's a fairy tale, and I just don't buy it. How could baseball's owners, a bunch of loudmouth, self-made millionaires with a taste for public attention (hence the decision to purchase a baseball team) have negotiated and stuck by this secret pact and then breathed not a word of it, not even to this day? Think of the hundreds of people who would have had to have been "in the know" on this national conspiracy: not one of them has ever breathed a word? Where's the direct evidence of this conspiracy? Where are the secret documents, the smoking guns, the closed-door meeting notes, the tell-all book from somebody's assistant? The story is that, apparently, with nothing more than a wink and nod, all of baseball's owners toed the line, even though the incentive to "cheat" (by signing a free agent) and capture the riches and fame of a championship season was palpable and within easy grasp. Would all teams, even those struggling at the gate with fans starved for a winner, forgo the substantial chance to win it all? Why would these teams abide by this supposed agreement to fix salaries, especially if those teams that profited from the conspiracy got to keep their profits (the best free agent players) and never had to pay back the losers (the teams that went without improvement)? Why stick to a conspiracy that only benefitted your competitors, especially when those competitors had no means of punishing cheating clubs? Conspiracies don't last without a means of keeping cheaters in line. Yet somehow this conspiracy, in an industry whose every move to subject to intense press scrutiny, managed to remain a secret right in front of our noses.

The arbitrator(s) who heard the union's grievance found collusion. But that collusion was not shown by "direct evidence" (such as a written agreement, or testimony of telephone calls); instead, it was shown only "circumstantially." Circumstantial proof means that certain results or conditions are proved and those results or conditions are "consistent with" illegal behavior, although they don't necessarily prove it. For instance, if a man lies dead in a room and I'm the only person who had access to that room, then my access provides circumstantial proof of my guilt. The problem with circumstantial proof is that it relies on an inference from a fact, and the reality is that other, often equally compelling inferences are also available from that fact. So in 1986 when Jack Morris, a star pitcher, became a free agent and failed to get a decent offer, that fact circumstantially suggests the clubs were colluding. It also circumstantially suggests the clubs couldn't afford Morris. Both inferences are available: it requires a volitional decision to pick one inference over the other. I'm not saying circumstantial proof is worthless; I'm saying circumstantial proof without more is not very convincing.

The arbitrator rested his decision not on the few phone calls that were made between a few clubs, but on what he termed "conscious parallels" in clubs' decision-making. It's very hard to separate illegal (but tacit) parallel behavior from legal (and even explicit) independent decision-making that takes into account competitors' behavior. Both clubs and agents use bids from other clubs to gauge contract requirements and shape their offers. The Red Sox will bid in light of what they expect the Yankees will pay; indeed, agents inadvertently facilitate price fixing by acting as the conduits of bid information from club to club. When the Red Sox decide to limit their offer in light of the Yankees' bid, that's just good business. Multiply that good business to all competitor clubs, and it provides circumstantial (but merely circumstantial) evidence of collusion. It also provides circumstantial evidence of good business sense.

I'm not crying for A-Rod. He'll get paid plenty. But it is odd to me that commentators seem so eager to dismiss charges of collusion in this case, where collusion would be easy to accomplish and where clubs have every reason to commit it. It's even more odd that these same commentators are happy to embrace the standard line about the miraculous collusion of the 1980's. It all seems so backward to me.

By the way, the only reason it's "illegal" for owners to collude is that "concert of action" is prohibited in the collective bargaining agreement. It's not illegal in any other sense, given the exemption labor agreements enjoy from antitrust scrutiny. Why is this phrase in the CBA? Because the owners insisted on it in the 1970's after Mike Schmidt and Larry Bowa of the Philadelphia Phillies tried to market themselves jointly in seeking new contracts. Why did the owners worry about that? All it would mean is that Schmidt (the better player) would have taken a bit less to give Bowa more; who cares if Schmidt wants to pay Bowa part of his salary? Who cares if Texas was willing to pay part of A-Rod's salary? He only got the market price.

The Patriots Did Not Cheat

It looks pretty clear at this point that the New England Patriots, in violation of an NFL policy, stationed a video photographer on the sidelines during a game against the rival New York Jets. Apparently the photographer's job was to capture the Jets' defensive signals as they were relayed from the coaches to the players on the field, all with the hope of stealing their signs. I guess mechanically this could work, although I imagine it would be very difficult to decipher the Jets' signals, relay the defensive plan to the offense, and adjust the offensive play in time to take advantage of the information. But the difficulty must not be too overwhelming; otherwise why would the Patriots bother to try?

So this is cheating, right? The Patriots need to be severely sanctioned for gaining this illicit advantage, no? No. What the Patriots did is not cheating, at least not in any meaningful sense of the word. No illicit advantage was likely gained.

English is such a limited language. We have so few words to describe objects or events that sometimes our inhibited vocabulary confuses our thinking. I've read about the debate over how many words the Inuit natives of Alaska have for "snow." Turns out it's pretty limitless. But for English-speakers, we have only one word for snow, and we rely on adjectives (heavy, light) to try to characterize snow more specifically. Same thing for "cheating": we have only one word for "the action of intentionally breaking a rule." So an NBA forward who nudges his opponent out of the way in order to get a rebound is "cheating," as would be the forward who injects his opponent with a tranquilizer for the same purpose. Both are cheating in this broad sense, yet the latter is so much more violative of the ethics of the game (and the former is just playing the game) that it deserves a different term. We don't have one. So we'd call both of them "cheaters" and then would expect consistency and equality in the sanction imposed in response. The single vocabulary term misleadingly suggests an equivalency in the two players' conduct.

Sign stealing is legal in the NFL. It's perfectly permissible. Coaches, players, interested fans, television watchers, and anyone else among the thousands of folks observing an NFL game can study the histrionics of the coaches, note the defensive alignment, and steal the signs. No rule prohibits this. I'd be disappointed in a team if it didn't at least try to steal the signs: the field is only about fifty yards wide. If some assistant coach notices that, every time the opposing team's defensive coordinator waves his hands in the air the linebackers blitz, then I'd expect him to call the blitz out to the offense the next time he sees the sign. Again, no rule prohibits this. I'm sure attempted sign-stealing has been going on for as long as signs have been given.

The burden is on teams giving signs to take precautions with their signals. They have to use subterfuge, change signals, employ decoys and so forth to keep their opponents from learning their communications. Even coaches in youth baseball typically employ a fairly complex set of signs that is resistant to code-breaking. At the pro level the signs should be variable and subtle. Lawyers have the same obligation. When we speak with our clients we have to make sure the conversation is confidential and away from listening ears. If someone overhears the conversation then that someone can testify. It's the lawyer's fault for not properly protecting the information. The same standard, by the way, applies to everybody in life: if you want some information kept private then you have to keep it tucked away. Leave it out for others to see and you've lost your privacy.

All the NFL rule prohibits is using a photographer to facilitate the sign stealing. Admittedly the Patriots violated the rule. But let's not assume that the Patriots benefitted from the illegal photographer. Even if the Patriots' sign-stealing efforts were successful and paid off in identifiable advantages on the field, the Pats might have broken the Jets code even without the photographer. In the NFL, teams are allowed to view overhead photographs of the opponent's defensive alignment just before the snap and immediately thereafter. A knowledgeable coach with a clipboard and pencil could perform the same study of the opponent's signals, correlate them with the defensive photographs, and deduce the defensive calls. In short, the Patriots might have ended up with the same competitive advantage they (presumably) had anyway. Those people calling for the Patriots to forfeit games need to show how this videotaping produced an advantage that the Patriots wouldn't have gained legally. I doubt there was an advantage gained from the illegality.

In sports, it's not cheating unless you're caught. So the basketball defender who illegally nudges an opponent off his jump shot has not committed a violation unless the referee detects the nudge and calls a foul; the baseball batter who on a bunt runs on the inside of the baseline is not out unless the umpire calls obstruction; the football offensive lineman who holds the defensive end but gets away with it has done nothing wrong. Yet all these players have willfully and intentionally violated known rules of the game, and all of their violations potentially affect the competitive integrity of the game and the outcome of the contest. Does it make sense to call them "cheaters"? No, they didn't get caught, even if the replay shows their guilt, and even if the player admits to the truth after the game. So even assuming the worst, that the Patriots broke the rules against the Jets and have done likewise to opponents ever since Bill Belichick came to the team, the bottom line is that, for all those games prior to the Jets game, the violation wasn't called. The Patriots weren't caught; those games are over. As far as the Jets game is concerned, the illegal photographer was discovered in the first quarter and stopped at that time. The foul was called; the game wasn't affected. Whatever sanction the commissioner devises, he shouldn't touch any game results, from the Jets contest or otherwise.

So what is cheating in sports? Here's my rule: nothing done on the field of play is cheating. What happens on the field, even if it violates the rules of the game, is still the game. The game includes circumventing the rules to try to win. On the other hand, off-field conduct that results in undetectable on-field advantages, and that violates the rules, is cheating. Taking performance-enhancing drugs is cheating, as is violating the salary cap or employing professionals in an amateur game. But sign-stealing? That's as much part of the game as the home crowd yelling while the opponent's quarterback calls signals at the line. Both are allowed if done one way and against the rules if done another. And what should be the penalty if a team takes steps to artificially inflate the level of crowd noise during games? Forfeiture of game, loss of draft picks, large fines (what many recommended in response to the Patriots' photography)? No, crowd noise can be loud all by itself, resulting in the same disadvantage for the opponent. This isn't cheating; it's just gamesmanship.

Punishment for cheating is usually severe, and imposed without regard to whether or not the cheater gained by his act. As for gamesmanship, the usual remedy is to take away the gain. In football pass interference is called only if the defense "gained" by it; that is, the pass was "catchable." If the pass was "uncatchable," then the interference is not penalized because of no gain. The Patriots didn't cheat, and they didn't gain from their violation. The penalty should have been minimal.

Bill Belichick's Interpretation

In his answer to the NFL's accusation that he videotaped an opposing team's defensive signals during a game, in violation of a league rule, Patriots' coach Bill Belichick spoke about "my interpretation of the rules." Reading as much as we can into this reference, Belichick implied that the league rule prohibiting videotaping was a matter of some ambiguity, and implied further that his transgression, far from being willful, was more a matter of reasonable difference and misinterpretation. Some commentators, seeing no possibility for ambiguity or interpretation in the rule, have become so worked up over Belichick's conduct that they think the Commissioner's unprecedented punishment is too lenient. One commentator has even called for Belichick's lifetime banishment from the sport. This is what happens when people practice law without a license. Let's take a look at the rule and see if Belichick has a point. Does he?

Belichick indeed has a point. Whoever wrote this rule left a few matters in doubt. Should Belichick be banned just because someone working at the NFL lacks a command of the language?

The NFL's "Game Operations Manual," the source for the rule in question, states that "no video recording devices of any kind are permitted to be in use in the coaches' booth, on the field, or in the locker room during the game" and that "all video shooting locations for club coaching purposes must be enclosed on all sides with a roof overhead." Start with the second clause of the sentence, after the "and." This statement implies that some in-game video will be allowed for "club coaching purposes," and that video taken for this purpose, that is, for in-game use, must be video that originates from locations enclosed on all sides with a roof. Indeed, often we see players and coaches on the sidelines during NFL games examining photographs of formations and plays taken from vantage points presumably high in the stadium, from enclosed places. Now look at the first clause. It says no video recording devices are permitted to be "in use" during the game. But we already know that some video recording devices (those from certain enclosed locations) may be used during the game for "coaching purposes." So, for in-game coaching, a coach may only use the "enclosed location" videos.

What about for "out-of game" coaching, like during the practice week? The rule says "no video recording devices" may be "in use" "during the game": they may not be used, as the rule says, "in the coaches' booth, on the field, or in the locker room," at least not "during the game." The rule implies, fairly if not unambiguously, that teams may in fact make video recordings from locations other than the "enclosures" as long as those video recordings are not used "during the game." Indeed, that's the better interpretation of this rule. If the rule were "no video recordings allowed except those from the designated enclosures," then why do we need all the language concerning "in-game" use? Why the words about "the coaches' booth," "the field," and so forth? Under standards of legal construction, all words must be given a plausible meaning, if one is available. In other words, we are to try to avoid surplusage (wasted words). With respect to the NFL, the better interpretation of this mess of a rule is that some video recordings (those from enclosures) may be used during games, while other video recordings (from outside these enclosures) may not be used during games, but may be made and used otherwise.

Now, I realize that other, plausible interpretations of this rule are available. The rule may be intended to mean "no video recording except from enclosures" (if so, the rule has a lot of surplusage), or could mean "no video at all during games, but photographs are not video" (if so, even more surplusage), or perhaps "use" of video means "not only not watching video, but also not even making the video" (if so, then we need a lot more words defining "use"). I'm not saying Belichick didn't interpret the rules aggressively and in his favor. I'm also not saying taxpayers, lawyers and regulators don't do the same, every day. When one is dealing with a rule, what's not prohibited is impliedly permitted. Belichick took an aggressive position and paid the penalty for his interpretation. He admitted as much, and said he was punished for his interpretation. But please don't say the man had no leg to stand on here. Don't call him a cheater for adopting a plausible interpretation of a very ambiguous rule.

Now here's the rub: the NFL, apparently just before the season began, sent a memo from Executive Vice President of Football Operations Ray Anderson to the teams that "reminded" them that, "videotaping of any type, including but not limited to taping of an opponent's offensive or defensive signals, is prohibited on the sidelines, in the coaches' booth, in the locker room, or at any other locations accessible to club staff members during the game." Here's where all the overheated commentators get their "prohibition" idea, and conclude that Belichick violated a clear prohibition and thus is a cheater making up lame excuses about misinterpretation. Not so fast, please.

First, just what is the effect or significance of a memo from a league vice president? I would imagine the NFL employs quite a few people who have the title of vice president. Does a memo from a league VP have the effect of law? Is it equivalent in significance to the NFL's "Game Operations Manual" quoted above? Can the NFL, through some memo from a VP, simply amend the Manual just like that? No committees, no notice, no deliberations: just a memo that adds words and gives the rule a particular meaning, and it's done? Can a memo create a new rule that is instantly binding on all teams?

But, you say, the memo didn't announce a new rule. By its own terms it was just "reminding" the teams of the present rule. So it's just a reminder, not an amendment, and if so then the rule itself (the one in the Game Operations Manual) hasn't changed. Just because Mr. Ray Anderson, Vice President for Football Operations, characterizes the rule as a "prohibition" doesn't make it so. Indeed, even interpreting the rule as a prohibition, Anderson's memo mischaracterizes it. The memo says "videotaping of any type," including an opponent's signals, is prohibited from certain locations, namely from "the sidelines, from the coaches' booth, in the locker room, or from other points accessible to club staff members during the game." In other words, a team may, legally, videotape another team's signals: they just can't do it from these certain locations, or any location "accessible during the game." How is that a prohibition?

Now the memo's rule that permits videotaping of signals but prohibits those videotapes from being made from the sidelines may be a good idea, and maybe that should be the rule, but that's certainly not the Game Operations Manual Rule that the memo merely purports to "remind" everyone about in the week prior to the start of the season. In other words, the memo seriously misstates the rule, because the rule prohibits the in-game use (but not the making) of videotapes, or at least that's one plausible interpretation of it.

Which was the rule, the Manual or the Memo? If you're an employee at your job and a memo comes down from a company VP reminding you of a company rule, a rule that you already had in mind and had parsed through pretty carefully, and the memo's re-statement of the rule was at variance with what you had a right to believe the rule actually stated, which rule (the one in the authoritative document or the one in the memorandum) would you put your finger on as being the correct, binding rule? Which one would you follow? What if your job were a competitive one and money (or wins) was to be made by interpreting the rules in a plausible yet aggressive and self-interested way? Would you be a "cheater" for going by the rule in the official company policy manual instead of the inexact repetition by the company vice president? Would you choose to follow the Manual particularly when the VP's memo made it clear he was merely "reminding" you of the rule, not changing it? Isn't one entitled to think the rule hasn't changed when one sees the word "reminder"?

Why was this rule so ambiguous? It's only ambiguous if we assume the rule writers wanted to write the rule that VP Anderson recited in his pre-season memo. I don't think they did. The rule doesn't state the easy directive that "no video recording devices are allowed except those in the enclosures" for one simple reason: that's not the rule the writer of the Manual wanted, or maybe not even the rule the NFL wanted when (pre-Goodell) it first enacted this rule. That rule would be easy to state. The rule writer wanted to permit teams to record from anywhere, but not to allow the coaches to view the recordings during the game. How else could we explain the prohibition on video devices in the locker room? Under the NFL's interpretation of its rule, the Patriots would be banned from videoing Belichick's halftime speech. That's not the point of the rule. The point is no coaching use of video. That's why all the "coaching locations" are specified.

Look at it this way: under the NFL's interpretation, Belichick could legally have a video of the Jets' signals shot from the front row of the stands. (Indeed, that vantage may afford a clearer angle.) He may also use the products of that video during the game, so long as he is not standing in one of the three prohibited locations. This would be a silly rule. The rule is a directive to the coaches/team personnel. The aim of the rule is prohibit in-game viewing. The NFL wasn't worried about Belichick shooting a video, but was worried about using the fruits of that video during the game. Many commentators charged how brazen, arrogant and even stupid Belichick was to put his camera operator on the sideline in direct view of the Jets' staff. He wasn't brazen and is certainly not stupid. It makes much more sense to interpret Belichick's behavior as consistent with his explanation. He obviously thought he was doing nothing wrong and therefore had nothing to hide.

Every lawyer knows rules of prohibition (criminal statutes) are the hardest to write. I don't know why so often sports leagues turn to the criminal model. The NFL's Game Operations Manual is full of rules on how many towels to supply, location of game balls, and other matters mostly trivial to the competitive event. I would bet none of those rules are written like a criminal statute ("teams are prohibited from supplying fewer than 24 or more than 26 balls"). Just say the team must supply 25 and you're done. Here, if the NFL really wanted the rule to be "only two cameras," then just say so. Presumably, the NFL did not just say so because that is not the rule the NFL originally intended to create.

I'm not saying Bill Belichick didn't deserve a sanction. The league is entitled to interpret its rules, and even to do so after the fact, at a hearing in which discipline is the outcome. Courts do it all the time, especially in civil cases. My point is that the rule, the real one in the Manual, contains a lot of room for ambiguity and interpretation. My other point is that, no matter how one chooses to interpret the rule, there is no plausible interpretation consistent with the one given in the Memorandum issued pre-season. My final point is that our football commentators need to get off their high horse for a while and realize that people, be they taxpayers, lawyers, journalists or football coaches, need at times to interpret rules. That they do so in an aggressive way is actually a good thing, on balance: it makes us write better rules.

Chapter Eleven

Doing Justice in a Fallen World

Criminal law speaks in categorical terms to prohibit anti-social behaviors. But despite the attention given to criminal law, it is a mere sideshow when compared to the large bulk of laws that regulate most aspects of business, public, and private life. Outside the criminal world, lawmakers are more cautious: most legal rules read like guideposts instead of prohibitions, revolving around concepts such as "reasonableness" to shape behavior. The law's tentativeness reflects the limits of human knowledge and the limits of law: often a single rule does not fit every occasion, and a flat prohibition would not suit. Frequently lawyers deal with clients the same way. Instead of flat pronouncements about the borders of permissible behavior, the lawyer is limited to pointing out the deficiencies of the present approach and suggesting plausible improvements.

These essays don't purport to solve the intractable problems they address. When the law can't set a limit, it tries to identify the costs of a behavior or activity so that people will consider the costs and not just the benefits. Often the law and lawyers try to structure thinking, not determine it. Let's see how we can do on problems that defy simple resolution.

The Costs of Climbing

Last winter's story of the stranded climbers on Oregon's Mt. Hood was an unmitigated tragedy. One climber was found dead; the other two remain lost and are presumed dead. After weeks of effort, the county sheriff called off the search. The rescue effort was immense, involving hundreds of people, state and local government agencies, law enforcement, and many volunteer organizations. Although it's unpleasant whenever a tragedy generates a debate, a public debate nonetheless has arisen over the costs of the rescue. In my mind it's a legitimate question, although we discuss it at the risk of appearing callous. Nonetheless, should lost climbers have to pay for the costs of rescue?

First, the term "costs" needs a little definition. Many of the rescuers are volunteers; they certainly incur costs in time and materials, but they and their organizations are willing to give away these costs. We don't charge recipients for the generosity of volunteers, so these costs should not count. (They count in a social sense, of course, and should figure into any discussion of prohibiting certain sports or activities.) The salary of the governmental employees at all levels, however, must be included as costs. The claim that some climbers' groups have made that these costs should not count because "they're just getting paid anyway" goes too far. All employees on salary are "just going to get paid anyway," but that's not a reason for me to refuse to pay the plumber when I call him to the house. The lost climber is using the sheriff's services as much as I am when I call the sheriff about my neighbor's dog. Should I have to pay for the sheriff's services with respect to the dog? Yes, and I do when I pay taxes.

So we probably need to develop a rough taxonomy of costs, dividing those that arise from an ordinary and expected function of public employees (calling cops about barking dogs) and those that are in some sense extraordinary. Sometimes we get to use government services at no additional cost (police for local matters) and sometimes we get assessed added amounts (sidewalk built in front of our house). I'm thinking a police officer driving around town looking for a missing kid is an ordinary and expected police function; Air National Guard personnel firing up the Blackhawk helicopter ($5,000 per hour operating cost) seems to fit in the "extraordinary" category. We could think of other taxonomies (such as whether the government action is directed at a public or private benefit, or general or specific beneficiaries), but no matter how we define the issue, we'll need to identify those functions that might be subject to surcharge, were we to impose one. We'd also need to figure out whose functions "count." Surely we should include the salary of the airplane pilots circling the mountain, and probably also the deputy at the command station, but what about the dispatcher coordinating agents from the station house? Should we include office overhead? Since overhead is a charge routinely included in business charges, the presumption would be to include it here too.

Next, along with defining what we mean by costs, we'd also need to come to some agreement on what sports or activities should be subject to a rule requiring reimbursement of rescue costs. Let's start with mountain climbing. Should all climbers have to pay, or only those who attempt notably dangerous climbs, as did the climbers who were lost on Mt. Hood? They attempted to climb the north face; I'm told this is a dangerous climb any time, made particularly risky when attempted in the winter months when severe snow and wind storms are common. Although these climbers from New York and Texas were experienced, I live in Oregon, and locals have told me that these particular climbers were flat-out foolish to attempt this climb. I see Mt. Hood from a distance nearly every day. It looks so peaceful, yet it and other parts of Oregon's beautiful but rugged wilderness claim lives with regularity.[1]

Many people, not just climbers, need to be rescued from Oregon's forests. These forests are dense and vast; the federal government alone owns about 60% of Oregon, with much else owned by the state. Oregon is a big place inhabited by only 3.5 million people, most of whom live in Portland or the Willamette Valley to its

---

1. Mt. Hood is one of the most climbed mountains in the world. Overall, more than 35 climbers have died in the past 25 years while attempting to scale the mountain. "Mount Hood Climbers Reach Safety." 20 February 2007. *MSNBC.com.* http://www.msnbc.msn.com/id/17219953/.

south. The rest is all forest, mountain range, high desert, rugged coastline and wilderness. It's a huge outdoor playground but also a seductively dangerous one. So, that means Oregonians have to rescue (and pay to rescue) not only lost climbers, but also hikers, walkers, fishermen, hunters, boaters, surfers, kayakers, canoeists, dirt bikers, snowmobilers, mountain bicyclists and so on. You name it, if you can do it outside (and it's fun), then people will do that in Oregon and some of them will get lost or in trouble. Is climbing dangerous? Sure, at least it seemed so when I read Krakauer's book on Everest. But so is a lot of this stuff. Even driving at night in Oregon's mountains and forests is risky, as the sad plight of the Kim family so testifies.[2] Accidents happen.

Bad incentives loom either way. If we charge lost climbers the true costs of their rescue, climbers will perhaps choose not to ask or to delay asking for help even when it's needed, worsening their situation and making eventual rescue costs higher. But if we don't charge them, then we create incentives for inexperienced adventurers to get themselves in trouble without fear of financial reprisal. Probably these incentives cancel each other out; more likely the incentives don't matter much here at all. People do not usually gamble with their lives, at least not once the threat to the life becomes apparent, and so it's likely the rule of law is irrelevant to people's behavior. In other words, probably neither the skilled veteran nor the reckless adventurer genuinely believes he will get into life-risk-

2. James Kim and his family were on vacation in Oregon when they were attempting to head home and took a wrong turn. The family ended up on one of the back roads that were rarely plowed during the winter, ultimately ending up stranded in the snow. After nine days surviving in their car, the husband set out in his street clothes through the snow to find help for his family, and tragically died after trekking 8 miles. The wife and two daughters were rescued and spent one day in the hospital before being released. "Father's Effort to Save His Family Called 'Superhuman.'" 7 December 2006. *CNN.com*. http://www.cnn.com/2006/US/12/06/missing.family/index.html.

ing trouble; probably both, once that trouble is apparent, will take every step to remedy it, despite the prospect of financial costs.

Let's not shrink from what requiring lost climbers to pay for their rescue might mean. It means any one of the following: sending a bill to the rescued climber, or to his estate, should he not be found; requiring the climber to post a bond before departing; folding the costs of rescue into a license fee, or mandatory insurance, or permit, or a user's fee. Regardless of whether the climber pays before or after, the climber is still paying. A user fee and the like simply socialize the costs across a broader group, although it's limited to those who specifically engage in activity that at least bears a generic resemblance ("climbing") to the risks to which the Mt. Hood climbers subjected themselves. The costs could alternatively be socialized across the entire taxpaying public through a marginal hike in taxes. Just raising taxes is not a bad move here; all of us have some probability (however minute) of being in need of rescue some day, so we could plausibly consider a tax payment to be the equivalent of paying a user fee. But, of course, that is an overstatement: serious mountaineers and certain "thrill seeker" types put their lives more in danger than does, say, the average law professor, who's more likely to die from falling out of his chair while asleep than from tumbling off a cliff. One side note: if we do assess a seriously high user fee or insurance requirement on climbers and others, then to the same extent we are shutting off the comparatively indigent from engaging in outdoor recreation. Since outdoor camping, hiking, and other activities of this type have traditionally been the "vacation of the poor," imposing a fee for usage of our forests is problematic.

A few states (Oregon, Colorado and Utah) by law do create the possibility of assessing rescue costs. Oregon's statute is a joke because it caps reimbursement at $500 per individual. The Blackhawks use that much in oil. It also requires only negligent climbers to pay. Plus, the statute isn't even written properly. The statute simply says "a public body may collect," but who collects and how? The statute doesn't even provide a cause of action or assignment of liability. Anyway, no one's going to go to much trouble to prove negligence in a court of law just to collect a mere $500. Plus the climber can substantially negate a claim of negligence by showing he was carrying a cell phone (utterly useless, since we haven't yet filled Oregon's national forests with cell phone towers) or one of those locator devices, which could help in the right conditions, assuming trackers were nearby. (Let's not make the recent Mt. Hood climbers an example of the need for locators; those men were far out of reach of rescuers due to weather.)

Another issue to sort out is the definition of rescue itself. Just as we might ask climbers to be reasonable or non-negligent in assuming the risks of a climb, so we'd ask the same of rescuers. When should a rescue begin and end? What costs should be undertaken? If the climber is to pay, he might have an interest in a check being written on his account. In the days of Oregon's settlement, people who did not purchase fire protection didn't get the benefit of the fire department's services. Some people rationally chose to bear the risk of fire themselves, just as today some of us choose to bear the risks of earthquakes. Could climbers refuse rescue, on some form signed before embarking? Would we make people get rescued (and pay for that rescue) even when they didn't want it? What if a rescue attempt is made but is later shown to have been unnecessary when the bemused climbers walk into camp? On the other hand, what if the rescue is stopped, when modest further efforts might have been fruitful? Should the climbers still have to pay? You see, if we start collecting payments from climbers, and these payments become $50,000 instead of $500, then the survivors might want a judge or jury to second guess the conduct of the sheriff in directing the operation. Today we cheer rescuers. Do we want to make them defend their conduct in a court of law?

Finally, if we're going to seek reimbursement from lost climbers, we have to ask for what purpose. If we want reimbursement to refill depleted public coffers, then the present limitations on recovery in Oregon law make no sense. Oregon taxpayers undertake these expenditures on behalf of climbers who do not pay Oregon taxes. A far more substantial user fee or reimbursement charge would be needed even to begin to comprise true rectification. On the other hand, instead of compensation, state authorities may seek reimbursement in order to make these risk-loving people think twice about their intended conduct. If that's the case then we should make sure the collection fee is equal to all the costs of the rescue, even those borne willingly by volunteers. The person causing the social problem should consider all the social costs his conduct will generate in order to decide if the conduct is truly worth it.

Collecting the costs of rescue is virtually impossible to implement. The difficulty of identifying the people to be charged, the sports or activities to be covered, and the amount to be collected are so significant that the problem defies resolution by a rule of law. Law has its limits. If we really think some of these sports or activities are so dangerous that no reasonable person would attempt them, then we should ban them, much as we have bare-knuckle fighting. But, if we're going to permit people to use our wildernesses for recreation, then we're letting people risk their lives on the promise that we'll make some plausible effort, or even an extraordinary one, to rescue them should trouble arise. Lots of people risk their lives, in the wilderness and elsewhere. We need to allow them that latitude. Indeed we profit from it, as those who push the envelope of human capacity help the rest of us learn about the contours of the envelope and thus live more safely within it. With the benefits from thrill seekers come the costs.

Donovan's Beef

University of Florida basketball coach Billy Donovan made a decision to work for the Orlando Magic and then changed his mind. Maybe he should have been more certain of his preferences before signing the contract, but the fact is he wasn't. He made a mistake and didn't know his own wishes until after the fact. So in a large fit of seller's remorse, he asked to undo the deed and go back to the job at which he's been most successful, having won consecutive national college championships.

Not an unusual story in the abstract. Employments are relationships, and relationships happen slowly, haltingly, with fits and starts. Yet, the law doesn't allow for relationships to happen slowly. Employment relationships are formalized by contracts, the same kind of legal documents the law uses to schedule a yard maintenance service or join the health club. A decision is made, a document is signed, duties arise, and changes of mind can carry consequences. It is interesting that the law tries to structure human relationships and club memberships in the same way. In other words, the law is an ass.

Commentators termed Donovan's conduct "unprofessional" and called for him to reimburse Florida for the costs of jet fuel it spent looking for a replacement, take a cut in pay, and agree to a large financial penalty should he break his new agreement. This thinking is wrong from the start: coaching a basketball team isn't a profession. I'm not trying to put anyone down, but there are but three traditional professions: law, medicine and the clergy. (Yes, even we mere teachers missed out on this exclusive club.) Yet we throw around the word "professional" nowadays to describe just about any occupation. It's just sloppy talk, but the problem with sloppy talk is that it leads to sloppy thinking. Professionals have a unique calling, required to act not in their own interests, but in the interests of another. Lawyers, for instance, have to make all kinds of personal and business sacrifices, and even turn away lucrative work, to serve their clients, even when those clients refuse to pay, ignore advice, and fire them. For the rest of us, the non-professionals, we are allowed and expected to act in our profitable self-interest, tempered only by the general norms of business ethics and good manners.

Donovan is not a professional and doesn't owe any professional duty to the University of Florida or to the Orlando Magic. He's just an employee, with the ordinary employee duties of loyalty to his employer. Employees, even those whose employment is formed by a written contract, don't have to take or continue in any job. The freedom to work or not work is subject to even greater legal protection than the freedom of speech. No court will make a person perform personal services, yet courts can and do enjoin speech and assess damages and even criminal penalties for wrongful speech. So if Donovan doesn't want to coach the Magic, he doesn't have to. He should be able to walk away.

Nor should he have to pay a penalty for his indecision. Unquestionably the University of Florida spent money recruiting Donovan's replacement; probably the Magic also had recruiting costs. Reportedly the Magic's fans also bought season tickets, and perhaps some of those purchases were made because of Donovan's impending arrival and exceeded ordinary sales. But in effect Donovan already has paid for some of these costs. Although the check for the jet fuel and so forth was written on Florida's account, Donovan paid too in terms of diminished salary. Because there are only so many top-level basketball coaching jobs in the nation, coaches (even at their high salaries) actually make less than they might otherwise were substitute positions (such as football coaching) available to them. But Donovan can't leave Florida to go to the NFL, only to the NBA or some other top college program. As a result, the costs of recruiting new coaches are effectively shared by the employer and the new employee. This is a particular instance of the general phenomenon known as tax incidence. Of course, the contention that basketball coaches bear at least some of their costs of recruitment is speculative; the answer would depend on the employer's and employee's comparative sensitivity to changes in the price of coaches. Admittedly too, a coach like Donovan in very hot demand probably "contributed" little to the costs of his recruitment. But other coaches in less advantageous positions do bear some of these costs. My point is, Florida and the Magic do in effect pass some of these costs onto others, and so in the struggle between management and labor it's a mistake to assume that management's nominal costs are the actual measure of its losses. So paying back the school or the Magic for its recruitment expenses ignores the fact that those employers are often able to pass those costs on to others, including fans.

Finally, I've seen it discussed that the Magic will demand of Donovan that, in exchange for "letting" him out of his contract, Donovan must agree to a five-year (apparently the length of his broken contract) prohibition on coaching for any other NBA team. Billy, this is crazy. Why should Donovan have to sign a non-compete agreement for a job that he's never going to fill? Why should the Magic obtain, for the trivial costs of its jet fuel, a valuable five-year exclusive option on the services of an in-demand young basketball coach? I can't imagine any judge who's awake enforcing such an agreement. The fact that the putative prohibition would be nationwide in scope only lessens its chances for judicial enforcement. Occasionally courts will issue so-called "negative injunctions" in personal services cases. These are shameful. While paying homage to the traditional prohibition on involuntary servitude, these judges, although not requiring the employee to fulfill the contract, prohibit the employee from providing similar services to any other employer. These courts assume that people are stupid, that we'll perceive a genuine distinction here. Of course there is none, which is why few judges will issue them. An injunction prohibiting Donovan from working for another team or college for the duration of his Magic contract would in effect require Donovan to coach the Magic or quit the business. No way a court would issue that injunction. How would the Magic be irreparably harmed by Donovan's refusal to coach? Are there no other coaches, such as Larry Brown, available who could coach a professional squad?

The Magic have only one "professional" choice here: cut Donovan loose and wish him well. Tentative, provisional relationships, including employment relationships, don't mesh neatly with the formalistic exactitude of the law. Yes, Billy signed a contract and now wants to change his mind. The lesson we should all learn from this episode is that contracts shouldn't stand in the way of the freedom of a person to give his labor on terms to which the person agrees. Unfortunately for the Magic, that agreement is in essence renewable every day.

I Pine for Wood Bats

I still love the feel of the wood bat in my hands, even if I only have a fungo bat for practice drills. The metal bats and the distinctive ping sound they produce can't match wood. With wood, everyone knows immediately from "the crack of the bat" how well the ball was struck. With metal bats, all hits sound the same. Yet all the tactile and aesthetic considerations don't override the primary aim of today's Little Leaguer in purchasing a bat: the kids want the bat that will hit the ball the furthest. And in my mind there's no question about performance; today's manufactured metal bats, fashioned out of alloyed composite materials, hit the ball harder than does the traditional wood bat made from ash.

Some states and localities have banned metal bats from their youth baseball leagues, and other states are considering following suit. These bans have been encouraged by parent organizations that cite to several tragic injuries (usually to pitchers, the closest fielder to a batted ball) from hard-hit line drives off of metal bats. Needless to say, the bat manufacturers are displeased, claiming that no valid evidence demonstrates that metal bats form a safety risk. Should metal bats be banned?

Surely the bat manufacturers would agree that their bats are better than they were in previous years, and certainly better than decades ago. And "better" includes the characteristic that these new bats hit the ball harder. These bats must perform better given their considerable expense. So here's what I can't figure out about the manufacturer's claim that there is no difference between wood and metal bats.[3] It may well be the case that a ball, when struck by a

---

3. In an interview with CBS news, Dr. Stephen Nicholas, identified as a sports medicine expert at New York's Lenox Hill Hospital, claimed a "ten to fifteen percent difference in speed" between a metal bat and a wood bat. "Do Metal Bats Pose a Greater Risk?" 27 July 2006. *CBSNEWS.com*.http://www.cbsnews.com/stories/2006/07/27/earlyshow/main1840638.shtml.

metal bat in its "sweet spot" or a wood bat in its sweet spot, comes off the bat at an identical velocity. But how often do batters, particularly in youth ball, square the ball at just the right spot? Not often. But here's the thing: everyone seems to agree that metal bats have a much larger sweet spot, and are, for their weight/length ratio, lighter than wood bats. What this means is that players swinging metal can use a larger bat (youth leagues vary in their restrictions on bat size), swing it harder, and hit the sweet spot more often. So the game is changed, and clearly pitchers and other fielders are in danger, more often than they would be in a game with wood bats. Instead of one or two really squared hits in a game, with wood bats, we have that many each inning. Batters using metal can make contact with the pitch all over the bat, such as on the handle or toward its end, and still hit line drives. With a wood bat, hits on those spots would likely crack the bat, or at least sting the fingers, and usually result in an easy out.

But banning metal bats may not be the only response to (what seems to me) an obvious case of the batted ball flying harder, and more often, than in years past. One only has to be in law school for about a week to realize that it takes two to tort. If pitchers are in danger from metal bats, then instead of banning the bats maybe the pitcher's mound needs to be moved back. When I see a team of 12-year-old boys playing on a 60-foot diamond (with the mound 46 feet away), the diamond looks too small and the players too big. A diamond appropriate for 9's and 10's is too small for 12's. Of course no remedy is faultless; baseball has inherent dangers. One claimed advantage of metal bats is cost-savings; although the bats are pricey, they supposedly last longer (although I think their very thin walls are vulnerable to easy denting). Maybe that cost savings should be redirected into building larger diamonds. Maybe also younger players should be segregated from older ones.

There are undoubtedly good reasons, probably having to do with cost, space and available coaches, that nine and ten year-olds are often in the same league with 12's. (Also, given other

children's interests, it's difficult to find enough kids to field competent teams at all levels.) For the better players, of any age, quick
reflexes are usually enough to defend oneself. But dangers lurk. Many
baseball injuries seem to result not from hard-hit line drives, but
from bad hops on grounders due to poorly maintained fields. All
of us have seen kids struck high on the body or the head from a
bad hop on a hard-hit grounder, even in a practice setting. Should
Little League ban bad fields? There is a rule against playing in
"unsafe" field conditions, but any veteran of youth baseball knows
that even decent fields are full of irregularities, "lips" on the edge
of the grass, pebbles in the dirt, and the like.[4] We're all just volunteers here and maintaining even a decent field takes a lot of coordinated effort.

The other problem with legislative bans on any dangerous
activity is data.[5] Probably the most dangerous sports activity for
children involves swimming in the backyard pool; perhaps routine

---

4. What's more, despite all of its claimed preference for safety, Little
League in my mind continues to allow the most dangerous activity I've
ever seen on a youth baseball field: coaches hitting grounders to players.
Now I realize that this practice activity is necessary for player development and game preparation, but its necessity doesn't change the fact that
it's dangerous. Some of these coaches, in an effort to "get them ready" for
higher levels of play, or perhaps out of a touch of anger, hit their grounders
quite hard. Boys get bruised, and we're lucky if it ends there. Should LL
ban this activity also, or limit coaches to soft grounders? Having grown men
rap hard ground balls directly at players standing on a typically uneven
baseball field creates a clear danger of injury. Some teams or leagues have,
in response, adopted rules requiring the wearing of fielding helmets
equipped with face masks. These contraptions provide protection, but
probably create bad fielding habits that, once the mask is removed at higher
levels of play, reveal themselves. I'm not against fielding headgear, but I
do wonder if the cost (in terms of discomfort, habits developed, etc.) is
worth it. Mopeds would be popular if helmets weren't required. Make a
kid take the mound in a helmet, face guard and heart guard, and do you
think kids would be excited to pitch? Maybe they'll just quit.
5. "The U.S. Consumer Product Safety Commission's National Electronic Injury Surveillance System reported 17 deaths identified nation-

exposure to the sun comes next. I would bet the odds of being catastrophically injured by a batted ball are very far down the list. So why should legislatures single out the particular danger of metal bats? Is it just a matter of whose injury or complaint manages to get itself political salience? Should we voters encourage our politicians to outlaw swimming pools, require big floppy hats, and so forth, until we get down the list to the metal bats issue? Now of course just because no state will ever outlaw swimming pools doesn't mean a state cannot address other, lesser dangers that are perhaps more susceptible to amelioration. But still, like swimming pools, metal bats do have their virtues; they are (supposedly) cheaper, and more importantly, they hit the ball harder. More fun for everyone.

All dangerous activities have offsetting benefits. Is the net effect of metal bats negative? Should we (or our legislatures) implicitly decide that the occasional grievous injury from a batted ball is a price "worth" paying so other kids can enjoy the fun of metal bats? (Obviously holding metal bat manufacturers liable for batted-ball injuries will drive the price of bats higher, meaning that those kids who get to enjoy the fun of metal will have to compensate those who are injured by that enjoyment.) The mounds aren't going to be moved back any time soon, nor will pitchers start wearing head gear and heart guards. Instead of an outright ban, the "lowest tech" solution might be for a group of parents from just one team (preferably a good, winning one) to buy their kids wood bats and win games anyway.

----

wide from 1991 to 2001 linked to batted balls: eight from non-wood bats, two from wood bats and seven not known. Eighteen deaths linked to thrown balls occurred over the same period." Carey, Jack. "Dealing with a Batty Situation: Wood vs. Metal." 2007. *USATODAY.com*. http://www.usatoday.com/sports/2007-06-03-bats-cover_N.htm.

Why Rugby Is Un-American

An Australian rugby player got hurt on the field, apparently as a result of someone's negligence, and sued for damages. So far, I understand. But his damages award was limited to $90,000 Australian (about $70,000 US) because, according to the way-down and under judge, the player had, since his forced retirement, made a boatload of money in real estate investment.

In American law, like that of Australia, there is a doctrine called "set-off" by which damages will be diminished to the amount the injured person "benefited" from the injury. This doctrine recognizes that our interactions with others may result in both costs and benefits, and that the plaintiff should only be awarded the net. But here's the limit: the costs and benefits must be to the same interest or same property. Think of the movie version of Spiderman, where the freak accident that befalls the young hero (a tort, if someone negligently caused it) produces costs (the spider bite hurt) and benefits (now the hero gets to shoot spider webs out from his forearms, a nice advantage in life). The same interest (health) is both harmed and helped, and so damages would be set-off by the realized monetary value of becoming a superhero.

The Aussie court's theory is that the rugby star's spinal cord injury enabled, in some causative way, the player to commence real estate speculation. He nearly had his neck broken, lucky bloke. Things are wrong in Australia. There's a reason the benefit, to be offset, must be visited upon the same "interest" as that harmed: it's the only way to be confident in the causative link between the gain and the initial injury. We don't "set off" an injured person's inheritance that happens to arrive after an injury because the injury did not cause or lead to the inheritance. So exactly how did suffering a spinal cord injury on the rugby pitch cause the player to become a skillful real estate investor? It didn't. Any skill or acumen the plaintiff has at investment was there already; suffering a spinal cord injury did not endow the injured person with additional insight.

The court's theory, a mere nod to the requirement that the harm and benefit be tied to the same interest, is that the injury "freed up time" and thus enabled the athlete to spend time in real estate. That is not a theory at all. Any life-threatening injury or illness has the wonderful benefit of freeing up time, simply because the lucky victim gets to lie around suffering and can't go to work. On the court's reasoning, any income-producing activity the victim was able to perform, even if it's painting landscapes with the brush in his teeth, should be set off from the award, since the injury freed up the time for the work. When your principle of law includes all possible activities, then it's not a principle at all, it's just an excuse to do what you want to do.

And what did this judge want to do? Not give damages to a millionaire. Okay, I understand the impulse, although it's debatable. But let's be honest and say that; let's not bring in set-off doctrine to reach a result the doctrine would actually reject. Should wealthy people, like professional athletes, not be allowed to recover damages simply because they're rich? Can the rest of us run around and negligently or recklessly injure and defame wealthy athletes and other performers, and then successfully defend the resulting lawsuits on the basis that the plaintiff has enough money and doesn't need any more? Pretty silly idea, if you think that damage awards have a role in stopping people from acting carelessly toward others. That's why the judge wasn't forthright about what I think was his true reason; the idea of denying money to wealthy plaintiffs seems hard to defend.

Sports Law as a Substitute for Morals

Many legal scholars have been writing lately about one particular function of law, namely that it fulfills an "expressive" purpose. This means that the law has a role in reflecting and in turn teaching what we collectively come to view as right and wrong. Nothing earth-shattering here, but I do think this particular function of law is on the increase and I do find this development troubling. Legal rules should not be in the business of implicitly teaching us what is right and wrong. Moral conduct and minimal legal requirements are two different things. The trouble with employing law to "express" rightful conduct is that minimal standards for community peace (the law) morph into prescriptive rules that reflect one particular version of "rightful conduct" in a particular situation. Law becomes ethics. We can differ about morals (and we do); law should reflect the unanimous consensus of all reasonable people, not a particular answer to a vexing and intractable moral question.

What does this have to do with sports and sports law? A lot. Sorry to sound alarmist, but law is taking over sports, and I'm not very happy about it. The latest debate in the sports world concerns the employment by women's college basketball teams of male practice players. The male players go up against the women's best squad to get them game-ready, the idea being that the men are better players than the second string on the women's team. The downside is obviously that the female players who sit during this portion of the practice do not further develop their skills and feel left out of the team. It would be a good debate, if anyone cared to discuss it on these terms. But the debate does not center on these competing costs and benefits. Instead, the primary focus of the debate, even in the popular press, is on a federal statute, Title IX.[6]

Federal statutes can, if we want them to, establish a principle to resolve some big issues or problems; they can require equivalency in athletic opportunities for men and women, for instance. But they don't do very well when the questions get too specific or detailed. How is law made? At some point, some federal judge or federal reg-

---

6. Also known as the Patsy T. Mink Equal Opportunity in Education Act, Title IX was enacted on June 23, 1972. Specifically, Title IX states: "No person in the United States shall, on the basis of sex, be excluded from participation in, be denied the benefits of, or be subjected to discrimination under any education program or activity receiving Federal financial assistance." "Title IX." 22 August, 2007. *Wikipedia.org*. http://en.wiki pedia.org/wiki/Title_IX.

ulator decides what point along a continuum of plausible outcomes constitutes a reasonable or appropriate standard of equivalency for opportunities for women, or when less than full participation is tantamount to exclusion from participation. Trust me, folks, lawyers and judges don't get any special training on what degree of equality is appropriate; law schools offer no training in wisdom. Yet we resort to a judge or lawyer to pick a point on the line and then we call it law. Law is not very pretty when you get close and see how it's made.

Why should non-lawyers turn to the law for answers to vexing social questions? Why should non-lawyers debate this issue in terms of Title IX, instead of in terms of what's best for the women's team? Questions about "what's best" are exactly the kind of questions the law typically does not answer. Very seldom does the law give dispositive answers to contemporary questions. That's not the function of law. The law sets minimal standards to facilitate cooperative living and minimize conflict. I was listening the other day to a talk radio discussion of the topic of male practice players, and the commentators, obviously not lawyers, were debating this issue exclusively in terms of Title IX and federal law. Again, lawyers have no special wisdom on whether or not women's teams are justified in employing male practice players. Quite the opposite: lawyers and lawmakers need non-lawyers to debate such issues in non-law terms and come to a resolution that we lawyers, if needed, can express in legal terms.

Non-lawyers, not law, should have a monopoly on the "expressive" function; non-lawyers need to teach lawyers about what is right, apart from the law. Is it right to bring in men for the women's team practice? That's a pretty good question right there. Why does everyone need to discuss this issue in legal terms, as if law had an answer and that law's answer is the right one? Why does everyone want to practice law? Law is supposed to reflect conventional morality, not create it.

I hate the NFL replay system. It's not so much the delay in the action or the desire to get calls on the field correct. I don't like the delay and don't have a strong need for perfect calls, but these aspects don't trouble me. What troubles me is what the television announcers say during the replay challenge. Accompanied by repeated viewings from multiple angles, the announcers fish around for the applicable rule (defining a "catch," or a "downed runner," or a "touchdown;" the NFL rules are pretty complex) and then apply that rule to the facts of the case ("see his knee, right here?"). Hey, they're practicing law (without a license)! I like practicing law, but I don't want to see a bunch of amateurs do it on live television on a Sunday afternoon. Now everyone gets to see how law is made (was the moving ball "juggled" and therefore not a "catch?"). It's tedious. It's also ultimately indeterminate. We could sit there all day and not agree on some of these calls. Even the reviewer's standard for overturning an on-field decision ("indisputable evidence") is a legal standard that is misapplied weekly. Who can blame these quasi-lawyers? They're referees and announcers. To do it right, the NFL should have a lawyer loosen his tie and sit in the booth, if we really want to watch law practiced.

All kinds of formerly moral or cultural decisions are nowadays filtered through law, from personnel decisions to medical treatment to college athletics. The demand for lawyers only grows. I'm working as hard as I can to produce lawyers just to keep up. Please don't complain about the number of lawyers in this country, at least not if you're someone who, by his political votes especially, furthers the hegemony of law and legal regulation into all facets of life. But however you vote, resist the senseless growth of law. Law can at times serve as the final answer to a vexing problem. But law should be resorted to only where thoughtful, civilized discourse apart from law can yield no consensus answer, and where a uniform "legal" answer is absolutely needed. A law court should be the place of last resort, not the first. I'm troubled when the first mention I've seen of the use of male practice players involves a lengthy discussion of Title IX. Is there anything else to say about this issue other than citing to a federal statute?

Racial Bias in Foul Calls

Even putting aside the game-fixing scandal involving Tim Don-aghy, this past off-season has not been a good one for the NBA's referees. An economics paper analyzing foul calls has claimed to find a bias among referees in calling more fouls against members of a "race" other than their own. (The NBA's own account of the data shows no discernible differences.)[7]

The majority of NBA referees are white while the majority of players are black. The study examines summary game data and the race of the players and officials; it shows a correlation between the mere presence of white referees with an increase in fouls. In other words, the study did not have specific data on which of the three referees working a particular game called particular fouls, only that the presence of white refs meant more fouls for black players.

Various explanations having nothing to do with racial bias may explain this data. The increased fouls may, in fact, have been called by the one or two black refs working a particular game. All the study proves is that games refereed by white refs are called "tighter" than games without them. I'm guessing (pretty confidently) that the white refs are also the more veteran refs, on average. In other words, one plausible interpretation of the data is that the NBA's veteran refs tend to call a slightly tighter game, giving out more fouls.

Another explanation is that black players may in fact commit more fouls than white players. Why? Let's assume black players in the NBA are, on average, better players than the white NBA play-ers. "Better" means better along all dimensions, including defense. Thus a coach will assign his best defensive players (black, on aver-age) to guard the opponent's best scorer (black, on average). Top scorers draw the most fouls. The study controls for a player's po-

---

7. Alan Schwarz. "Study of N.B.A. Sees Racial Bias in Calling Fouls." 2 May 2007 (*N.Y. Times*).

sition and all-star status, but that seems inadequate to me. Some players, even if not all-stars, are excellent scorers who are adept, even on entering the league, at drawing fouls. These black scorers will tend to be guarded by black defenders (again speaking of averages). These black defenders will be whistled for a greater number of transgressions. This effect could be magnified if, as is often claimed, certain referees favor certain star players. Think of Dick Bavetta sending Dwyane Wade to the free throw line at every conceivable opportunity: the poor player guarding Wade (presumably a black) will be assigned these fouls.

Why does a study that shows an enhanced likelihood of fouls suffered by blacks prove racial bias? I watch a lot of NBA games. It is not at all uncommon to see but two whites on the court at any one time, and often they are guarding each other (for example, opposing centers). So when two black players get involved in a tough charge/blocking call situation, why is the fact that a foul call is made (either way) instead of not made evidence of bias against a player on account of his race? A black player will be unhappy in either case, either from the foul being called or not called. If a foul is called, then by definition it will be assigned to a black player. I would think conclusions of the sort the authors claim would require one to examine plays where whites and blacks are involved in contact, and the foul is called against the black disproportionately. Yet the author of the study concludes that "if you spray painted one of your starters white, you'd win a few more games." The study does not seem to support that conclusion.

Most NBA teams feature a lot of "isolations" in their offenses. (We have Pat Riley, Mike Fratello and other control-freak coaches to thank for this wonderfully entertaining style of play.) The way it works is this: take your offensively challenged players, tell them to stand as far away from the basketball and the hoop as possible while still being over the half-court line, then give the ball to your superstar, let him dribble around for a while, go one-on-one, and then shoot. Who are these isolation stars? Kobe Bryant, Paul Pierce, Lebron James (blacks). And who stands around on the outside

watching play, just like us at home? Usually the less-skilled big people, which often means the centers, which means Chris Dudley-
types (whites). (Forgive the gross generalizations, but that's what
this story is about.) Now granted, with the recent rule changes and
the arrival of Mike D'Antoni, isolation offense is on the decrease (my
prayers answered). But with that said, clever offensive coaches (Doc
Rivers, Phil Jackson, for instance) are able to design offenses that
still get the ball to the star player in isolation situations. These iso-
lating blacks are being guarded by fellow blacks. These isolators are
very skilled at drawing fouls; these top defenders play physically
and thus are vulnerable to fouling. Where's the racism? The story
might just be that blacks get the ball more and play a more physical game, and that white (veteran) refs detect fouls within that physicality more often than non-whites. But it's the physicality to which
they respond, not the race.

Whites may be better at drawing fouls. "Flopping" is a special
(and specially hated) part of the game. For the uninitiated, flopping
means pretending you've been fouled (basically by dropping to the
floor in a screech of pain as the offensive player brushes past on his
way to the basket). The greatest (worst) flopper in history was Vlade
Divac, who I'm assuming qualified as "white" (he is Serbian) in the
study. Divac was hated (at least by me) for his skill at pretending
to be fouled, with success. In today's league, Manu Ginobili of the
Spurs (who is Argentinian) is probably also called "white" in the
study and is the current cinematic protagonist of the thespian flopping all-stars. Who else can flop? Kirk Heinrich of the Bulls is a
master, as is Shane Battier of the Rockets, as is Matt Harpring of
the Jazz. I'm not sure about this, but most of those players would
be classified as "white." Maybe whites are good at flopping? Maybe
some players (who may be white) learn to flop in order to mask
defensive deficiencies or overcome speed disadvantages, and thus
find a way to contribute to team victories without scoring? Maybe,
after a lifetime's learning, they get good at it? This study could be
subtitled, "Whites Good at Flopping; Refs Buy It."

What is "white" anyway? Did the study label Europeans as white?

If so, European players for years have been described by NBA scouts as "soft." "Soft" means that they shy away from physical contact on both ends of the floor. Well, if this stereotype is true and these white players are settling for jump shots or playing half-hearted defense or not going hard for rebounds, then won't they be less likely to commit fouls? Is the study really showing that referees favor whites, or is it showing that whites (Europeans/South Americans) commit fewer fouls in the first place?

It may well be that the authors were able to control for all the factors I mention and have indeed uncovered an instance of unconscious racial bias. But I do doubt, in the fluid and confused environment of an NBA game, the referees have time to form and exercise a racial bias, even an unconscious one, as they call fouls. The games move very fast, and the whistles are immediate. I don't think it's even possible to see race in that context.

Chapter Twelve

The Fun of Games

I recommend law school to nearly everyone who expresses an interest. Legal training provides tremendous discipline, both in terms of one's work ethic (law school is hard) and more importantly in terms of one's mental processes. Legal thinking at its best is rigorous, compressed, analytical, and useful no matter what the subject.

Of course it's precisely this "legal acumen" that gets lawyers into trouble. It's hard at times to turn off the routine skepticism and argumentativeness of law practice when one goes home at night. For many lawyers, learning to return to normal, to stop "lawyering" (yes, we use it as a verb) every situation we encounter and everything we observe comes only from practiced diligence (and from much yelling by our spouses). For the rest of the lawyers, we never learn. We're lawyers 24/7. It's all we know. So when we watch sports or complain about bad calls against our favorite team, we do it like lawyers, consulting the rule book (yes, I have all of them at home), applying law to facts, questioning motivations and perceptions, and making arguments.

Needless to say, we are lots of fun to have around.

The Myth of Tanking

The Boston sports media and many of my fellow Celtics fans have convinced themselves that the NBA's historic Boston franchise was "tanking" its 2006-07 season. "Tanking," as best I can figure out, means that the Celts were purposely losing games in order to improve the team's draft position. Some writers have given this claim an economic twist, suggesting that tanking games in basket-ball is easier and more productive than it would be in football.

The problem is that the Celtics were not tanking games, nor were the NBA's other losing teams. They were rationally respond-ing to the incentives their place in the standings gave them. They were not trying to lose; they were just indifferent to winning.

One reason people think they see tanking is that they see the teams playing their stars less, or even shelving them with the type of minor injuries that players might ordinarily ignore. This be-havior, however, should not be confused with tanking. In all sports, teams languishing toward the end of a losing season will similarly rest star players. It's an opportunity to give younger players some needed experience and also serves to lessen the strain and chance of injury for the stars. Both the younger players and the stars will be in better position to compete the following season. Hence los-ing baseball teams will commonly shut down star pitchers toward the end of a losing season; a losing football team might even give a start, or significant playing time, to the youthful backup quar-terback. Why should we expect the Celtics and other losing bas-ketball teams to behave any differently?

One perceptible distinction, which upon examination amounts to no real difference at all, is that NBA teams will claim minor in-juries to star players in order to justify the stars' non-participation. (Perhaps even some of these injuries are faked or exaggerated.) Why don't we see such dubious injuries in other sports? The answer is that the NBA commissioner has a history of fining teams who do not play available stars or who play them sparingly. The only way a coach can rest a star like Paul Pierce without incurring the wrath of the commissioner is to exaggerate an injury and put Pierce on the injury list. By contrast in baseball, for instance, the season for star pitchers can be ended peremptorily in favor of giving the prospect a chance to start a game, all without so much as a whim-per of complaint from the commissioner's office.

The other reason fans thought the Celtics were tanking was

because the fans wanted (at least to a certain extent) the Celtics to lose in order to maximize the team's chances of drafting a top player, such as Greg Oden or Kevin Durant. They expected the Celtics' players and coaches to have the same desire. The theory of "selection bias" suggests that these fans saw what they expected to see. They expected the Celtics would throw games, they saw the Celtics benching Pierce and playing Gerald Green, and so they concluded that fact was evidence of tanking.

Despite being asked about it every day, the Celtics coaches and players adamantly maintained that they were not playing to lose. Were they lying? Let's try a little lawyering here. What we have, if the media and fans were right, was a massive conspiracy kept hidden by young men of varied schooling and maturity whose lives take place under constant public scrutiny. Think how many people would have to coordinate their efforts to lose a basketball game on purpose. Players would have to shoot to come close (to avoid shot-clock violations) but they would have to miss: I'm just guessing here, but I doubt the Celtics have, since they started this alleged tanking, taken fewer shots per game than before (in fact I would bet they've taken more, with Pierce, a slow-down player, on the bench). So we have a team taking just as many shots that has to find a way to miss more of them, and these misses have to come from hungry, hustling young professionals intent on making their mark and making their money in the most competitive athletic league in the world. A league, by the way, although not quite a tournament payoff (where the best players get the lion's share), but still pretty darn close, and as such, giving every young player, especially a talented one like Gerald Green (who by his slam-dunk appearance seems eager for stardom), a rare chance to shine. Why in the world would Green miss shots so that the Celts could draft some college player who may take his spot, his money, his shots, his stardom? Why would Green and the other scrub players be in on the fix, even assuming one could easily fix a game? I mentioned shooting, but players would have to perform less than their best in all facets of the game.

Is it true, as has been argued, that the NBA is particularly prone to tanking teams because it's easier to lose a basketball game on purpose than it is a football game? Just the opposite. If I had control of a pro football team and wanted it to lose, a few quiet words to the starting quarterback would do the trick. A meaningless late-season NBA basketball game is comparatively difficult to fix. One could try by getting to the leading scorer or point guard. But in a late-season game featuring a lot of scrub players, a point guard throwing the ball into the stands or a shooter missing multiple shots is likely to be pulled from the game. Unlike his treatment of a star, who will be given every benefit of the doubt to "shoot his way out of it," a coach will show less patience with a sub. Plus, who's to say a particular sub will play a major role in the team's fate that night? With Pierce, you know he'll be at the center of the offense, especially in an important game. No, if you want to fix a basketball game and it's a late-season game featuring scrub players, you'll need to involve a big part of the team to make it work.

Yet this amazing team-wide conspiracy happens every NBA season, right under our noses, (and in Boston, no less, a town teeming with aggressive sports reporters) and yet not once has any direct evidence of the conspiracy been unearthed! These NBA kids have more discipline than the Mafia. Never has a player admitted, "Yeah, I missed the tying shot, but Coach gave me the sign to make sure we lost." Never has a coach, even in the most candid moment, allowed that he was instructed by the GM to improve the team's draft position. How is it possible that no one's ever talked? Is player loyalty that deep, even years later after trades are made or players retire? Or were the players never told? Can the coach, through idiot play calls or crazy substitutions, help bring about his team's losses, without the players ever knowing? Everyone tells me the NBA is a player's league, with the role of the coach overrated and ineffectual. So now he's in total control? I watch a lot of Celtics games. Doc Rivers' lineups usually feature the typical balance of rebounders, ballhandlers and shooters. (Indeed, I thought Rivers' lineups were sometimes a little crazy back when the team was still in the playoff hunt.) The team runs the same basic offensive sets they've run all season. Nothing's changed. Really, could these giant conspiracies engaged in by losing teams go on, year after year, without a single shred of direct evidence (apart from the perceptions of fans) ever once breaking free, except for perhaps the occasional stray comment that these same zealous "conspiracy" fans twist into a direct admission of complicity?

Of course not. The "tanking" claim is preposterous. The irony is that everyone knows it. It's become a common observation that tanking games is just not worth it. The incremental addition to a team's number of ping-pong balls does little to increase a team's chances of getting the top picks. The odds are still against a team, even the worst team in the league, from landing either of the top picks.[1] It makes little rational sense to tank; why would teams do it? Aren't the teams, their coaches and managers, as rational as we? (No, they're more rational, apparently, since these commentators admit tanking is pointless but claim they see it anyway.) Why engage in this massive conspiracy to achieve an aim that is nearly worthless?[2]

Watch the "tank" games: the players are hustling, looking for all appearances like young players seeking a contract; the coaches are yelling; the contests are competitive. No one's trying to lose.

---

1. As indeed happened in the draft after this season, when neither of the two teams with the worst records and therefore the most ping pong balls (Boston and Memphis) wound up winning the lottery for the top picks.

2. And it didn't happen in "the old days," before the weighted lottery. The lottery and ping-pong balls were introduced in response to the "perception" of tanking, not it's alleged reality. I know it doesn't happen, even when the incentive to tank is palpable. Last season, the Celtics came down to their final game against Miami, and a loss would have guaranteed Boston the sixth slot (depending on the lottery) in the next draft. All they had to do was lose. They won. That win only cost the team Brandon Roy, the NBA's Rookie of the Year.

What's Wrong with Tony Kornheiser

The hiring of Tony Kornheiser for the Monday Night Football announcing team continues an unfortunate trend. Increasingly, commentators don't talk about the game they are supposedly covering. Instead, they talk about "sports issues," usually sports law issues, while the game goes on in the background. Both baseball and football give us the worst of this, as the many dead spots during the action give ample room for the commentators to pontificate about the state of the game, the commissioner's doings, player-manager disputes, and the like. The last MNF team, John Madden and Al Michaels, distracted the viewer constantly from game action, especially when the score became even a little one-sided. It's as if the commentators prepare with talking points instead of game film. But why employ ex-jocks or former coaches to try their unpracticed hands at this brand of meta-commentary when one can get a pro? Hence the hiring of a full-time, experienced opinion-maker like Mr. Kornheiser.

Maybe it's just personal preference. I don't want to watch the sports reporters or Bryant Gumbel when I tune in to a football game. It's the game match-up that draws me, not a chance to hear Kornheiser preach or Dennis Miller offer canned one-liners. The constant argument is distracting. I used to go to a church that played music during the recitation of prayers. Who thought this up? Who thinks this is a good idea, to say to the audience we're going to do one thing, lure them to the activity of that thing, and then, while doing that thing, distract them with something else? Ads for MNF hype the upcoming game and its stars; they don't say tune in to hear someone give brief, offhand opinions on difficult issues of sports law. I no more want to hear Tony speculating on the legality of mandatory drug testing while a halfback runs off tackle than I want to hear soft rock music kick in while I'm reading from a prayer book. It's also frustrating. Joe Theismann or now Ron Jaworski can explain how a quarterback reads defenses, but neither is very adept at trading arguments with a professional writer who in high school had his head in Latin conjugations while the quarterbacks had their arms around a cheerleader.

No, the fair opponent for Kornheiser's attempts at quick intellectualisms would be the nemesis who helped make his career, Michael Wilbon. I enjoy PTI. I love MNF. I also have a TIVO. If for some bizarre reason I want to watch the two shows simultaneously I could make it happen. There might be a few folks for whom this sounds appealing, but I suspect not many. I like my expert football commentators to be expert in football.

What a Lawyer Can Do About the Ryder Cup

No good news from the K Club, site of the last Ryder Cup competition.[3] Once again the United States got drubbed by the Europeans. Maybe they have better golfers than we do. But American lawyers can't be beat. Can we figure out a lawyer's solution to the American problem?

Start with the selection process. It's terrible. American golf stars at the time of the last competition included John Daly, Fred Funk, Fred Couples, Corey Pavin, Justin Leonard, Davis Love, Tim Herron, Brad Faxon and Billy Andrade; not one was on the team. Wouldn't a selection of players from this list have helped the U.S. team more than some of the journeyman pros who made up half the squad? I'd take Daly over JJ Henry; Daly's birdie/bogey binges are killers in stroke play but ideal for team matches. Players like

---

3. The Ryder Cup is a three-day competition made up of two teams; Europe and the United States. The format is match play between two teams of twelve. Match play is a scoring system which uses units per hole, not per stroke. The player who has the lowest score on a hole is given one point. If the two players tie, then each get a half. The team with the greatest number of points at the end of the tournament wins. "Ryder Cup." 20 August 2007. *Wikipedia.org*. http://en.wikipedia.org/wiki/Ryder_Cup.

Couples, Funk and Pavin, although past their primes, are still play-ing competitive golf. If you had to bet your fortune on someone to beat Henrik Stenson and David Howell in singles play, would you pick Davis Love and Tim Herron, or Vaughn Taylor and Brett Wet-terich? Me too. Yet somehow the U.S. picked the latter team, who combined to lose 9 and 7. Rule Change #1: Institute a fan vote. These players are popular for a reason. I guarantee you the fans would have picked a better American team.

The selection process is flawed because it's based on the wrong measure. It's complicated, but in brief, the current points system favors players who win or finish high in tournaments near in time to the coming Ryder Cup competition, no matter the relative im-portance of the tournament. So if JJ Henry wins at Hartford he has a great chance to make the team, which he did. The winner of the BC Open got more points than the runner-up at the contem-poraneous British Open. In short, the system looks for the hot pro and favors these backwater tournaments where few of the top play-ers compete. But golf isn't played in streaks, and the Ryder Cup isn't played in seclusion. Great players can work on their games to prepare for big tournaments. Count only the big tournaments. To me, a player like Daly, with two majors' trophies in his trunk, should be an automatic. Plus I like to watch him play. Rule Change #2: Ig-nore the BC Open; start with winners of majors who are still play-ing well, then take winners of the "near-major" tournaments, like the Players Championship. If you need any more, take Fred Cou-ples. Or just use a fan vote; we'll do the job.

For the Junior Ryder Cup matches, the kids must have a U.S. citizenship. Oddly, the rules for the grown-ups are less conspicu-ous. At one point, Ryder Cuppers had to be "native-born," but the rules were eventually changed to require citizenship, as best I can determine. Hey, lots of golf pros have taken U.S. citizenship, including Greg Norman, Aaron Baddeley, and Annika Sorenstam. They want to enjoy our sunny tax havens, so let's make them wear those silly shirts and play for the team. Plus, the Ryder Cup is a big deal: ex-posure, fame, and eventual fortune. We let it be known that accepting U.S. citizenship makes one eligible for the Cup, then we'll see a team with Ernie, Vijay, and maybe even a Euro or two (Paul Casey lives in the U.S.). The American team captain can stop worrying about color-coordinating the outfits and start issuing passport applications. But be careful; we don't want to lose Tiger Woods to Thailand. Rule Change #3: Let all Americans play. Ours is a generous country.

At the Movies (and Little League Baseball)

The best part of being a lawyer is putting all that expensive legal education to work in everyday settings, like dealing with the customer-service hotline for the appliance dealer or, better yet, movie criticism. While we lawyers have no clue about cinematography or visual effects, we do understand the (il)logic of human behavior. Ever been watching a good suspense movie and, right as the hero was about to open the door behind which the killer lurked, some jerk said loudly, "that would never happen!"? That's your lawyer, or will be one day.

So the other night I was watching a movie with my young boys. The story involved a peaceful, fun-loving American family whose otherwise nondescript existence was abruptly interrupted by an alien invasion. After much resourceful fighting, and a large dollop of improbable movie luck, the panicked humans were able kill the last of the homely alien critters and, presumably, return to their normal lives. But I couldn't help but wonder why the humans' first reaction to the aliens' arrival had been to fight. Why start a war with the little green monsters without first considering the likely benefits and costs of the planned action? In short, why didn't this wildly impulsive human family first consult their lawyer, to take advantage of the lawyer's trained habit of considering all possible aspects of any problem?

If aliens did launch an invasion of the Earth, as I paused the movie to ask my sons, why not let them come aboard? They only want a colony, after all. Why must we always presume that one alien colony will inevitably lead to a complete takeover? In most of the alien invasions I've seen in the movies, there's only one inter-planetary "mother" spaceship, and maybe a few zippy little attack vehicles. Even allowing for chronic over-crowding, how many crea-tures do most mother spaceships hold? Plus, the newbies are from another planet. Shouldn't we inquire about their comparative pref-erences before we start sending futile attack fighters after them? If we took the time to get to know them, we might be surprised. Sunny river valleys with cool summers might be highly distasteful to our new friends. The sparsely inhabited, vegetation-free moon-scape of western Idaho, on the other hand, might be just the thing to make our strange new Americans feel right at home. "Oh, it's the high desert you want," we'd craftily say to them. "We've been sav-ing that special land for future generations of very wealthy people. We love those freezing winters and the constant winds from Canada. But, since you green thingies seem so nice and all, we'd be willing to let you have these picturesque acres, for a suitable price."

Plus who knows what alien bodies, consisting of non-biological inert matter, might be hungry for. Styrofoam, soiled baby diapers, and rocks, not grain and wheat, might be alien dietary staples. This is exactly the stuff we're trying to get rid of! After a short interim, states would begin to compete for alien colonies, offering tax breaks and unlimited access to landfills as lures. We might be able to make a ton of money off bewildered alien invaders unfamiliar with the twists and turns of American capitalism.

But there could be a few social problems. One small problem might be just coexisting in our crowded urban centers with the aliens in this movie, whose bodies consisted of large blobs that lacked skin and had to count on unreliable energy fields to remain conterminous. Imagine the inevitable workplace issues, as co-work-ers got covered with slime from diaphanous beings. Plus human labor wages might begin to lag if these super-aliens outperformed us. Social relations will create even trickier situations: what will we say when the precious apple of our eye falls in love with a one-eyed scaly creature sporting tentacles, antennae and no audible means of communication? "Daddy, I know it will take some getting used to, but Zorg and I love each other."

The other social integration problem would be with our youth sports (which is exactly the issue my youngest brought up: how would we compete with them?). Recently I was asked about returning again to coach the local Little League baseball team. Alien offspring, those green mini-monsters, would put our young boys and girls on the bench. (And how would the age and size restrictions that permeate youth sports be applied to weightless beings who live for light years?) Maybe I'm cynical (like I said, I've coached), but here's where we'd draw the line and fight.

Last year's Little League team, like all the many other years I've coached, began the season with twelve happy young boys. The children laughed, competed, and for much of the season had a great time on their way to finishing third in the league. Not so for the parents. All the parents of the kids temporarily on the bench wanted their superstars in the game, if only in the outfield; all the outfielders' parents demanded their boys play the infield, those of the infielders to play catcher, the catchers to pitch, and the pitchers, to pitch more. The parents were miserable, and their misery eventually infected their children, who became, well, little human monsters. (Only my son was happy. He got to pitch nearly all the time.)

So I understand why we defend the Earth. We must keep the alien invaders off the planet to protect our youth sports. Even our usual legal remedy against losing out at sports, self-interested legislation or, in a pinch, activist judicial usurpation, would be unavailable. Anticipating the Earthlings' resort to political machinations or judicial redress, the aliens would engage in vigorous pre-election alien cell division, producing millions of voting offspring to seize control of our state and national legislative, executive, and judicial bodies. That's not a big deal, of course; someone has to volunteer for distasteful public service. But once alien political control resulted in overturning our brand new "humans-only" sports laws, the aliens would dominate all sporting contests. Immediately, human-Americans would take to the streets, rioting, forming factions and revolting, just like James Madison figured.

Madison's boy played third base.

Super Observations

I killed the better part of a day watching the 2006 Super Bowl. Since my team wasn't in it, I was able to take a few notes.

First, I have heard this enough: "I look forward to the day when we won't mention the skin color of the man who coaches the Super Bowl winner." Wait a minute, everyone, I think we're there. I couldn't help but notice how Lovie Smith and Tony Dungy had pat, stock answers to the "first-black-to-win" question. Their answers were reflective and had a sense of history, at least they seemed so the first time they were provided. The newspaper accounts had a similar dull repetitiveness, as if the article writers had little to add but had to write anyway. The sheer repetition of the observation reduced the entire point to banality; the stories were made even less compelling by the fact that it was a foregone conclusion some two weeks ago that a black man would coach the winning team. When the point becomes entirely banal, then I guess that means we've reached a place where it's no longer interesting or newsworthy to mention the skin color of the winning coach. We're cured! Congratulations, America.

The Bears are probably the fourth or fifth best team in the NFL right now. I'd put the Colts, Patriots, and Chargers all in front of them for sure, and we could argue about the Ravens and, of course, the Seahawks. The Bears are a good team, but several offensive weapons short of the top three teams. Not counting the linemen (and no one does, so why should I have to? Let someone else worry about the linemen), I don't think there's even one offensive player on the Bears who for sure starts for the Chargers or Colts. I think Muhsin Muhammad starts at receiver for the Chargers (probably) and for the Patriots (for sure), but anybody on the waiver wire can start there for the Patriots, so that's not a big credit to the Bears. The Bears kept complaining that no one gave them a chance against the Colts, and they were right: they had no chance.

Speaking of the Patriots, how is it that they're not in this game? Why aren't those two bogus penalties called against the Pats' defense held up as the controversial reason that the Colts, and not the Patriots, are in the big game? The first bogus penalty was the pass interference call against a Patriots' defensive back that gave the Colts the ball on the one-yard line, setting up the easy tying touchdown. Pass interference? The defender never touched the receiver! The television announcer acknowledged there was no contact but termed the defender's conduct illegal "face-guarding." But even TSLP, a casual fan, knew to a moral certainty (yes, I'm often morally certain about football penalties from the comfort of my sofa) that face-guarding is no longer illegal in the NFL! The rule was changed several years ago. You would think the announcer would know the rules. And friends, despite what these ex-jocks in the booth tell you, the rules are really not all that complicated or all that lengthy. There's even a somewhat abbreviated version for fans, in digest form. (I keep it by my side during games, right next to the remote control.) Take a few minutes to read the rules and become more expert than the guys who are paid tons of money to think and talk about nothing other than football. I've seen the networks carrying golf telecasts have on staff a rules expert to chime in on rules issues, even though in professional golf rules questions seldom arise. Given the comparative multitude of NFL replay and rules issues, shouldn't CBS have employed a similar rules expert, or even better, an experienced lawyer? TSLP is available for all future Super Bowl telecasts, and promises to laugh like a drunken fool at all the lame studio jokes.

The second bogus call was the 15-yarder for "roughing the passer" that resulted from a blitzing linebacker running past Peyton Manning with his, the blitzer's, hands in the air (to deflect the pass or to wave to his family, I wasn't sure which) and one of those hands grazing, merely stroking, almost tenderly, the side of poor Peyton's helmet. Not even the gifted thespian Manning felt enough contact to go into his customary "I'm shot!" act. Yet the referee called the serious penalty, propelling the Colts deep into New England territory, setting up the final winning touchdown. Two outrageous calls that should be prominently mentioned every time the Colts are referred to as the 2006 NFL Champions. These were the most controversial officials' decisions since, umm, the Tuck Rule was invoked at some historic moment in the distant past that I cannot now bring to mind. Let's move on.

The NFL made a big point to keep this Super Bowl from being watched in places other than homes and bars. For instance, the NFL has used its copyright over game broadcasts to bully a number of churches, which had planned to host Super Bowl parties as fun social events and fund-raisers, into canceling their plans. Bad move, NFL. The Super Bowl has become so lucrative for the league precisely because fans have made the event into an excuse for a national party day. That's why the television network gets over two million dollars for a commercial spot! Do the TV folks like the idea of the NFL telling viewers to turn off their sets?

The moment Tony Dungy elected, in the final minutes of the game, not to kick the easy field goal to add three points to the margin of victory, the people at my party reacted in one of two ways. It was a couples party, by the way. Exactly one-half of those present (the half that watched the half-time show, and that's about all) said, in effect, "how nice of that coach not to add meaningless points." The other half of the room (the ones who had spent the afternoon yelling at the television set) quickly started asking each other about the point spread, the total number, and other betting angles.

I'm not making anything out of this, just making a small anthropological observation for the benefit of science. It does amaze me how people watch the same event and so often see such a different thing.

Index